Consumer Society

Consumer Society

CRITICAL ISSUES AND ENVIRONMENTAL CONSEQUENCES

Barry Smart

Los Angeles | London | New Delhi
Singapore | Washington DC

First published 2010

Apart from any fair dealing for the purposes of research or private study, or criticism or review, as permitted under the Copyright, Designs and Patents Act, 1988, this publication may be reproduced, stored or transmitted in any form, or by any means, only with the prior permission in writing of the publishers, or in the case of reprographic reproduction, in accordance with the terms of licences issued by the Copyright Licensing Agency. Enquiries concerning reproduction outside those terms should be sent to the publishers.

SAGE Publications Ltd
1 Oliver's Yard
55 City Road
London EC1Y 1SP

SAGE Publications Inc.
2455 Teller Road
Thousand Oaks, California 91320

SAGE Publications India Pvt Ltd
B 1/I 1 Mohan Cooperative Industrial Area
Mathura Road, Post Bag 7
New Delhi 110 044

SAGE Publications Asia-Pacific Pte Ltd
33 Pekin Street #02-01
Far East Square
Singapore 048763

Library of Congress Control Number 2009934785

British Library Cataloguing in Publication data

A catalogue record for this book is available from the British Library

ISBN 978-1-84787-049-0
ISBN 978-1-84787-050-6 (pbk)

Typeset by C&M Digitals (P) Ltd, Chennai, India

CONTENTS

ACKNOWLEDGEMENTS

I would like to thank colleagues and students who have contributed to the development of various sections of the book and Doug Kellner in particular for his detailed comments on the manuscript as a whole.

In Chapters 2, 5, 7, and 8 I have drawn on and developed material from two essays, '(Dis)interring postmodernism or a critique of the political economy of consumer choice', published in *Reconstructing Postmodernism Critical Debates* (2007) edited by Jason Powell and Tim Owen, and 'Made in America: the unsustainable all-consuming global free-market "utopia"', published in *Globalization and Utopia: Critical Essays* (2009) edited by Patrick Hayden and Chamsy El-Ojeili. I would like to thank the respective editors for their comments on the essays. Also the analysis in one section of Chapter 5 benefited from helpful comments I received from Roland Robertson and Richard Giulianotti on an earlier journal article 'Not playing around: global capitalism, modern sport and consumer culture', published in *Global Networks* (2007).

Finally, I would like to thank Chris Rojek for his editorial advice and support, Jai Seaman and Katherine Haw for providing help whenever I needed it.

We must not forget that the boiling heat of modern capitalistic culture is connected with heedless consumption of resources, for which there are no substitutes.

Max Weber, the Congress of Arts and Science, Universal Exposition, St Louis, 1904

Too much and too long we seem to have surrendered personal excellence and community values in the mere accumulation of material things. Our Gross National Product, now, is over $800 billion dollars a year, but that Gross National Product, if we judge the United States of America by that ...counts air pollution and cigarette advertising, and ambulances to clear our highways of carnage. It counts special locks for our doors and the jails for the people who break them. It counts the destruction of the redwood and the loss of our natural wonder in chaotic sprawl. It counts napalm and counts nuclear warheads and armored cars for the police to fight the riots in our cities. It counts ...the television programs which glorify violence in order to sell toys to our children. Yet the gross national product does not allow for the health of our children, the quality of their education or the joy of their play ... It measures neither our wit nor our courage, neither our wisdom nor our learning, neither our compassion nor our devotion to our country, it measures everything in short, except that which makes life worthwhile.

Robert F Kennedy, the University of Kansas March 18th 1968
http://www.jfklibrary.org/Historical+Resources/Archives/Reference+Desk/
Speeches/RFK/RFKSpeech68Mar18UKansas.htm

We know that our present mode of life is without future; that the children we will bring into the world will use neither oil nor a number of now-familiar metals during their adult lives ... We know that our world is ending; that if we go on as before, the oceans and the rivers will be sterile, the soil infertile, the air unbreathable in the cities ... We know that for a hundred and fifty years industrial society has developed through the accelerated looting of reserves whose creation required tens of millions of years.

Andre Gorz (1975) *Ecology as Politics* *

And to those nations like ours that enjoy relative plenty, we say we can no longer afford indifference to suffering outside our borders; nor can we consume the world's resources without regard to effect, for the world has changed, and we must change with it.

Barack Obama, 44th President of the USA, Inauguration Speech, January 20th 2009

* Reproduced with permission from Pluto Press, www.plutobooks.com

1

CONSUMING: HISTORICAL AND CONCEPTUAL ISSUES

The twentieth century has been termed 'The American Century' (Luce, 1941; Evans, 1998). This designation seems especially appropriate in respect of contemporary consumer culture and associated consumer lifestyles, for as the twentieth century developed the global reach and influence of American consumerism increased markedly. With the growth of American economic and cultural influence, particularly in the latter half of the century, American consumer brands, culture, and lifestyles increasingly were being exported to and adopted by the rest of the world, albeit inflected in various ways by local customs and practices (Ritzer, 2005; Brewer and Trentmann, 2006). American corporations, consumer goods, cultural forms, and styles exerted an increasing influence over people's lives and corporate brands, commodities, and services associated with the likes of Ford, Coca-Cola, Disney, McDonalds, Nike, MTV, Microsoft, Starbucks, and numerous other commercial enterprises became cultural universals, immediately recognizable features of the consumer landscapes of a growing number of people around the world. If consumerism had its initial roots in Europe in the seventeenth century, as the fruits of conquest and colonization gave rise to increasing material wealth and a growth in the range of products available for consumption (McKendrick et al., 1983; Brewer and Porter, 1993), the 'imitation' that quickly took hold in the American colonies, and then in an independent USA, became from the late nineteenth century the 'real thing', a way of life to which, in due course, more and more people around the world have aspired, albeit while also at times attaching local meanings and values to the commodities and services purchased and consumed (Glickman, 1999; Beck et al., 2003; Breen, 2004; Brewer and Trentmann, 2006).

In the closing decades of the twentieth century there were accumulating signs that America was no longer the manufacturing powerhouse that it once had been and the growing economic prowess of Japan and the 'Asian Tigers' led observers at the time to speculate on America's relative decline, as in the early twenty-first century did the emergence of China and India as economic powers. However, if American manufacturing is no longer the driving force that it was early in the twentieth century, and especially in the immediate aftermath of World War II, America has sustained its place at the epicenter of global consumer culture. In 2006, consumer purchases accounted for 70% of US gross domestic product (GDP) the closest competitors in the GDP consumer stakes being the UK (61%), Italy (59%) followed by other EU member states France and Germany and then Japan (approximately 55%) (Meyerson, 2008). From being a leading exporter of manufactured goods in the first half of the twentieth century America increasingly has become an importer, a 'nation of shoppers', buying goods produced predominantly overseas, a significant number of which are 'outsourced' by American corporations that have abandoned a commitment to manufacture and 'heavy capitalism' in favor of brand enhancement, product promotion, and the mobility, flexibility, and financial benefits of 'light, consumer-friendly capitalism' (Bauman, 2000: 63; Klein, 2001; Arvidsson, 2006).

As the twentieth century drew to a close 'the emergence of China, as the new workshop of the world' (Anderson, 2007: 6), began to be a focus of growing interest, increasing expectation, and rising concern. As China's production and consumption of commodities, goods, and services rapidly rose, so speculation grew that it would soon overtake America as the primary catalyst for global economic growth, its anticipated annual growth rate, combined with its projected level of consumer expenditure, being expected within decades to contribute more to global economic expansion than that of America (Bin Zhao, 1997; Shenkar, 2005). India, Asia's fourth largest economy in the early years of the twenty-first century, was also developing rapidly, its economic growth rate, second only to China, averaged 8% for the period 2003–2006 and the signs of a burgeoning consumer culture, catering for a rapidly expanding middle class with increasing disposable incomes, were becoming ever more apparent. A report in *The New York Times* in 2003 described consumers inside an Indian shopping mall, young people at Barista Coffee, the Starbucks of India, families wandering through department stores, shopping at Marks & Spencer, Lacoste, and Reebok, dining with their children at McDonald's, or buying food at the Subway sandwich shop. While poverty continues to be a big and serious problem in India with around 80% of the 1.1 billion population living on 25 rupees (30p) a day or less (Warner, 2007), following the opening up of the economy another increasingly prosperous India has emerged, one that is 'based on strong industry and agriculture, rising Indian and foreign investment and American-style consumer spending by a growing middle class [between 250 and 300 million in number], including the people under age 25 who now make up half the country's population' (Waldman, 2003; see also Farrell, 2007).

What appears to be occurring in Asia has been described not as the emergence of China but its re-emergence. Before 1800, Europe and America were not the driving forces of a developing world economy, rather the dominant regions were in Asia and it has been suggested that if 'any economy had a "central" position and role ... it was China' (Frank, A.G. 1998: 5). In addition, in this period the Indian subcontinent was itself 'highly developed and already dominant in the world textile industry' and this contributed to its very significant 'balance of trade surplus with Europe' (Frank, A.G., 1998: 85). In consequence, the recent rapid economic growth of China and India, and their increasingly influential participation in global consumer culture, may signify the beginning of an historic process of reorientation of the global economy away from the West and towards Asia, perhaps a restoration of Asia as the epicenter of the global economy, or the development of a bipolar or tripolar global economy (Chen and Wolf, 2001; Virmani, 2005).

One illustration of the growth of American or Western-style consumer activity in China and India is the increase in private car ownership. In 2004, in China the requirement to register bicycles ended and cycling became increasingly equated with the poor, with those unable to afford car ownership, those largely excluded from a growing consumer culture. In Beijing, the annual cycle tax was cancelled, bicycle lanes converted into car lanes, and 2 million cars given priority over around 4 million bikes. Between 1978 and 2006 the number of cars and vans on China's roads increased more than 20-fold to 27 million and in Beijing alone in 2006 car ownership was increasing at a rate of 1000 every day (Watts, 2009; BBC Asia-Pacific News, 2008). In India, a comparable pattern is emerging as a growing middle class aspire to car ownership and car manufacturers move in to nurture and satisfy the demand for auto-mobility, the best example of which is the production by Tata of a 'people's car', the four-seater 625 cc Nano, the world's cheapest car (Madslien, 2008). Given that 'a large Indian middle class ... has internalized Western consumer and celebrity culture even more avidly than its Chinese counterpart' (Anderson, 2007: 8) it is no surprise to find observers projecting that the consumer market in India may in due course exceed that of China (Engardio, 2005).

A consumer lifestyle – consumerism – that initially emerged in Europe, in England, in the seventeenth century, developed and achieved maturity in America, has subsequently become in the course of the twentieth century the most persuasive and pervasive globally extensive form of cultural life, one to which more and more people around the world continue to aspire. Before giving consideration to broad aspects of the historical trajectory leading from seventeenth century England through twentieth century America and, with the globalization of economic life, on to the growing number of other locations around the world that have embraced Western consumer lifestyles, including centres of development in China and India (Kalish, 2005, 2007; Shenkar, 2005; Farrell, 2007), brief clarification of key terms and consideration of the pivotal relationship between production and consumption is warranted.

Consumption and Consumerism

Consumption is a cultural universal, a necessary aspect of human exist-ence, a practice that has constituted a prominent part of social life in all societies throughout human history (Douglas and Isherwood, 1979). Mundane consumption is a necessary and routine part of people's lives, as is the exercise of choice in respect of a variety of relatively inconspicuous or ordinary products and services intrinsic to the maintenance of every-day life (Bevir and Trentmann, 2008). Consumption is closely articu-lated with another culturally universal and no-less essential practice, production, and to achieve an effective understanding of consumption analysis has to take production into account. As two radical critics of nineteenth-century political economy observed, consumption is a neces-sary corollary of 'the existence of living human individuals' and production for consumption is synonymous with material life itself:

> the first premise of all human existence and, therefore, of all history ... [is] that men must be in a position to live in order to be able to "make history." But life involves before every-thing else eating and drinking, housing, clothing and various other things. The first historical act is thus the production of the means to satisfy these needs, the production of material life itself. (Marx and Engels, 1976 [1845]: 41–2)

The relationship between consumption and production, alluded to in this statement, is complex and varied, has changed over time and undoubt-edly will continue to do so. Production and consumption continue to be articulated in a number of ways. The very process of production itself involves consumption, 'is immediately consumption' (Marx, 1973: 90), in the sense that, of necessity, materials and resources are used and energy and other capacities are expended in the course of making things and/or providing services. But where things are made and services are located is also subject to change. With the globalization of forms of economic production, manufacturing of consumer goods, and provision of consumer services have been increasingly outsourced or off-shored from wealthier, more developed, 'consumer' societies to less wealthy, less developed, 'producer' societies, creating distance between producers and consumers (Klein, 2001).

In a parallel manner the process of consumption can also be seen to be productive in so far as the act of consuming produces a range of effects and consequences, as in the mundane senses referred to above where the consumption of foodstuffs produces life, maintains and develops the body, reproduces energy and other bodily capacities, or where the consumption of a service may produce an ability, or an extension or development of the same, as in sports training and coaching, or in educational courses. While on the 'supply side' production creates the things, the objects, the services that are integral to the act of consuming, on the 'demand side' the process of consumption 'creates for the products the subject for whom they are products' (Marx, 1973: 90). The implication being that it is only in the act or process of consumption that a product truly achieves realization – 'a garment becomes a real garment only in the act of being worn ... the product ... *becomes* a product only through consumption' (Marx, 1973: 91). A further respect in which Marx considers consumption to promote production is that through use, through the act of consuming, 'consumption creates the need for *new* production' (1973: 91), creates the motive by reproducing the need, not only for products, which have been used up or consumed and need to be replaced, but also for other related new products offering additional and/or complimentary functions as, for example, is the case with accessories for mobile phones, computers, and many other commodities.

In addition to producing objects and/or services for consumption, production, in the broadest of senses, also stimulates consumption by generating needs, wishes, desires, and fantasies in respect of goods and services, effectively creating the consumer, and powerfully influencing, if not determining, how a particular good and/or service is to be consumed (Marx, 1973: 92–3). It is here at the nodal point of the articulation of production and consumption that a particularly distinctive modern way of life – *consumerism* – a way of life that is perpetually preoccupied with the pursuit, possession, rapid displacement, and replacement of a seemingly inexhaustible supply of things, first emerged, rapidly developed, and subsequently has grown to become global in scope and influence. It is a way of living that revolves around the wanting of things, the longing for things, the purchasing of things, a way of life in which having, desiring, and wishing for more and more things have become significant preoccupations for late modern subjects whose identities are increasingly bound up with what and how they consume. As critics have commented, consumerism represents 'the crass elevation of material acquisition to the status of a dominant social paradigm' (Princen et al., 2002: 3).

Analysts of modern consumer activity and the development of consumerism as a way of life have drawn a number of distinctions between 'consumption' on the one hand and 'consumerism' or 'consumer culture' on the other (Slater, 1997; Miles, 1998; Gabriel and Lang, 2006; Bauman, 2007b). While consumption has been present throughout all human history, and necessarily so, 'consumerism' or 'consumer culture' is argued to be a more modern phenomenon and is considered to have developed initially in the West in the late seventeenth and early eighteenth centuries (Braudel, 1974; McKendrick et al., 1983; Slater, 1997). For example, in France through the course of the seventeenth century, markets, especially at fairs and carnivals, were becoming an increasingly prominent source of consumer activity and historians have noted that in England early in the eighteenth century there were increasing signs of a growing propensity to consume and traces of a developing commercial interest in the value of advertising, marketing, and sales techniques (McKendrick, 1983).

There is a considerable body of historical evidence that reveals a steady growth in the range of goods being consumed in the West *before* the advent of the Industrial Revolution, in particular, commodities obtained through overseas voyages of discovery and 'colonial exploitation', such as 'coffee, tea, tobacco, imported cloths and dyes, new foods (potatoes, tomatoes), fruits', commodities that demonstrate that the 'west was a master consumer of imperially expropriated commodities before it was a consumer of goods it produced itself' (Slater, 1997: 18–19). The appearance in this period of a growing variety of consumer goods, including different forms of clothing and materials, crockery, decorative or non-essential manufactured items such as broaches, buckles, and pins, as well as cards, toys, and puppets, constitutes evidence of changing preferences and tastes on the part of consumers and households to obtain goods through the market by becoming more productive and dependable workers and signifies the early development of consumer culture, the emergence of consumerism as a way of life (Vries, 1993: 117; see also Campbell, 1987). The increasing proliferation and purchase of such commodities from the eighteenth century onwards has led analysts to refer to a 'consumer revolution', which along with the Industrial Revolution is considered to have inaugurated a process of transformation in and through which consumer activity has been accorded a critical economic significance and a prominent, if not central, position in contemporary social life, leading in due course to contemporary society being designated a 'consumer society' (McKendrick et al., 1983: 9; Miles, 1998: 6).

Although consumer culture has a history that extends back into the eighteenth century, if not earlier, it is only with developments from the late nineteenth and early twentieth centuries that those early traces began to be given a more substantial and coherent form and through the subsequent growth of mass production and mass consumption came to be recognized as constitutive of a distinctive way of life – 'consumerism' – that has continued to grow in influence to become, from the late twentieth century, truly global in scope and extent.

On Consumerism

It is developments from the period 1880–1930 that have been identified as particularly influential in promoting the growth of consumer culture, as inaugurating a series of qualitative changes that might be said to have ushered in a new age of consumption, to have given birth to consumerism as a distinctive way of living to which more and more people have aspired, initially in Europe and North America but subsequently across the rest of the world (Slater, 1997; Miles, 1998; Gabriel and Lang, 2006).

In drawing a series of distinctions between different possible meanings of consumerism Gabriel and Lang comment that it was from the 1920s in America 'that the meaning of consumption ... broadened ... to resonate pleasure, enjoyment and freedom ... [moving] from a means towards an end – living – to being an end in its own right' (2006: 8), to being not just a way of life, but in effect increasingly synonymous with the primary purpose of modern life, providing meaning to social existence. Consumerism is represented by Gabriel and Lang (2006: 8–9) as:

(1) A moral doctrine in developed countries.
(2) The ideology of conspicuous consumption.
(3) An economic ideology for global development.
(4) A political ideology.
(5) A social movement promoting and protecting consumer rights.

With the exception of the last category all of the 'distinct uses' listed are closely interrelated aspects of an ethos of consumerism that gathered momentum throughout the twentieth century with the accelerating global diffusion of the economic logic of modern capitalism. The identification of consumer activity, the pursuit and purchase of commodities and services as constituting a virtual duty, as embodying a 'moral doctrine', as articulated with 'freedom, power, and happiness', and as signifying 'the good life', is integral to the political economy of a form of life that requires a continual cultivation of new markets and a parallel perpetual (re)generation of consumer demand. The several 'meanings' distinguished are the inextricably inter-connected moral, social, economic, and political dimensions of consumer culture, of consumerism as a way of life that has become global, 'natural', quite simply the way the world is thought to be and cannot be imagined otherwise.

The final meaning of consumerism distinguished represents a response to a number of different consequences of a way of life that revolves around increasing consumption of goods and services, and represents far more than merely a social movement operating to promote and protect consumer rights, as Gabriel and Lang indicate by drawing attention to the growing concern about 'unbridled consumption in a world of finite resources and a fragile natural environment' (2006: 9). Concerns about the consequences of consumer culture, the impact of a way of life that is predicated upon the increasing use of what are in many instances finite resources and materials, and that leads to the production of growing volumes of waste, as well as potentially irreversible climate changes, are matters to be considered at length below.

The rapid growth and expansion of consumerism through the course of the twentieth century was the product of a number of factors. Technological and organizational innovations in production raised output significantly and reduced unit costs. In the early decades of the century the benefit was initially experienced in reductions in working hours, as well as relatively modest increases in consumption. From the early 1940s, rather than having more free time, people were inclined, encouraged, indeed exhorted, to continually consume more goods and services and more, it seems, was never enough (Schor, 1992; Siegel, 2008). Commercial corporations following an economic logic of market expansion and market creation, extending their operations to become transnational enterprises producing and/or promoting global brands, have contributed significantly to the global diffusion of consumerism, as have the growing number of advertising agencies, marketing organizations, and communications media that have become the creators and bearers of commodity sign values and promoters of brand identities (Ewen, 2001; Klein, 2001; Dawson, 2005; Barber, 2007). Global brands have successfully penetrated local cultures and enticed people around the world to consume this or that commodity by generating persuasive and appealing promotional lines and marketing messages, for example, 'It's the real thing' (Coca-Cola), 'Just do it' (Nike), 'Impossible is nothing' (Adidas), or the zeitgeist defining, 'because you're worth it' (L'Oreal), which effectively exemplifies the narcissistic individualism central to late-modern, materially acquisitive consumer culture.

Mass Production and Mass Consumption: Fordism

In respect of innovations in production that raised output significantly while simultaneously reducing unit costs of consumer goods, Fordism, a term which derives from Henry Ford's early twentieth-century, radically engineered Model T automobile assembly production line, warrants a prominent place insofar as it is widely acknowledged to have 'signalled the transformation of consumerism from an elite to a mass phenomenon in the 20th century in advanced capitalist societies' (Gabriel and Lang, 2006: 10; see also Miles, 1998: 6–7). Fordism describes the introduction in industry of particular production practices, including a detail division of labor that radically simplified tasks, standardized components, and sequentially organized machinery to facilitate a coordinated productive flow in the form of an assembly line (Harvey, 1989).

With Fordism there was a significant transformation of the organization of production, a rationalization of the labor process that simultaneously led to a loss of worker control, an increase in the productivity of labor and a reduction in unit costs, a relative shift in the balance of production from producer to consumer goods, and an absolute increase in the volume of commodities produced. The increased output of standardized goods – mass production – made possible and necessary a parallel growth in consumer demand. The prospect of increasing living standards and the provision of 'mass consumption' have been regarded as compensation for a deterioration in the work experience associated with Fordist rationalization, with consumerism being described as a 'bribe ... for accepting intensive rationalization, alienation and utter lack of control over ... work life' (Slater, 1997: 188) and as 'reward for accepting potentially alienating work' (Gabriel and Lang, 2006: 189). This is perhaps best exemplified by Henry Ford's decision in January 1914 to respond to high labor turnover associated with the imposition of rationalized production by offering his workers the incentive of a doubling of their pay to become more efficient, harder working, and more productive (Raff and Summers, 1987).

The proliferation of goods produced through the adoption and deployment of Fordist rationalization led not only to the cultivation of 'local' or 'national' consumer markets, but also to increased international trade and an accelerated pursuit of global consumer markets for the burgeoning quantities of goods being manufactured. As one perceptive observer remarked at the time on the impact of increasing productive capacity:

> Production has played many parts in history; it has taken vari-
> ous forms. The form which it takes in this, the Machine Age, is
> strange and new. Consumptionism is a new necessity ... Through
> the centuries the problem has been how to produce enough
> of the things men wanted ... *the new necessity is to make men want
> the things which machinery must turn out if this civilization is not to
> perish.* (Strauss, 1924: 578–9, emphasis added)

For this observer of a rapidly developing mass production/mass consumption
American society it is advertising that constitutes 'the circulatory system
of twentieth century industry', that influences and shapes consumption
(Strauss, 1924: 583). Consumers may not directly engage with advertising
copy, they may not stop to focus on advertisements in the newspaper, on
the billboard/hoarding, and/or, as has become increasingly the case of
late, on the screen, but Strauss remarks that advertisements are 'doing
their work just the same ... bringing about the desired result', namely
stimulating 'the appetite for more things of every kind', and creating
a world which is 'dominated by things', a world in which all relationships are increasingly being reduced to the commodity form, effectively
treated as thing-like (1924: 586, 581, 587).

  However, advertising was merely one, albeit important, factor recognized by Ford when he reflected on the consumer market benefits of
worker productivity schemes that improved workers' wages. If mass production commodities were to be actualized then there had to be a mass of
consumers. Ford had recognized that it was in his interest for his producers to be able to be consumers and for that a combination of an appropriate level of income and availability of credit would be necessary (Harvey,
1989). This period extending from the late nineteenth century through
to the 1920s might be considered the 'take-off phase' for mass consumerism (Robertson, 1990). What changed with mass production was the
requirement, the necessity, for an increase in the scale of consumption,
an increase in both the number of goods being consumed and the speed
or rate at which things needed to be consumed (Ewen, 2001). With the
growth of mass production, and the necessary cultivation of mass consumption, consumer activity began to occupy an increasingly prominent
place in social life (Bauman, 2007b).

  Fordism was more than a system of mass production, it has been described
as 'a total way of life', one which, of necessity, included relatively standardized forms of mass consumption. Fordism held relatively firm until the
economic recession of the mid-1970s led to forms of economic restructuring and rationalization, promoting alternatives to large-scale, relatively rigid mass production systems that took advantage of innovations in
information technology to introduce 'labour processes, labour markets,
products, and patterns of consumption', which have been described as

'flexible', 'post-industrial' or 'knowledge-intensive', and in respect of work and employment aspects in particular, 'insecure' (Harvey, 1989: 135, 147; see also Lash and Urry, 1994; Beck, 2000). The more flexible, post-industrial or knowledge-intensive economic order which developed from the mid-1970s gave, as Harvey notes, 'much more autonomy to the banking and financial system relative to corporate, state, and personal financing' and in making significant improvements in 'communication and information flow' and distribution techniques it presided over a dramatic increase in the velocity of circulation of 'commodities through the market system' and the volume of consumer activity (1989: 164, 285).

Flexible Production and Consumption

Mass production and mass consumption have not disappeared, but the deployment of information technologies and other organizational innovations in production, distribution, and retailing have promoted greater manufacturing and marketing flexibility, and commodity choice, by making shorter production runs for niche or micro-markets and tastes, or provision for specialized forms of consumption, economically viable and profitable. The increases in product ranges and product turnover as durability has been diminished by acceleration in engineered obsolescence, alongside increased segmentation of the consumer market and the prospect of 'greater volatility' in respect of consumer preferences, has led some analysts to designate new forms of consumption 'post-Fordist' (Lash and Urry, 1994: 274). Taking stock of some of the more significant developments in consumption that have accompanied the emergence of greater flexibility, Harvey describes two particular trends. First, how increasingly fashion, styling, and design have been deployed beyond luxury or elite markets 'to accelerate the pace of consumption not only in clothing, ornament, and decoration, but also across a wide swathe of lifestyles and recreational activities (leisure and sporting habits, pop music styles, video and children's games, and the like)' (Harvey, 1989: 285). Second, an increase in the consumption of a range of services, including 'personal, business, educational and health services', as well as entertainment, leisure, recreation, sport, and other ephemeral services, the reduced lifetimes of which increase turnover and promote an acceleration in capital accumulation compared to more durable material goods. A major consequence of the developments identified by Harvey in respect of production has been an increased emphasis being placed on 'the values and virtues of instantaneity', insofar as instant, fast, and disposable goods promote acceleration in both 'the turnover of goods in consumption' and capital accumulation (1989: 286).

A flexible and faster-paced 'society of consumers'

In one analysis of the transformations to which modern forms of life have
been subject as work has been displaced from its 'linchpin role' and consumer activity and associated 'wants, desires and longings' have grown
in significance to become, in the course of the latter part of the twentieth
century, the 'principal propelling and operating force of society', a contrast is drawn between what is represented as an earlier 'solid' phase
of modernity and a later 'liquid' phase (Bauman, 2007b: 28). The solid
phase of modernity is exemplified by the 'society of producers', a form
of social life in which goods are sought and desired for the 'comfort and
esteem' they can deliver, where emphasis is placed upon stability, permanence, and reliability, and pursuit of security through orderly, durable,
and long-term forms and arrangements is favored. It is permanence or
stability and continuous reliability that are identified as foundational values in the 'solid modern society of producers' (Bauman, 2007b: 31). This
form of social life is contrasted with the ways of living, the preoccupations,
preferences, and values that emerged with and developed out of the
'consumerist revolution' and that subsequently have come to predominate
in contemporary social life (Campbell, 1987).

In the 'light' of 'liquid' modern society of consumers it is argued that
stability, permanence, and durability are no longer assets but liabilities,
obstructions to be swept away by the relentless torrent of innovation, the
endlessly meandering tributaries of fashion, styling, and design, and the
'ever rising volume and intensity of desires … and speedy replacement
of the objects intended and hoped to gratify them' (Bauman, 2007b: 31).
The solid, stable, more secure and, by implication, 'heavy' and slower
society of producers is overtaken, surpassed, by the lighter, more mobile
and flexible, and faster-paced 'society of consumers'. Bauman argues
that the promotion, nurturing, and continual regeneration of 'wants,
desires and longings' associated with the 'advent of consumerism augurs
the *era of "inbuilt obsolescence" of goods offered on the market* and signals
a spectacular rise in the waste disposal industry' (2007b: 31, emphasis
added).

While the contrast drawn between the two 'ideal types' – a 'solid' phase
of modernity/'heavy' capitalism/'society of producers' and a 'liquid' phase
of modernity/'light' capitalism/'society of consumers' – is illuminating
there are important underlying continuities that have contributed significantly to the particular transformations identified. Underlying a
relative shift in emphasis from a society of production with traditional
imperatives to labor and produce, to a society of consumption with a
social logic that revolves around consumer activity, a view initially introduced by Baudrillard (1998) and elaborated and extended by Bauman,

it is the persisting pursuit of increases in economic growth and capital accumulation that has promoted the relative shift of emphasis in social and economic life from production to consumption (Sklair, 2002).

Writing in the mid-nineteenth century before the advent of mass production methods and the generation of a mass market for consumer goods, Marx and Engels identified the distinctive transformative logic of the modern capitalist mode of production, emphasizing the need for a 'constant revolutionizing of production … [and] constantly expanding market for its products … over the whole surface of the globe' (1968[1848]: 83). They drew attention to the relentless character of the processes of transformation, which are intrinsic to such a competitive economic system, one which has as its primary objective continual capital accumulation and, its necessary corollary, an ever expanding global consumer market for the continually increasing volume and range of goods being produced. 'All that is solid', fixed, and stable has indeed been rendered fluid as production and consumption have been subjected to relentless transformation, leading to the development of a more mobile, flexible, and faster-paced 'consumer society' and 'uninterrupted disturbance of all social conditions' (Marx and Engels, 1968: 83).

Approaching the mid-twentieth century Schumpeter introduced a notion of 'creative destruction' to conceptualize the processes earlier identified by Marx and Engels, describing it as the 'essential fact about capitalism', as a 'process of industrial mutation … that incessantly revolutionizes the economic structure *from within*, incessantly destroying the old one, incessantly creating a new one' (1975[1942]: 82). Schumpeter presented creative destruction as a defining feature of capitalist economic life and described it as a 'fundamental impulse that sets and keeps the capitalist engine in motion [that] comes from the new consumers, goods, the new methods of production or transportation, the new markets, the new forms of industrial organization that capitalist enterprise creates' (1975[1942]: 82). A 'perennial gale of creative destruction' leads to new consumers, commodities, technologies, sources of supply, and types of organization and it is around these, rather than in respect of price, that competition becomes increasingly orientated. Moreover, as will be considered later, products and/or by-products of complex processes of creative destruction may, in turn, prove to be more 'destructive' then 'creative', inviting, if not warranting, the designation 'destructive creations' (Calvano, 2007; see also Beck, 1992).

The economic system Marx and Engels and Schumpeter analyzed has of course changed in a number of important respects, but it remains firmly wedded to 'creative destruction' for precisely the reasons they outlined and from the late nineteenth century 'consumerism' became an increasingly essential cultural corollary, vital for engendering continual increases in consumer demand, which became more and more necessary as productivity grew rapidly through the twentieth century.

However, in the course of the late twentieth century the consequences of rising consumption and associated developments in consumer lifestyles became a focus of increasing concern as evidence indicating a variety of undesirable outcomes began to accumulate. The technical, social, and aesthetic engineering of product obsolescence, the production of commodities deemed unnecessary, wasteful, and/or damaging to the health, well-being, and welfare of users and their communities, and broader, frequently less-detectable, indirect, and delayed detrimental effects on the environment attracted increasing analytic attention and criticism (Gorz, 1983; Bahro, 1984; Princen et al., 2002; Gardner et al., 2004; Gardner and Prugh, 2008; Jackson, 2009).

Increasing turnover of commodities, aided by advertising images, marketing narratives, and the cultivation of brand loyalties that promote the idea that consumer activity – pursuing, purchasing, using, having, and more importantly *being seen to have* a particular product – produces satisfaction and promotes happiness, is an essential part of modern social life and constitutes the foundation of our consumerist economy. Happiness, as Baudrillard notes, 'is the absolute reference of the consumer society' (1998: 49), but this 'happiness' is not to be confused with 'inner enjoyment', rather it is bound up with the *visible* attainment of consumer goods and directly or indirectly, discursively and vicariously shared experience of consumer services; it is associated with a display of consumer activity and its proceeds; with a presentation of signs or evidence of consuming achieved. This is a happiness that is signified by and invested in the world of consumer objects. It is an 'enforced happiness', a diminished happiness, a market contrived simulation, not happiness 'in the full sense of the term' (Baudrillard, 1998: 50). Elaborating on this theme Baudrillard adds that:

> There is *no question for the consumer … of evading this enforced happiness* and enjoyment, which is the equivalent in the new ethics of the traditional imperative to labor and produce. Modern man spends less and less of his life in production within work and more and more of it in the production and continual innovation of his own needs and well-being. He must constantly see to it that all his potentialities, all his consumer capacities are mobilized. If he forgets to do so, he will be gently and insistently reminded that he has no right not to be happy. (1998: 80, emphasis added)

The issue of happiness is a matter to which I will return in a wider discussion of consumer choice and the consequences of consumerism, but it is worth noting at this juncture that the reduced time spent in production referred to by Baudrillard only applies to *some* modern men and women, primarily in wealthier countries, but also in privileged locations secured in metropolitan environments in less wealthy and less developed countries, and to a substantial degree has been made possible by the globalization of economic production and the increasing amount of time other men and women in poorer parts of the world spend in manufacturing activity, working under very difficult and often dangerous conditions for low wages, with little if any employment, safety, and health legislation to protect them (Klein, 2001; Labour Behind the Label, n.d.). It is also appropriate to add at this point that in the USA in the period from the 1950s to the present, although productivity rose 400%, the hours worked by many Americans steadily increased as well (Rauch, 2000). As a study of the growth in working hours in America demonstrates, it is precisely in the cause of mobilizing an essential consumer demand for rising productive capacity, ensuring workers have the rising income required to retain a place on the consumer treadmill, that working hours have increased (Schor, 1992). Certainly in the homeland of consumer culture, the USA, the contrast originally developed by Baudrillard in the late 1960s now appears radically overdrawn, for the pursuit of consumer happiness has subsequently required a growing number of Americans to spend more and more of their lives in production within work If this fact is coupled with the increasing levels of indebtedness that have been a corollary of the pursuit of the consumer dream, then it is clear that there are very good grounds for *not* being happy with a way of life that costs so much yet arguably ultimately delivers very little of what it appears to promise.

There are interesting comparisons to be explored between American, UK, and continental European experiences of the consequences of consumerism and the 'work-and-spend' cycle. For example, towards the end of the twentieth century it was noted that manufacturing employees in the USA were working 320 more hours a year than their equivalents in some European countries (Schor, 1992). Working hours began to increase significantly in America from the early 1970s, a period that is synonymous with the pursuit of flexible accumulation, deregulation, and restructuring of labor markets, erosion of trades union influence, and a reduction in wage rates (Harvey, 1989; Schor, 1992; Castells, 1996: 274–5; Luttwak, 1999: 205). The UK pattern parallels American experience rather than that of other European countries, with reports suggesting that its labor force has the second-longest working hours in the developed world, just behind the USA. Full-time workers in the UK put in the longest hours in Europe, 43.6 a week, compared with an EU average of 40.3. Furthermore, since 1998 the number of people working over 48 hours a week has increased from 10% to 26% and one in six of all workers is working more than 60 hours a week (Bunting, 2004). The UK has emulated the USA in respect of the other side of the work-and-spend cycle, with consumer expenditure reported in 2006 to represent 61% of GDP, second only to the figure of 70% recorded in the USA (Meyerson,

2008). The data on the consumption of materials in the USA over the period 1900–1995 provide further confirmation of the accelerating growth of consumption from 1970. While over this period as a whole the consumption of materials in America increased from 161 million metric tons to 2.8 billion metric tons, over 50% of the materials were consumed in the period from 1970. Moreover, while in 1900 approximately 50% of the materials consumed were from renewable resources (e.g. wood, fibers, and agricultural products) this had declined to 8% of total consumption by 1995 (Matos and Wagner, 1998).

In Europe from 1970, in some quarters at least, people were being exhorted to 'work less, live more' (Gorz, 1982: 134) and legislative moves were being made to reduce the length of the working week to enable modern *citizens* to enjoy the fruits of greater economic productivity by spending less and less of their lives engaged in production within workplaces. But in America the emphasis increasingly was being placed on modern *consumers* working more in order to be able to spend more, buy more, have more (Schor, 1992; Luttwak, 1999; Bunting, 2004). However, by the beginning of the twenty-first century concerns that had been articulated at various moments in the course of the previous century by analysts critical of the consequences of modern industrial civilization (Penty, 1922; Roszak, 1972; Schumacher, 1973) were being given greater credence by the accumulation of scientific evidence confirming the damaging impact of modern consumer lifestyles on the environment (Princen et al., 2002; Starke, 2004, 2008, 2009; Giddens, 2009) and people were being exhorted to 'consume less, live better', 'consume less, live more', and to recognize that institutional complacency was making worst-case climate change scenarios increasingly likely (Porritt, 2007; DiCaprio, 2008; Armstrong, 2009).

On the Separation of Production and Consumption

Population growth, increasing industrialization, and rising manufacturing productivity in the course of the nineteenth century, along with enhanced mobility associated with developments in transportation, and rapid urbanization that transformed many market towns into developing cosmopolitan cities, provided the context for the emergence of a distinctive consumer culture. Through the nineteenth century the availability of ready-made goods increased steadily, especially as 'ready-made clothing and pre-processed convenience foods' became cheaper and more abundant (Schlereth, 1989: 343). Markets were displaced by small stores and streets of shops, and later in the century mail order catalogues emerged, department stores began to be established, and increasing attention was given to the display and presentation of goods and the decoration of retail premises to further entice consumers. As towns grew and the space to grow fruits and vegetables and raise livestock disappeared populations of wage earners became increasingly dependent on the purchase of ready-made goods. Towards the close of the century even those living in rural environments were purchasing 'more of the goods and services that they had once either produced for themselves or simply had done without' (Schlereth, 1989: 341) and as the purchase of ready-made and convenience goods increased so 'the distance between producer and consumer grew' (Bronner, 1989: 42).

Reflecting on the factors that contributed to the development of consumerism and, in particular, the formation of America as a mass consumer society, William Leach observes that:

> Before 1880, consumption and production were, for large numbers of people, bound together, with men and women, and children living and toiling closely with one another ... in local or regional economies ... Most Americans knew where the goods and wealth came from, because they themselves produced them, knew their value, and understood the costs and sufferings required to bring them into existence ... After 1890 the institutions of production and consumption were, in effect, taken over by corporate businesses. Business, not ordinary men and women, did most to establish the value and the cultural character of the goods – in this case the new machine-made goods. At the same time, merchants, brokers, and manufacturers did everything they could ... to *separate* the world of production from the world of consumption. (1993: 147, emphasis in original)

The historical transformations identified by Leach led to an increasingly distinctive and seemingly separate consumer world in which women were mainly responsible for shopping and where in the absence of any involvement in the production of goods the '"true" value ... meaning or worth of any commodity' became difficult to determine beyond the problematic measure of price and the enticing images conveyed through advertising copy (Leach, 1993: 148). It was in this context that consumer conduct began to be equated with freedom. Consumption was considered to offer an attractive and appealing opportunity for self-expression, was deemed to constitute a vital source of fulfillment, and represented for many people compensation for the drudgery, erosion of control, and loss of meaning encountered in their workplaces. Whereas work was increasingly experienced as alienating, the world of consumption appeared to offer self-realization, fulfillment, even liberation. The production of a seemingly limitless range of new goods appeared to offer the prospect of new possibilities, new meanings, and new forms of human expression and being.

While industrial capitalism promoted a separation of the life-worlds of production and consumption, and increasingly with the globalization of production distanced 'producers' from 'consumers', consumption has remained closely articulated with and dependent upon the logic of capitalist economic production (Klein, 2001). As Marx observed, 'production produces consumption (i) by creating the material for it; (ii) by determining the manner of consumption; and (iii) by creating the products, initially posited by it as objects, in the form of a need felt by the consumer. It thus produces the object of consumption, the manner of consumption, and the motive of consumption' (1973: 92). The separateness of the world of consumption has been an outcome of the way in which the capitalist economy has developed, the ways in which economic production has been reorganized. As distance developed between production and consumption, between producers and consumers, so the contribution made by workers, the conditions under which they labored, and the treatment and remuneration they received were increasingly obscured from view. As Leach notes:

> By 1910 more and more people were less and less aware about how things were made and who made them. Besides, who would want to know these things in a culture already disposed to encourage self-indulgence, self-gratification, and self-pleasure? To acknowledge suffering caused by capitalism under these new conditions would be to arouse one's own guilt and to cause one's own distress. But the separateness of consumption made it easy to deny the suffering. The outcome was a greater tendency toward selfishness and a corrosive moral indifference. (1993: 150)

The developments in question occurred within a period identified as one dominated by the promotion of market forces and relations, the implication being that it was the 'market view of society ... which "fragmented" life into the producers' sector that ended when his product reached the market, and the sector of the consumer for whom all goods sprang from the market' (Polanyi, 2001[1944]: 266). The market view of society, the idea of the self-regulating market, of social relations being embedded within the economic system, and 'the running of society as an adjunct to the market' (2001: 60) are defining statements of economic liberalism. By the 1940s, increasing awareness of the damage to the social fabric inflicted by the self-regulating market had largely discredited economic liberalism and greater regulation and control was being exercised over economic life. The primacy of society over the economic system seemed to have been secured according to Polanyi who commented that 'the market system will no longer be self-regulating', that society would not in future be 'constricted by economics' and that the 'passing of market-economy can become the beginning of an era of unprecedented freedom' (2001: 259, 260, 265).

While the 'market utopia' lost some of its appeal for a time after 1945, in the closing decades of the twentieth century, in response to problems of reduced levels of capital accumulation and economic 'stagflation', there was a return to economic policies promoting market forces, what was termed 'free-trade', and the idea of market self-regulation. With the turn to 'neo-liberal' economic policies in the mid-1970s the idea of freedom was once again diminished by being equated with 'advocacy of free enterprise', exercise of consumer sovereignty, and expression of consumer choice. As had been the case in the earlier 'liberal' manifestation of the market-economy analyzed by Polanyi, 'No society built on other foundations ... [was] said to deserve to be called free' and, in turn, 'freedom that regulation creates ... [was frequently] denounced as unfreedom' (2001: 265).

Neo-liberalism advocated unbridled entrepreneurial freedom, free markets, free trade, and a radically reduced state, and vigorously promoted consumerism. Deregulation, privatization, market forces, and consumer choice became the watchwords of neo-liberalized states as they extolled the virtues of economic globalization and sought to provide the appropriate institutional setting within which economic growth could be maintained and corporations could significantly increase rates of profit by generating increasing consumption of goods and services (Gorz, 1985; Bourdieu, 1998; Harvey, 2005). With increasing economic globalization there has been an erosion of the economic sovereignty of nation-states, as well as a transformation of the relationship between national economies, and between 'sovereign' states and international corporations. The promotion of 'free trade' and the formation of a global marketplace has served to further increase the distances between producers and consumers, as Klein (2001) documents in her discussion of the off-shoring of manufacturing industry from the consumer heartlands of North America, Europe, and Japan to contractors in distant locations. Many companies have closed down their factories in preference for overseas sourcing of product lines and the redirection of resources to innovative product research and development activity, and marketing and branding campaigns to cultivate consumer demand. Klein refers to the running shoe company Vans closing their factory in California and 'contracting production in South Korea' and describes how Adidas 'closed down everything' and retained only one small factory as a 'global technology centre ... [making] about 1 percent of total output' (Klein, 2001: 198–9).

Economic globalization has not only extended the distance between producers and consumers it has virtually severed any evident connection between the two in that 'many of today's brand-based multinationals now maintain that the location of their production operations is a "trade secret" to be guarded at all costs' (Klein, 2001: 201). The reason frequently given for such secrecy is to prevent competitors 'taking advantage', but it is also apparent that the global disconnection that now exists between producers and consumers is necessary to preserve the appeal, desire, and carefully cultivated sign value and artfully contrived enchantment of branded consumer goods manufactured, in some instances at least, under conditions that consumers certainly would not contemplate accepting in their own workplaces and awareness of which might well lead to a consumer boycott. Increasingly consumer goods are manufactured in low-wage cost locations, in 'free trade zones' or 'export processing zones', in countries such as Bangladesh, China, El Salvador, Indonesia, Kenya, Mexico, the Philippines, Sri Lanka and Vietnam. It is in these locations that goods are manufactured for multinational corporations, including the likes of Nike, Gap, IBM, Levi's, Reebok, and Walmart. Within specially designated production zones there are frequently 'no import or export duties and often no income or property taxes either', no unions, long working days, low wages, and little if any concern is shown for the health or welfare of workers (Klein, 2001: 205, 210–26). In addition, evidence from Asia and the Indian sub-continent has revealed that child-labor is routinely being used by sub-contractors employed by suppliers to produce low cost fast-fashion commodities for high street retail stores in wealthy countries (Hawkes, S., 2008; McDougall, 2008; Labour Behind the Label, n.d.).

Workers in export processing zones, located primarily in the southern hemisphere, generally will not be consumers of the goods they produce for there is a huge discrepancy between their minimal, at times barely subsistence, rates of pay and the inflated prices attached to the goods that they have made when they go on sale in shops and stores, primarily but no longer exclusively in northern hemisphere countries. The one world forged through economic globalization is very heavily stratified, marked by wealth and riven with income inequalities that are increasing, and 'remains sharply divided between producers and consumers … [moreover] the enormous profits raked in by the superbrands are premised upon these worlds remaining as separate from each other as possible' (Klein, 2001: 346–7). The increased distances opened up between producers and consumers through economic globalization serve to conceal the inflated market value of manufactured commodities, 'the riches of the branded world', from producers, the corollary of which is that the attention of consumers needs to be drawn away from any serious reflection on the exploitative conditions of production, 'the squalor of production', by investment of resources in marketing and branding and cultivation of enchanting and spectacular retail displays and environments (Klein, 2001: 347; Dawson, 2005). As Klein observes:

> for the system to function smoothly, workers must know little of the marketed lives of the products they produce and consumers must remain sheltered from the production lives of the brands they buy. (2001: 347)

The 'out-sourcing' of manufactured goods has become an increasingly prominent feature of the global economy and has served to increase the distance between the respective life-worlds inhabited by producers and consumers (Luttwak, 1999; Harvey, 2005).

Fusion of production and consumption

The increased distancing of production from consumption and producers from consumers, which has been a consequence of the development of the capitalist market economy and its globalization in particular, does not quite tell the whole story. In a few, relatively exceptional, information technology constituted environments production and consumption have become at times more difficult to distinguish. For example, within the knowledge-intensive software environment of Web 2.0 it is suggested that creativity is often collaborative and that the distinction between production and consumption does not hold. Rather than producers and consumers Alex Bruns (2007) refers to 'the rise of the informed or active ... user' or to 'user-as-contributor', exemplified by forms of citizen journalism such as Indymedia and Slashdot, as well as 'user-led content creation' in respect of multi-user online gaming. The implication is that the practice of making, constructing, or creating in the Web 2.0 environment is of a different 'productive' and 'consumptive' order and this leads Bruns to refer to a 'participatory mode' in which those involved are both users and producers of information and knowledge.[1]

In some respects this may appear to represent a return to an earlier idea introduced by Alvin Toffler in *The Third Wave* (1983). Toffler argued that the information technology revolution, computers, and telecommunications would radically transform the nature of production and promote a transfer of productive activity from the workplace to the home. To a limited degree his perception of the potential impact of information technology has been borne out by the subsequent transformation of productive activity, but his expectation that the end of the market economy was in prospect and that a return to production for self-consumption, or 'pro-sumption' as he termed it, would replace exchange has not transpired in practice, to the contrary there has been an increasing encroachment of the market into more and more areas of people's lives as the scale of commod-ity consumption has grown and the pace has accelerated (Smart, 1992: 78–81; Bruns, 2007: 2).

In some specific instances the transformation of production through deployment of information technology has allowed consumers to be able to exercise a degree of influence, albeit within a predetermined or edited range of design and performance options, and thereby become more involved in determining the specification of products which they order and purchase. Such products can be considered 'customized', but this represents merely an extension to a larger number of commodities of a relatively longstanding consumer goods industry practice, 'made to measure' or made to customer specification, in which colors, shapes, designs, and other features of particular commodities, including clothing, furniture, and now other goods such as computers, may be determined by consumer choice from within a range of possibilities. It represents a qualification of mass production, if not a movement away from it to smaller batch, niche, or more personalized production, but it does not represent a radical transformation of either the logic of the economic system, or the respects in which production and consumption are articu-lated, and it does not warrant a confusing conceptual conflation of the terms production and consumption any more than does the proliferation of forms of 'self-service' in which consumers take on tasks which in the past 'were done for them' (Ritzer, 2005: 37). The fact that customers can determine, within option ranges prescribed by commercial corpora-tions, some of the specifications of the products they elect to purchase, or that self-service has become a more common feature of a number of industries (e.g. ATM banking, supermarket food shopping, fast food 'restaurants', etc.) are developments that reflect the necessity of continu-ing to innovate in a competitive economic marketplace in order to gen-erate increasing consumer interest and sales, reduce staffing costs, and raise turnover.

Where there do seem to be grounds for recognizing a significant transformation in respect of the articulation of production and con-sumption, as well as the relevance of the designated roles of producer and consumer, is in respect of an at present relatively restricted range of goods and services which are 'of an intangible, informational nature', it is here that a 'shift away from ... industrial, and towards postindustrial or informational economic models can be observed' (Bruns, 2007: 3). But once again there is no necessity for the introduction of terms which serve simply to obfuscate rather than clarify the exceptional form of articulation between acts of creation and use concerned. Reference to the collaborative and participatory nature of Web 2.0 content creation and development is sufficient and helpful, introducing notions of 'produser' and 'produsage' less so (Brun, 2007: 3).

A Consumer Age

The major transformations associated with the emergence of a consumer age led not only to an increasing distance between producers and consumers, but also to much greater significance being accorded to consumption. What has been identified by social analysts as a transition from a producer to a consumer society in the late twentieth century is firmly rooted in a series of transformations that were taking place from at least the late nineteenth century. Indeed, a consumer culture was forming throughout the nineteenth century as wage earners increased in number and ready-made goods became more widely available, market buildings were replaced by streets of smaller shops, department stores were established, increasing consideration was given to the display of goods, advertising grew in scope and intensity, and mail order purchase came on stream allowing those out of town consumers to achieve inclusion in the emerging consumer society. As one critical observer has noted, this 'transformation requires a subtler conceptual framework than simply the notion of a shift from a Protestant "producer culture" to a secular "consumer culture"' (Lears, 1989: 77 n8). The persuasive idea of a 'passage from producer to consumer society' along with the notion that 'the aesthetics of consumption ... now rules where the work ethic once ruled' (Bauman, 1998: 24, 32) has inadvertently served to encourage analytic attention to be focused on consumerism, choice, lifestyling, and identity matters to the all too frequent neglect of significant continuing complex articulations with production and in particular the continuing influence exerted by an overarching economic logic directed to the achievement of rising rates of capital accumulation through the generation of increasing economic growth and rising levels of consumption of goods and services (Warde, 1997; Harvey, 2005).

The development of an institutional basis for a consumer society, particularly in the USA in the period from the late nineteenth century through to the 1920s, was a necessary corollary of the rapid increase in productivity following the growth of industrial manufacturing. As manufacturing capacity increased and the economic environment became increasingly more competitive worries began to be expressed that production might outstrip 'available markets' and in consequence consumption began to be accorded an 'independent character' and the economic significance it warranted (Leach, 1993: 162, 147). Increasingly there was recognition that the problem was no longer how to produce enough of the things people needed and wanted but how to get people to want to purchase the increasing number and range of things which were being produced with the development of industrial manufacturing (Strauss, 1924). Commercial corporations began to recognize 'that they would have to develop methods to entice the public to consume those products that were … [becoming] available in abundance' (Renouard, 2007: 55). As one observer noted:

> The first condition of our civilization … is that we must turn out ever larger quantities of things, more this year than last, more next year than this … The problem before us today is not how to produce the goods, but how to produce the customers. Consumptionism is the science of compelling men to use more and more things. Consumptionism is bringing it about that *the American citizen's first importance to his country is no longer that of citizen but that of consumer*. (Strauss, 1924: 578–9, emphasis added)

The great 'abundance of commodities', a product of the growth of industrial manufacturing, created a requirement for an extensive retail and distributive network, which in turn led to the development of a range of new stores and purchasing possibilities and to commercial organizations directing increasing attention to lifting 'constraints on the expression of consumer desire' and devoting resources to 'expanding that desire' (Leach, 1989: 101).

From the early nineteenth century America changed from being the 'Land of Comfort', in which the majority of men were self-employed, property owners, producing 'foodstuffs and raw materials', enjoying a degree of prosperity and 'relaxed work habits', to becoming the 'Land of Desire', in which a growing number of men and women were employees engaged in disciplined labor working in 'factories and … big corporate bureaucracies' (Leach, 1989: 101). As the increase in productivity associated with the growth of industrial manufacturing raised fears about the prospect of overproduction, so distribution and marketing became matters of concern and increasing attention was directed towards the need to produce a 'new consumer consciousness' and promote a diffusion of desire for consumer goods and services, beyond an already privileged 'leisure class' to the population as a whole through 'advertising, display and decoration, fashion, style, design and consumer service' (Leach, 193: 37).

In this period it was not just in America that there were growing signs of an emerging consumer society. In the UK in the course of the nineteenth century the beneficial impact of new industrial technologies was evidenced by the greater availability of mass produced goods and, as a result of developments in transport that improved the distribution of goods, coupled with the growth of advertising and innovations in retailing, 'a seemingly endless stream of things ... could be acquired by the consumer' (Flanders, 2006: xvi). Technological innovations transformed not only how things were being produced, the methods employed in production, but also what it was possible to produce. For example, with the development of machinery to rivet soles to shoes, men's footwear with their heavier soles became easier to produce and between 1863 and 1893 the lines produced by Clark's more than doubled, rising from 334 to 720 (Flanders, 2006).

Through the eighteenth century there had been a steady increase in material possessions, in the 'acquisition of things', among all classes in England and between 1785 and 1800 'the rate of consumption of what had been considered luxuries and were now regarded as ... necessities ... increased at more than twice the rate of population growth' (Flanders, 2006: 26). By the middle of the nineteenth century, as living standard was being equated with possessions owned and goods consumed, across Europe and America arcades and department stores, and a variety of other means of consumption, were being established at an increasing rate and the signs of a burgeoning consumer culture were becoming increasingly evident.[2]

Department Stores and the Development of Consumer Society

The department store as a site of consumption can be considered a modern equivalent to the Greek agora or the medieval marketplace. From the mid-nineteenth century the department store has developed into a truly transnational institution and in many respects exemplifies the 'global development of consumer society' (Sedlmaier, 2005: 9). The first department store is widely considered to be Le Bon Marché in Paris, originally established in 1838 and which by 1852 had a range of departments selling a variety of consumer goods. However, a less well known enterprise, Bainbridges, founded in 1838 in Newcastle upon Tyne, was sorting its goods and receipts into 'departments' as early as 1849, a few years before the Paris store, and might therefore legitimately claim to be the original department store, but other contenders for the title have also been identified (Ross, 2008).

The establishment from the mid-nineteenth century of department stores in England has been described as a product of the development and convergence of two retailing transformations, specifically the increasing prominence of larger, 'middle-class haberdasheries and drapery shops' with plate-glass windows and gas lighting and the 'expansion of working-class

Figure 1.1　Macy's in Herald Square, New York City (photo Jess Powell)

purchasing power' signifying a growing market for ready-to-wear clothing, which served to encourage 'the development of mass-production methods' (Flanders, 2006: 85). What is particularly worthy of note is the change in scale that was occurring at this time. Ready-made clothing had been available at a price from the late eighteenth century as had an interest in clothing and fashion, but with the emergence of department stores in the late nineteenth century consumer goods were displayed in great abundance. Such stores 'stressed the quantity and quality of the goods they stocked, their wide variety, and the level of expertise of their staff in both acquiring these goods and selling them, as well as the design and layout of their shops'(Flanders, 2006: 110–11). By 1880 the primary source of innovation in department store development and design and the principal catalyst for the growth of consumer culture was America.

The first department store to emerge in America was Zion's Cooperative Mercantile Institute (ZCMI), established in 1868 in Salt Lake City (Mencimer, 2001). Macy's, the better known American establishment, was originally founded in 1858 as a dry goods store but by 1877 had become a department store 'occupying the ground space of eleven adjacent buildings' (see Figure 1.1). In 1902, it moved to its current location, Herald

Square on Broadway and 34th Street and with expansion in 1924 'became the "World's Largest Store," with over 1 million square feet of retail space' (Macy's Inc., n.d.). From the late nineteenth century, department stores rapidly developed across America and with their extensive range of consumer goods, imaginative displays, persuasive advertising, fashionable merchandising, and promotion of style and service they seduced consumers to spend and dominated the retail marketplace.

Reflecting on the wide-ranging transformations which accompanied the development of America's new industrial mass production capitalist economy and mass consumer culture, Leach remarks that the 'impulse toward expansion, concentration, and even incorporation that overtook the rest of the economy' had no less of an impact on merchandising as chain stores, mail order catalogues, and department stores in particular eliminated smaller competitors in 'the retail wars of the 1890s' (1993: 19, 16, 26–32). Although there was expression of discontent about the increasing influence and economic advantage accruing to large-scale merchandising and a degree of resistance from small retailers, by the beginning of the twentieth century department stores in America were being commended for turning America into 'a nation of large consumers'(1901 Federal Industrial Commission cited in Leach, 1993: 30). One indication of the rapid growth of consumption and influential part played by department stores in the process is provided by the sales figures recorded by Macy's in 1920 which revealed that 'it was selling each day what it took … a full year to sell in 1880' (Leach, 1993: 280).

Department stores were established in the late nineteenth and early twentieth centuries in a number of countries, including Australia, Canada, New Zealand, Japan, and China. David Jones was the first purpose built department store to open in Australia in 1877 and in 1890 they began to distribute mail order catalogues; T. Eaton & Co. established as a dry goods and haberdashery store in 1869 subsequently launched a mail order catalogue in 1884 and in the 1930s became Canada's largest and most successful department store generating 60% of all department store sales, finally succumbing to bankruptcy in 1999.[3] Smith & Caughey is the oldest New Zealand department store, originally established by Marianne Smith as a drapery store in 1880. Japan's first Western-style department stores grew out of kimono retailers, Mitsukoshi in 1904 being the first and Matsuzakaya following in 1910. An important later source of department store growth in Japan were the railway companies, which from the 1920s built stores linked to their railway termini, one prominent example being the Mino-Arima Electric Railway Company established in 1907 which became the Hankyu Corporation in 1918 and in 1929 opened the first Hankyu Department store (Hankyu Inc., n.d.). Department stores were founded in China early in the twentieth century, prominent examples being Wing On (Hong Kong 1907; Shanghai 1918), Sincere (Shanghai 1917), Sun Sun (Shanghai 1926) and The Sun (Shanghai 1936) (Mayhew, 2004; Harper et al., 2005).

The development of department stores, along with a range of other retailing innovations, contributed significantly to the growth of consumerism and expansion of consumer choice. The big department stores with their galaxy of consumer goods, devotion to display and, where appropriate, presentation of spectacular exhibits, and provision of a network of services that ranged from 'new kinds of consumer credit (charge accounts and installment buying)', restrooms, and restaurants, to the employment of staff to 'fuss and fawn over patrons' (Leach, 1993: 112), played a key role in the cultivation of consumerism, the mobilization of consumers, and the promotion of consumer choice. The institution of the department store, as George Ritzer (2005: 94) the American sociologist of consumer culture notes, provided a significant early example of the seductive appeal of spectacular retail displays of a growing range of consumer commodities and it constitutes 'one of the most important and immediate precursors' of later ways of marketing goods and services and enticing consumers to make purchases.

From the mid-nineteenth century, department stores have provided impressive architectural structures containing attractively designed spaces and displays of a wide range of desirable goods, structures which a number of analysts have described as cathedral-like or designated as 'cathedrals of consumption' because of perceived religious affinities (Corrigan, 1997; Jaumain and Crossick, 1999; Ritzer, 2005[1999]). Whether the metaphor is warranted is debatable, but the global proliferation of department stores and shopping malls, and a growing variety of other ways of retailing goods and services, alongside the increasing volume and accelerating velocity of consumption in the closing decades of the twentieth century and early years of the twenty-first century, indicated that an increasing number of people around the world had been converted to consumerism, had succumbed to 'the gospel of consumption' (Kaplan, 2008). However, the financial crisis and 'credit crunch', which began in the summer of 2007 in the USA and led, in due course, to global economic recession, falling stock market values and property prices, and rising unemployment, precipitated a dramatic decline in consumer confidence and the resources required to fund consumer expenditure, causing some observers at the time to speculate that credit-driven hyper-consumerism, which from the 1970s had provided the neoliberal capitalist economy with dynamism and growth and late modern lifestyles with purpose and meaning, might no longer be sustainable (Benady, 2008; Soros, 2008).

Notes
1. Indymedia is the online 'network of individuals, independent and alternative media activists and organisations, offering grassroots, non-corporate, non-commercial coverage of important social and political issues' (http://www.indymedia.org.uk/). Slashdot is a comparable but information technology focused news site which describes itself as 'news for nerds, stuff that matters' (http://slashdot.org/).
2. Department stores were being established in Europe from the late 1830s and the first store was established in America in the late 1860s a few years after Isaac Singer had established the Singer Sewing Machine Company as a franchise network to sell its sewing machines to the public. The Great American Tea Company, which quickly became the Great Atlantic & Pacific Tea Company (A&P), was established in 1859 and provided the template for the development of other chain stores across the country. By the late 1890s '1,200 mail-order concerns were [already] competing for the patronage of more than 6 million customers' across America (Leach, 1993: 57, 44, 26). Shopping centers started to be developed from the 1880s, the first open shopping mall being established in the early 1920s near Kansas City, and the first enclosed mall in 1956 in Edina Minnesota (http://history.sandiego.edu/gen/soc/shoppingcenter.html 13/3/08).
3. For further details see the 'Story of David Jones', http://www.davidjones.com.au/about/story_of_djs.jsp; 'Smith & Caughey's: About Us', http://www.smithandcaughey.co.nz/Default.aspx?tabid=88; 'Eaton's: the history and legacy of a Canadian institution', http://www.eatons.com/ and McQueen (1998).

2

CONSUMER CHOICE: RHETORIC AND REALITY

The figure of the consumer occupies a prominent place in contemporary social life, economic analysis, and political rhetoric. Within economic analysis consumption has long been presented as the end or point of production and the interest of the consumer promoted as taking precedence over that of the producer (Smith, 1976[1776]). As J.K. Galbraith noted, within 'virtually all economic analysis and instruction, the initiative is assumed to lie with the consumer' (1969: 216). The growth in productive capacity that accompanied the development of industrial capitalist economies in the late nineteenth century and through the twentieth century led to understandable concern being expressed about the need to generate effective consumer demand for the rapidly increasing range and volume of goods and services becoming available. As productive capacity increased and consumer culture grew in intensity and reach, within economic analysis and political rhetoric, increasing reference began to be made to the importance of the consumer being able to exercise choice and pursue his or her interest in and through the market.

Economic Analysis and The Sovereign Consumer Subject

In some formulations within economics the consumer has been represented as 'sovereign'. The notion of consumer 'sovereignty', drawn from the political realm, was employed initially within neo-classical economics but returned to prominence late in the twentieth century in neo-liberal economic and political thought when renewed emphasis was placed on the importance of adhering to free market principles and keeping state intervention to a minimum (Harvey, 2005: 20–2). The concept, originally introduced in the 1930s by William Hutt, attributed a dominant economic role to the consumer and served to legitimate the idea of the 'free market', within which unimpaired choice could be exercised by 'sovereign' consumers. Within economics it has continued to be assumed that 'power lies with the consumer', that there is a 'unidirectional flow of instruction from consumer to market to producer', indeed it has been suggested that in the market economy there is 'always a presumption of consumer sovereignty' (Galbraith, 1969: 216). Alongside the idea of consumer sovereignty, two related notions, of 'consumer choice' and 'consumer confidence', have increasingly become the focus of social and political comment and economic analysis. Lending further weight to the significance that has been accorded to consumption and the figure of the consumer, in the closing decade of the century within sociological discourse it was being argued that identity, status, and social inclusion were increasingly bound up with participation in consumer activity rather than involvement in production, occupation, or work, and that in our 'society of individualized consumers' freedom was increasingly 'grounded in consumer choice' (Bauman, 1998, 2000: 82–4).

Consumer choice is now regarded as an unquestionable virtue, an indisputably beneficial product of the market economy, and an exemplification of the freedom that is considered to be a corollary of modern capitalism (Friedman, 1982). Although the origin of the term is generally attributed to William Hutt's 1936 book *Economists and the Public: A Study of Competition and Opinion* (Hutt, 1940; Persky, 1993), it is in the work of the 'neo-Austrian school' economist, Ludwig von Mises (1881–1973), that the notion of consumer sovereignty receives its most explicit formulation. Mises was categorical about the economic significance of consumers: it was not entrepreneurs or producers who ultimately determined the course of economic affairs but consumers. As he remarked in characteristic fashion:

> Neither the entrepreneurs nor the farmers nor the capitalists determine what has to be produced. The consumers do that ... The consumers patronize those shops in which they can buy what they want at the cheapest price. Their buying and their abstention from buying decide who should own and run the plants and the farms. They make poor people rich and rich people poor. They determine precisely what should be produced, in what quality, and in what quantities ... The consumer is in a position to give free rein to his caprices and fancies. The entrepreneurs, capitalists, and farmers have their hands tied; they are bound to comply in their operations with the orders of the buying public. (1996[1949]: 270–1)

From this neo-classical standpoint it is the interests expressed, influences exerted, and wishes articulated by consumers that predominate in the market, it is they who 'determine the direction of all production processes and the details of the organization of all business activities' (1996[1949]: 270–1). For Mises, entrepreneurs and owners of the means of production are 'virtually ... trustees of the consumers', they do not rule consumers or have power over them, but to the contrary serve them (1996: 273). Producers are portrayed as dependent on the 'supremacy of consumers', as needing to comply with 'the wants of the consumers' and accommodate to 'the sovereignty of the consumers' (1996: 287). In direct contrast to the view of economic life that presents producers, entrepreneurs, and the owners of property as in possession of economic or market power Mises comments:

> All market phenomena are ultimately determined by the choices of the consumers. If one wants to apply the notion of power to phenomena of the market, one ought to say: *in the market all power is vested in the consumers* ... Ownership of material factors of production as well as entrepreneurial or technological skill do not – in the market economy – bestow power in the coercive sense. All they grant is the privilege to serve the real masters of the market, the consumers, in a more exalted position than other people. Ownership of capital is a mandate entrusted to the owners, under the condition that it should be employed for the best possible satisfaction of the consumers. (1996: 648, emphasis added)

While Mises did briefly acknowledge that 'an infringement of the supremacy of ... consumers' might arise from 'monopoly prices' (1996: 358), ultimately he regarded this as an empirically rare eventuality and he was far more concerned about what he saw as the negative impact on consumers of growing government interference in the market economy.

The notion of consumer sovereignty outlined is controversial on at least two counts. To begin with it suggests that consumers, through the exercise of choice, possess a power and influence to coerce in the marketplace that is comparable to the power possessed and exercised by sovereign political agents within the polity. This comparison is at the very least overstated and ultimately hard to sustain, as Murray Rothbard acknowledges in the course of a lengthy endorsement of the market and the significant part played by consumers:

> The term 'consumers' sovereignty' is a typical example of the abuse, in economics, of a term ... appropriate only to the *political* realm and is thus an illustration of the dangers of the application of

metaphors taken from other disciplines. 'Sovereignty' is the quality of ultimate political power; it is the power resting on the use
of violence. In a purely free society, each individual is sovereign
over his own person and property, and it is therefore this self-sov-
ereignty which obtains on the free market. No one is 'sovereign'
over anyone else's actions or exchanges. Since the consumers do
not have the power to coerce producers into various occupations
and work, the former are not 'sovereign' over the latter. (2001:
561, emphasis in original)

In addition to sovereignty being an inappropriate metaphor there
is a more significant substantive objection to the influence attributed
to consumers. While consumers routinely do exercise choice and decisions to buy or not to buy particular goods and services undoubtedly
have significant implications for producers and commercial enterprises, choices made by consumers are in respect of given ranges of
goods and services produced within economic circumstances and market conditions and subject to cultural processes and influences which
consumers have not chosen. As a critic of nineteenth-century economic
liberalism noted of the structural constraints on human agency, people
make history, but 'they do not make it just as they please; they do not
make it under self-selected circumstances chosen by themselves, but
under circumstances, existing already' (Marx, 1963[1852]: 15). What
is produced does not derive from consumers' needs, rather consumers
are drawn into a 'circle of manipulation' (Adorno and Horkheimer,
1997: 121) in which products are 'tailored for consumption ... and ...
to a great extent determine the nature of consumption' (Adorno, 1991:
85). Consumers do exercise choice and make decisions about purchasing goods and services, but do so subject to a variety of influences,
including manufacturing, retailing, and marketing strategies, as well
as fair trade and environmental campaigns, and not under conditions
of their own choosing (Gabriel and Lang, 2006). As Adorno remarked
in a series of critical reflections on consumer culture, '[t]he customer is
not king, as the culture industry would have us believe, not its subject,
but its object' (1991: 85).

Today's consumers encounter a consumer culture that is highly individualistic, very materialistic, and continually subject to transformation
through the perpetual generation of new fashions and styles and the
relentless development of new product lines and services, which are
enticingly promoted through increasingly innovative advertising, marketing, and branding campaigns, frequently fronted by celebrities from
the iconic worlds of entertainment and sport. It is a highly stratified
consumer culture, one that is differentiated according to inequitably

distributed access to a variety of essential resources, including not only income, wealth, and credit, but also information about consumer products, their potential benefits, and attendant risks. Furthermore, the circumstances in which consumers now exercise their choices include a range of concerns expressed about the potentially damaging impact of consumerism on individuals and communities, as well as worries about the environmental sustainability of an increasingly materialistic way of life which has been producing increasing quantities of waste, rapidly depleting scarce resources, and contributing significantly to global climate change (Simms et al., 2006; Jackson, 2009).

The primacy accorded to the consumer is a fundamental feature of neo-classical economics and the account of social and economic life it has generated generally has constituted the reality 'for legislators, civil servants, journalists, television commentators ... indeed all who must speak, write or act on economic questions' (Galbraith, 1975: 23). Indeed, insofar as social scientific discourses reflexively transform the contexts they analyze, the concepts, theories and findings generated within the discourse of economics 'could not, and did not, remain separated from the activities and events to which they related ... [but] have become integral to what "modern economic life" actually is and inseparable from it' (Giddens, 1990: 41). When the Fordist–Keynesian configuration that had been formed in response to the 1930s crisis of capitalism, a crisis precipitated by economic depression and lack of effective demand for goods and services, itself ran into difficulty in the 1970s as economic stagnation and rising inflation took hold, political administrations in the USA, the UK, and New Zealand, and subsequently elsewhere around the world, (re)turned to neo-classical policies and associated assumptions about social and economic life. Once again the emphasis in economic policy and political rhetoric was placed on the benefits of 'free' markets, the virtues of consumer freedom and consumer choice, and the need to address problems that were considered to derive from 'inappropriate' or 'excessive' forms of state intervention through the introduction of various 'privatization' initiatives and a range of other quasi-market measures. In due course, such policy measures achieved consolidation as 'neo-liberalism' which became 'a new economic orthodoxy regulating public policy at the state level in the advanced capitalist world' (Harvey, 2005: 22; see also Bourdieu, 1998: 2003).

Critical Reflections on Neo-classical and Neo-liberal Economics

In a series of critical reflections on economics J.K. Galbraith notes that it was another, radically different, era when the discipline was establishing its place within the field of knowledge. In the nineteenth century a substantial number of people were still employed in agricultural work, business organizations were small and more responsive to changing market prices, indeed could be considered 'subordinate to the instruction of the market' (1975: 24). Galbraith comments that it could be argued that, to a degree, economic theorizing at the time accurately reflected the realities of economic life. While acknowledging that subsequently there has been a necessary recognition within the discipline of the significance of some later economic transformations, including the impact of the development of 'monopoly – or, more precisely, oligopoly' on markets in particular, Galbraith contends that economics has 'remained the captive of its origins' (1975: 24). A significant number of the established, yet increasingly questionable, assumptions of economic inquiry have remained in place, notably 'the consumer [has] remained sovereign', 'consumer choice [has] continued to control all', and in consequence the discipline of economics is described by Galbraith as having 'slipped imperceptibly into its role as the cloak over corporate power' (1975: 24).

In Galbraith's account of the realities of economic life in the 1970s a sense is conveyed of growing social disquiet and political dissent, with universities, represented as 'increased greatly in size and complexity' and operating as an 'increasingly independent force', being identified as a potentially significant factor (1975: 25). The impression given is of growing public awareness of the unduly excessive power and influence exercised by large commercial organizations, paralleled by increasing public recognition that what may be promoted as an expression of consumer choice, as reflecting need, desire, or fantasy, may well satisfy private corporate commercial interest, but does not necessarily correspond to, or represent, the public will, or serve the public interest, or for that matter, as we now know, lead individual consumer subjects to achieve a greater sense of satisfaction, contentment, or happiness (Schwartz, 2005). As Galbraith commented at the time:

> People can be persuaded and scholars can persuade themselves that General Dynamics or General Motors is responding to the public will so long as the exercise of its power does not threaten public existence. When ability to survive the resulting arms competition or breathe the resulting air is in doubt, persuasion is less successful. Similarly when houses and health care are unavailable and male deodorants are abundant, the notion of a benign response to public wants begins to buckle under the strain. (1975: 25)

The signs identified are of a growing social imbalance in respect of resource allocation and associated attribution of value between private and public goods and services. Emphasis is placed increasingly on the interest of the private consumer pursuing satisfaction and seeking to experience pleasure through participation in consumerism, generally to the detriment of the quality of public sphere provision.

Galbraith is critical of the emphasis placed on ever-increasing production of goods and services for private consumption both within the economic system and in the discourse of economics. A corollary of the prominence accorded to economic growth and ever-increasing production of goods and services, of which Galbraith is critical, is the continual growth in the resources devoted to advertising, marketing, and salesmanship to cultivate appropriate increases in consumer wants and desires. With increasing affluence consumer needs, wants, and desires for a substantial number of goods become contrived, are in effect 'dependent on production ... depend on the process by which they are satisfied' (Galbraith, 1963: 134, 136). Furthermore, the preoccupation with achieving increases in production for private consumption, and the allocation of resources that involves, proves especially costly as far as the provision of public services is concerned. In Galbraith's view, when public services fail 'to keep abreast of private consumption' within a community and 'private goods have full sway ... [then an] atmosphere of private opulence and public squalor' prevails (1963: 211).[1]

If there was a degree of public disquiet about signs of social imbalance associated with the growth of corporate power in the period in question discussed by Galbraith, it was effectively neutralized – distracted, deflected, and/or dissolved – by the turn, following the mid-1970s economic crisis of 'stagflation', to neo-liberal, free-market economic policies, which emphasized the virtues of market forces and deregulation, further valorized the pursuit of private interest, and promoted a consumerist vision of the good life, within which 'consumer choice' constituted the supreme value, while simultaneously proceeding to introduce radical reductions in the public sector and public provision through the implementation of expenditure cuts and privatization measures represented as 'modernization' that would deliver greater 'efficiency' and value for money (Gorz, 1985; Bourdieu, 1998, 2003; Harvey, 1989, 2005). In these circumstances, and in response to what has been described as 'industrial need', the character of universities did indeed change, but not as anticipated. A rather different transformation of teaching and research institutions occurred and the production, status, and value of knowledge changed accordingly (Lyotard, 1984; Smart, 2002).

Within the field of higher learning increased emphasis began to be placed upon 'improving the system's performance'. This led to a redirection of institutions of higher learning, primarily towards provision of the skills and training considered to be necessary to optimize national economic performance within an increasingly competitive global capitalist economy. Universities were transformed into more vocationally orientated training establishments serving student 'consumers' and a burgeoning commercial corporate world (Lyotard, 1984: 49–51). Rather than becoming 'independent forces' the critical role of educational and teaching institutions has been compromised as they have become more and more subservient to governmental vocational policy measures and commercial corporate and military-defense interests and required to contribute to 'the increased reproduction of capital' (Lyotard, 1993[1970]: 47; Smart, 2002; Giroux, 2007).

Consumer representations

The representation of the consumer within neo-classical economics, as 'in ultimate command' in the economic system, is paralleled by the representation of the citizen within democratic political theory, as in 'ultimate authority over the production of public goods – over the decision to have more expenditures for education or for weapons or for space travel' (Galbraith, 1975: 29). The impression conveyed by both representations is that it is consumer-citizens who make informed and authoritative choices and that their expressions of choice are effective. However, in economic life, and arguably political life too, it is increasingly a global 'moneyed oligarchy' that in practice exerts most influence, contrary to the idea promoted through constitutional theory that 'the people exercise sovereign power' (Baran and Sweezy, 1970: 159). Recognition that oligopoly, the prominence of a few firms or commercial organizations exercising influence over prices, was an increasingly common if not 'normal form of market organization', did lead to a minor modification of the neo-classical model, but not to any significant amendment of understandings of the structure, motivation, or operation of the business firm, or for that matter to any reconsideration of the 'sovereign' role attributed to the consumer. To the contrary, as Galbraith notes, the misleading notion that the consumer has 'sovereign' status has continued to prevail and it is assumed that:

> The message of the consumer in the form of increased or diminished purchases is still transmitted to the market; this is still the instruction, the only instruction, to which the firm and industry respond. This instruction tells them where they can find the greatest possible profit, which is their sole interest. *So the consumer is still in control*. (1975: 32, emphasis added)

While the 1930s 'Great Depression' did lead to a minor amendment of the 'subsidiary role' accorded to the state within the neo-classical model of the self-regulating market economy, recognition of the need for greater overall management of the economy and an increased role for the state that was a significant feature of Keynesian economic policy did not significantly change the view of the importance of the market, or the necessity of firms responding to 'the sovereignty of the user'. Ultimately, as Galbraith notes, the 'Keynesian and neo-classical faith are one; both depend on the same view of the power of the market' and the significance of the consumer (1975: 39).

A number of criticisms of the neo-classical system are expressed by Galbraith, including that it is 'not a description of reality' and that it serves to guide 'attention away from inconvenient fact', but he adds that while it remains 'the available doctrine' its hold is not secure (1975: 42–3). Galbraith's work was directed towards overturning what he designated as the 'accepted sequence' outlined in established economic thought, in particular explanations of economic processes in which the figure of the 'sovereign' consumer, exercising freedom of choice and orientated towards maximizing satisfactions, is represented as pivotal. Notwithstanding the eagerness with which some observers have embraced an almost celebratory notion of consumerism, recognizing consumers as empowered, as liberated, as deriving pleasure and enjoyment, and as generating meaning and identity through consumer activity, the criticisms outlined by Galbraith in the course of his discussion of the complex relations of power in which consumers actually exercise choice retain considerable contemporary relevance. Indeed many of the critical observations he outlines in his 'revised sequence' are shared, if not explicitly endorsed, by later analysts who have developed comparable criticisms of the global neo-liberal consumer economy which emerged in the closing decades of the twentieth century (Bourdieu, 1998, 2003; Chomsky, 1999; Klein, 2001; Dawson, 2005; Harvey, 2005).

For example, in the 1990s Pierre Bourdieu presented a series of critical analyses of neo-liberalism, of the renewed emphasis placed within economic policy on the alleged benefits of promoting free market forces, private enterprise, financial deregulation, flexible – 'insecure' – labor markets, and consumer choice. Neo-liberal policies assumed, and sought to further promote, 'the undivided reign of the market and the consumer, the commercial substitute for the citizen', and simultaneously introduced measures to reduce the role of the welfare state (Bourdieu, 1998: 25). The economic regime established through these policies was one in which the primary goal, maximizing profitability, was pursued by means of the increasing deployment of information technology and the simultaneous subjection of employees to processes of labor-force downsizing, deregulation, casualization, and unemployment, producing what has been termed a 'political economy of insecurity' (Beck, 2000). Reflecting on the implementation of such neo-liberal policy measures Bourdieu comments that:

The companies, which offer no security to their employees and contribute to instituting a *consumerist vision of the world*, herald an economic reality akin to the social philosophy inherent in neo-classical theory. It is as if the … individualistic, ultra-subjectivist philosophy of neo-classical economics had found in neo-liberal policy the means of its own realization … the conditions for its own verification. (2003: 30, emphasis added)

It is to an analysis of this 'consumerist vision of the world' that discussion below is directed, a vision that effectively elevates the consumer to sovereign status, possessing freedom and exercising unimpaired choice, not only in the commercial marketplace, where the pursuit of private interest has long held sway, but increasingly within the public sector, where privatization policies and the imposition of internal markets or quasi-market mechanisms, misleadingly represented as 'modernization', have been accompanied by political rhetoric extolling the presumed benefits to be gained by an extension of 'consumer choice' to health and education provision in particular (Clarke, 2006). In his critical analysis of neo-liberalism and global order Noam Chomsky comments that 'we have to begin by separating doctrine from reality' (1999: 19), as we do if we are to give effective critical consideration to the pivotal notion of consumer choice.

Consumer Choice

It has been argued that our society now warrants the designation 'consumer society' in so far as identity and status are acquired and social inclusion or integration is achieved primarily through participation in consumer activity (Bauman, 1998). As noted earlier the suggestion is that whereas the work-based modern industrial capitalist society of the nineteenth and early twentieth centuries 'engaged its members *primarily* as producers' later twentieth century 'liquid' modern societies have increasingly engaged their members primarily 'in their capacity as consumers' (Bauman, 1998: 24, emphasis in original). The controversial implication is that there has been a relative shift of emphasis from production to consumption, a 'passage from producer to consumer society' (Bauman, 1998: 24), and that this is exemplified by the increasing prominence accorded to consumer activity and consumer choice. It is also argued that this shift of emphasis is reflected in the ways in which individual identity and satisfaction now appear to be less and less bound up with job, work, and career and more and more with lifestyle, consumption, and shopping (Sennett, 2001).

The passage from producer to consumer society is considered to be marked by a diminution of the significance of the work ethic and a corresponding valorization of consumption. It is consumer spending rather than waged work that is now considered a 'duty', the 'spending-happy consumer' (Bauman, 1992: 50), rather than the disciplined worker for whom work or labor constituted a calling, who is now a necessity, whose 'confidence' to spend is deemed so vital to economic wellbeing. Where economic deregulation, competition, and market forces are widely promoted, it is consumer choice that is accorded a special significance as 'the consumer society's meta-value, the value with which to evaluate and rank all other values' (Bauman, 1998: 58). Consumerism, a 'market-mediated mode of life', a form of life that recognizes no limits and now encompasses public as well as the most personal and private domains of everyday life, trades on and continually promotes the value of consumer choice, exercise or expression of which by individuals, under conditions that have tended to receive less critical analytic consideration, is generally represented as an exemplification of freedom (Bauman, interview; Rojek, 2004: 304).

In a wide-ranging analysis of the figure of the consumer Gabriel and Lang list some of the positive features that have been attributed to the idea of consumer choice. These include: (1) its assumed value to consumers – 'all choice is good', the more the better, and that consumer capitalism delivers 'more choice for everyone'; (2) its instrumental value to the economy – 'it is the driving force for efficiency, growth and diversity'; as well as (3) its implied political value, 'a social system based on choice is better than one without; choice is the supreme value' (2006: 26). Consumers are continually making choices, routinely so in the course of trivial, mundane, everyday consumption, but as a number of analysts have remarked what is expressed as 'choice' is shaped and influenced by a variety of factors and processes (Galbraith, 1969: 1975; Dawson, 2005; Gabriel and Lang, 2006). In particular analysts have drawn attention to the beguiling activities of cultural intermediaries in advertising, marketing, and branding who have sought to encourage individuals to conceive of themselves primarily as consumers and have attempted to stimulate them in their flights of fantasy to literally buy into the notion that a sense of self-worth, self-identity, and happiness can best be achieved in and through the consumption of an endless chain of things (Galbraith, 1975; Gorz, 1989; Klein, 2001; Dawson, 2005).

At times in the closing decades of the twentieth century it seemed as though policymakers were at a loss to imagine much else beyond the vagaries of market forces driving a globally extensive neo-liberal capitalism and stoking the 'infernal' dynamism of its 'culture of consumption' (Jameson, 1991: 206). The inability to imagine anything else has not been helped by an analytic tendency to marginalize matters of production, including the production of consumer subjects and the cultural value system within which priority is accorded to the figure of the consumer expressing choice. In contrast, an analytic focus that situates consumption in the context of production offers the prospect of exposing the limitations of market rhetoric, in particular the notion at the heart of the neo-liberal position that the 'free' or deregulated market effectively coordinates and organizes the activities of large numbers of individuals pursuing their economic interests in a manner beneficial to all the parties involved, and the inadequacies of consumer orientated models of contemporary social life which are a corollary (Jameson, 1991; Princen et al., 2002; Harvey, 2005; Schor, 2002, 2005).

Reflecting on neo-liberal economic rhetoric in the closing decade of the twentieth century Frederic Jameson commented that 'no free market exists today in the realm of oligopolies and multinationals', that the reality of economic life is radically different (1991: 266). Generally the parties involved in market exchange relations are, on the one hand, individual consumers, miscast as sovereign figures in the myths propagated within economic analysis, and, on the other, large and powerful corporations with the capacity to invest substantial sums of capital not only in the design, planning, and manufacture of goods or provision of services, but also in respect of the intermediary practices of marketing, advertising, branding, and celebrity endorsement deemed necessary to cultivate an appropriate level of demand by stimulating desires and wishes and promoting flights of fantasy on the part of consumers. The equation frequently drawn of the free market promoting increases in consumer choice and consumer freedom has always been contentious for, as Jameson argues:

> the market as a concept rarely has anything to do with choice or freedom since those are all determined for us in advance, whether we are talking about new model cars, toys, or television programmes: we select among those, no doubt, but we can scarcely be said to have a say in actually choosing any of them. (1991: 266)

An increasing number of people around the world now experience a proliferating range of choices in their everyday lives, but equally a significant number of people are bearing the costs of what can only be described as over-consumption in North America, Europe, Australasia, and increasingly in some parts of Asia (Worldwatch Institute, 2004, 2006). As the twentieth century drew to a close there were substantial global inequalities in the consumption of all manner of commodities with the wealthiest one-fifth of the world's population, who accounted for 86% of total private consumption expenditures, consuming 45% of all meat and fish, 58% of total energy, and 84% of all paper, while owning 87% of the world's vehicles. In contrast the poorest fifth of the world's population were responsible for a mere 1.3% of total private consumption expenditure, consuming 5% of all meat and fish, 4% of total energy, 1.1% of all paper, and less than 1% of all vehicles (United Nations Development Programme, 1998: Summary).

With the seemingly limitless extension of the commodity form more and more areas of people's lives have become subject, either directly or indirectly, to the logic of the market, to the enticements of an associated culture of consumption and, as a corollary, to the necessity of choosing, of exercising consumer choice. However, it is important not to forget that the mooted 'passage from producer to consumer society' is not experienced by, or accessible to, all people and that in many parts of our economically globalized world a *necessary* corollary for a substantial number of working people, one involving little if any choice, has been an increasingly rough passage from forms of subsistence, yet relatively independent, agricultural and/or craft work, to extremely poorly paid wage labor in frequently oppressive, unregulated, urban workshops, or export processing zones (Klein, 2001; Labour Behind the Label, n.d.). In short, the experience of people living, for the most part, in late modern, wealthy, cosmopolitan societies, those socially engaged primarily as consumers, is to a significant degree predicated on the largely enforced engagement of men, women, and indeed a good many children, as low-paid producers in the less wealthy countries that still account for the majority of the world's population, one example being Bangladesh where garment workers making clothes for popular retail stores in the UK were found to be working for 5p an hour and doing 80-hour weeks (War on Want, 2006a, 2007).

There is a very high premium placed on consumer choice in wealthy, late modern, neo-liberal 'consumer societies', but the value consumption is accorded is in substantial part economic, as is demonstrated by the significance attributed to the figure of the consumer, whose continuing 'confidence' to exercise choice by spending income or running up debt through credit has been proclaimed to be far more important to the well-being of the economy than a readiness to save or invest, as the response to the global economic recession that began in 2008 and the pervasive panic to do 'whatever it takes' to get consumers shopping to excess once again, served to confirm, simultaneously illustrating Jameson's point about the inability of politicians and policymakers to 'imagine anything else' beyond a return to the 'infernal' dynamism of consumer capitalism.

In Japan in the 1990s and early 2000s when consumer worries about the health of the economy, unemployment, and taxes were regarded as having eroded 'consumer confidence', the consequent weakness of consumption, that is people's apparent reluctance to spend, was identified as a major factor in the country's economic stagnation (Lopez, 2000). In a broadly comparable manner it was reported in 2003 that in the UK and USA consumer confidence had reached new lows and as a result fears were expressed concerning the likelihood of a global economic recession (O'Mahony, 2003). In 2008 in the wake of the sub-prime mortgage crisis in America and the ensuing global 'credit crunch' and associated economic recession, consumer confidence in the UK was reported to have reached its lowest ever recorded level and in the USA it was reported that 'consumers remain extremely grim about short-term prospects' (Hopkins, 2008; The Conference Board, 2008). The downward trend continued in the first few months of 2009 with consumer confidence in the UK being recorded as falling yet again to a new low while in the USA in February an all-time low of 25 (1985 = 100) was recorded (Nationwide, 2009; The Conference Board, 2009). What emerges from reports on the volatile phenomenon 'consumer confidence' is that consumer expectations – unfounded, irrational, speculative, or soundly grounded as they might be – are represented as pivotal to the modern capitalist economy, geared as it is to economic growth and the continually increasing (over)production and (over)consumption of goods and services. Consumer confidence is deemed of paramount economic importance, for the fate of the current organization of the global economy hangs on a continuing growth in the consumer activity it promotes. In a radically different and even more fundamental sense the fate of global ecology is also bound up with consumer activity, but in this instance it is with its transformation, its reorientation, redirection and moderation, at least in the over-consuming societies, rather than with its continuing growth.

Identity

Exercising consumer choice is deemed to have social and psychological value for consumers insofar as it constitutes a means for pursuing 'pleasurable sensations'. It is considered to provide a way of coping with, and to an extent is experienced as compensation for, the uncertainties and insecurities of everyday life, and perhaps above all, for a number of sociological and cultural studies observers, serves as the medium through which a sense of self-identity can be 'fashioned' and 'lifestyled'. Bauman (1998) identifies a striking correspondence between individual identity, unstable, fragmented, and continually in the process of 'becoming' as it is deemed to be, and the qualities intrinsic to what he has described as a 'postmodern' consumer society, in particular the temporary and transitory character of consumer commodities. The correspondence in the qualities increasingly associated with consumerism (temporary and transitory) and identity (flexible and provisional) in late modern societies, as well as the prominence accorded to consumer activity, flow from the implementation of neo-liberal economic policies and the associated generation of a political economy of insecurity.

Neo-liberal economic policies have: (1) radically transformed the world of work and the place and meaningfulness of a job in the lives of many working people, particularly those who find themselves in poorly paid, insecure, part-time forms of employment, often designated as 'McJobs' (Beck, 2000); (2) contributed to dramatic reductions in commodity turnover time through programmed product obsolescence or 'retirement'; and (3) significantly increased the volume and range of commodities and services produced and available for consumption. While a semblance of identity may now be purchased through individualized consumption, any sense of self-achieved in this manner is destined to be temporary, for the consumer process, and advertising, marketing, fashion, and popular culture lifestyling in particular, effectively contribute to the instability of identity through the perpetual generation and relentless promotion of new products, images, and values suggestive of further possible new identities and lifestyle choices. In short, the prominence of neo-liberal capitalist commodity production and associated 'market segmentation of multiple ad campaigns and appeals reproduces and intensifies fragmentation and destabilizes identity which new products and identifications are attempting to restabilize' (Kellner, 1992: 172).

Increasingly the resources employed in the process of identity formation – shaping what we think, or imagine, we might want to become and how we might want to represent ourselves – derive from the consumer marketplace. But while a degree of choice may be exercised in relation to the purchase of consumer goods and services, the range of things in respect of which choice is exercised are largely predetermined and the financial, informational, and other resources such as time required to make a free and informed choice are, for the majority of people, subject to significant limitations. Even the uses to which chosen commodities are put, and the place or meaning they may be accorded in people's lives, are continually exposed to the seductive influences and suggestive powers of advertising, marketing, and branding to which continual increases in corporate financial resources have been directed, reflecting the persisting systemic necessity of continually stimulating fantasies, arousing desires, and reproducing a willingness in people to consume at an increasing rate, which is vital to the well-being of an economy perpetually dependent upon a logic of growth (Ewen and Ewen, 1992; Ewen, 2001; Klein, 2001; ZenithOptimedia, 2008b).

Advertising and the Mobilization of Young Consumers

As one analyst of the conditioning of consumer activity has observed, in the USA people are exposed on average to 3000 advertisements each day, the purpose of which is to promote and sell brands, generally by associating products with exciting and socially attractive lifestyles and/or prominent celebrity figures (Schwartz, 2005: 53–4). It has been estimated that across the world in excess of $US400 billion is spent on advertising each year to try to influence consumer choices. The inference is not that the consumer is a mindless moron or a cultural dope, but rather that advertising frequently does have a significant impact on consumption, on the choices consumers make by mobilizing them in particular ways (Galbraith, 1969; Baran and Sweezy, 1970; Ewen and Ewen, 1992; Miller and Rose, 1997; Sutherland and Sylvester, 2000; Ewen, 2001; Klein, 2001; Dawson, 2005).

For example, research conducted in the USA on young adults and alcohol advertising indicates that there is a strong positive link between exposure to alcohol advertisements and choices made by teenagers and young consumers to increase their levels of drinking (Snyder et al., 2006) and Juliet Schor's (2004) study of the commercialization of childhood reveals the impact of increased advertising of a variety of consumer products and services, including promotion of alcohol and tobacco products and restricted rated films, specifically targeted at children and young people. Children are an important market segment because they possess considerable immediate spending power, exercise a significant influence over household expenditure choices, and finally their status as future potential 'brand loyal' adult consumers makes them an appropriate target for corporate market building, which goes some way towards explaining the significant growth in advertising industry expenditure directed at children, with estimates ranging from US$100 million in 1983 to US$12 billion in 2000 rising to between US$15–17 billion by 2007 (Shah, 2008a).

In the UK and across Europe as a whole research has revealed a growing range of media and sophisticated marketing methods and techniques employed by corporations in sales strategies directed towards children, the objective of which is to attempt to influence their consumer choices in general and their eating choices in particular. The latter constitutes a particularly controversial issue because considerable resources have been directed to the promotion of consumption of foods that are high in fat, sugar, and salt (Matthews et al., 2004; Which?, 2006). New technologies and marketing techniques have led to children being exposed each day to an increasing number of messages promoting unhealthy foods – 'We've identified more than 40 different ways that food companies market their products to children. Some marketing is clear to parents ... but many techniques are more hidden or underhand' (Which?, 2006). One report describes 12 particular marketing ploys involving text messages, Internet, computer games, websites, screen-savers, toys and puzzles, adventure playgrounds, product placement, and stars and celebrities, who are increasingly being employed to cultivate tastes and stimulate appetites for particular foods in children (Which?, 2006). The success of these food marketing techniques in influencing consumer choices has been argued to have contributed towards, if not produced, significant social consequences in the form of rising levels of obesity and associated health problems in children and adults who have acquired a taste for food containing unhealthy levels of fat, sugar, and salt (Schlosser, 2001; Shah, 2006).

The evidence of the impact of advertising on consumers suggests that the 'freedom' expressed in consumption often amounts to little more than a choice between brands, that caught up in 'the frenzy of buying and acquisitiveness to which the ... profusion of commodities gives rise' (Baudrillard, 1998: 27) 'choice' merely means that the dutiful consumer might have chosen to consume otherwise. The available range from which a choice is made, the potential uses, and the meanings that might be accorded to commodities, are powerfully influenced by the 'entire process of the production, distribution, [and] retailing ... of goods' (Philo and Miller, 2001: 66). From a very early age children are constituted as consumers, they are socialized to consume through targeted advertising that is designed to promote the achievement of a sense of selfhood and status through the ownership of things, instill brand loyalty to secure future consumer sales, and generate 'pester power', that is a significant influence over levels of parental expenditure (Hansen et al., 2002; Williams, 2006; Shah, 2008a). Immersed within a dynamic culture of consumption which has become part of the fabric of everyday life, consumers may experience their 'distinctive behaviours as freedom, as aspiration, as choice' (Baudrillard, 1998: 61), but in practice we consumers are being perpetually mobilized by an array of persuasive commercial techniques and seductive images conveyed through sophisticated media that continually stimulate and regenerate the wish to consume, and we remain ever-dependent on the market for the necessary means to do so, the endless procession of attractive 'new' commodities, rapidly proliferating range of appealing services, and available streams of credit on which we have come to depend.

Private Consumption, Public Services, and Choice

Reconciling the interests and rising consumer appetites of private economic subjects with demands for higher public expenditures to improve the provision of public services was identified by Schumpeter (1954[1918]), early in the twentieth century, to present a fiscal challenge to the 'tax state'. A deteriorating social imbalance between private consumption and public services (Galbraith, 1963: 1985) has presented contemporary societies with a recurring dilemma, namely how to reconcile consumer 'appetites which resist curbs on acquisitiveness either morally or by taxation; a democratic polity which increasingly demands more and more social services as entitlements; and an individualist ethos which at best defends the idea of personal liberty, and at worst evades the necessary social responsibilities' (Bell, 1976: 248–9). From the late 1970s the deployment of neo-liberal economic policies led to a series of interventions, represented as 'progressive' and promoted as necessary 'reform' and essential 'modernization', to transform the public sector by introducing market forces and principles along with a variety of costly auditing mechanisms, which were presented as the means for delivering efficiency and value for money. The logic of the marketplace and the figure of the consumer, exercising what has been presented as 'freedom of choice', are no longer confined to the commercial sector or the private sphere of the economy, they are now increasingly being invoked in respect of the public sector. As formerly non-market spheres of public life such as education, health, and welfare services have become subject to quasi-market mechanisms, so, in turn, students, patients, and welfare clients have been reconstituted in political discourse and media reporting as consumers or customers.

The choice agenda has served to legitimate the introduction of quasi-market forces within the public sector. Choice and market forces have been presented as innovations that will deliver a modernization of the public sector as a consequence of providers of education, healthcare, and welfare being required to respond to the demands of public service 'consumers'. Modernization in respect of the public sector is generally depicted in terms of greater efficiency, equated with reduced costs and selected measures of improvement in performance, which, in turn, are considered to signify enhanced levels of productivity and an improvement in standards achieved (Winters, 2006). Choice seems now to intrude into virtually every aspect of peoples' lives as a variety of lifestyles, products, and services are made available and aspects of peoples' lives that were insulated from market forces and entrusted to public sector professionals have been exposed to the market and, as the political rhetoric suggests, transformed into consumer choices.

The New Labour rationale for foregrounding the figure of the consumer in public sector 'modernization' programs was that the development of a more diverse society and a vibrant consumer culture had so transformed people's expectations, that the centralized and standardized 'one size fits all' provision associated with the public services was no longer fit for purpose and compared poorly with the more flexible and consumer orientated operation of the private sector of the economy which promoted consumer choice as a self-evident virtue (Clarke, 2006). While there was recognition that the public services needed increased funding it was argued that people wanted to be able to exercise choice and that by giving them the capacity to do so public services would be improved. As Prime Minister Blair remarked:

> In reality, I believe people do want choice, in public services as in other services … It is one important mechanism to ensure that citizens can indeed secure good schools and health services in their communities … Choice puts the levers in the hands of parents and patients so that they as citizens and consumers can be a driving force for improvement in their public services … We are proposing to put an entirely different dynamic in place to drive our public services; one where the service will be driven not by the government or by the manager but by the user –/the patient, the parent, the pupil and the law-abiding citizen. (Cited in White and Wintour, 2004)

Increasingly within the public sphere individuals are being promised 'choice' and are exhorted to welcome the prospect of being able to exercise their consumer sovereignty by registering their preferences for this or that service, although no guarantee is given of preferences being met. For example, in respect of health and medical services it has been argued that patients should be offered a choice of hospitals at which they might receive treatment and in education that parents should be given a choice of schools for their child or children. Frequently the notion of choice invoked in these contexts by politicians represents little more than a rhetorical device serving to legitimate the introduction of a range of policy measures designed to introduce market forces and mechanisms into public sector institutions. It is far from clear what patient or parental 'choice' amounts to in practice in the case of public sector provision, or for that matter whether choice is actually desired or being sought in regard to public services (Clarke, 2006). Indeed one critic has commented that the 'overabundance' of options which now confronts individuals in contemporary societies is more likely to be experienced as a 'tyranny of choice' than as freedom (Schwartz, 2005).

Within education schools, colleges, and universities are now routinely audited and ranked in terms of various criteria, as in the health sector are hospitals, ostensibly to allow former citizens of a welfare state now recast as consumers in a market society to have information that will allow them to choose the particular provider and/or provision which they feel might more effectively meet their specific needs and requirements. But behind the mantra of choice there lie a number of significant matters that need to be considered further.

Health

In response to the creeping privatization of the National Health Service which became an increasing feature of New Labour health policy in the UK from the late 1990s, one critical observer, drawing attention to research undertaken by the Consumer Council, argued that:

> people don't want a choice of hospitals, any more than they want a choice of fire brigades. What they want is a hospital near them that is as good as any other in the country. The real reason for the focus on choice ... is that you can't have a market without choice-making consumers. The truth is ... we are not being given a market in healthcare to satisfy our wish to choose between hospitals, we are being induced to choose between hospitals in order to make them compete with each other, instead of cooperating as they did in the past. (Leys, 2006a)

This view has received support from other surveys of patients which indicate that 'choice is not seen by the public as the greatest NHS priority and [that] the vast majority put a good local hospital ahead of choice of provider' (Winters, 2006: 14).

While there is, on the one hand, strong political rhetoric about patients as consumers and of the need to give 'choice' in respect of health provision and NHS services in the UK, exemplified by political discourse that transforms patients from citizens who are 'treated' into consumers or customers who are 'served' in hospital wards, there are, on the other hand, a number of examples where policy measures and associated differences in resource allocation between organizations responsible for delivery of medical and health services have served to reduce or prohibit 'consumer' choices. For example, in 1999 in the UK the National Institute for Clinical Excellence (NICE) was established by the New Labour administration ostensibly to drive up clinical standards in the NHS, its specific terms of reference being to review the clinical and cost effectiveness of treatments. However, in a number of critical instances its judgments about clinical effectiveness have been heavily influenced by assessment of the cost-effectiveness of treatments, their value for money according to relatively arbitrary financial criteria (i.e. withholding of approval for drugs that cost more than £30,000–48,000 for a year of good quality life), and in consequence NICE increasingly has come to resemble an economizing mechanism, a medical treatment rationing organization, with the choice agenda and potential benefit to patient well-being being considered very much secondary to cost, if not relegated from consideration altogether.

Because the NHS will not make a treatment available until it has received NICE approval, which may take a considerable length of time, if it is forthcoming at all, a number of cases arose where patients were advised by clinicians that their conditions would be alleviated, quality of life enhanced, and/or length of life potentially increased, by use of a non-approved drug. Where patients exercised choice to pay privately for the cost of clinically recommended non-approved treatment, in many instances they found that they were subsequently heavily penalized for their expression of choice by the withdrawal of any NHS treatment they were currently receiving at no cost and confronted with the requirement in future to pay full cost for all their treatment. In response to growing public concern about the matter and following a commissioned report on improving access of NHS patients to medicines, the Health Secretary announced a number of policy changes, including that in future patients would be allowed to pay privately for treatment with drugs which had not been approved for use within the NHS without losing their entitlement to continuing free NHS care. This represented an acceptance of a key report recommendation, namely that 'no patient should lose their entitlement to NHS care they would have otherwise received, simply because they opt to purchase additional treatment for their condition' (Richards, 2008: 5, recommendation 8). It was also accepted that greater flexibility should be exercised by NICE in appraising more expensive drugs for terminally ill patients and that the 'timeliness' of the NICE appraisal process should be improved.

In the UK, the context in which the notion of the patient as consumer and the associated choice agenda exist is one marked by significant differences in spending priorities between primary care trusts (PCTs). In 2006, analysis of Department of Health data on spending on individual disease areas by individual PCTs revealed 'very large variations in the amount spent per head of population and the proportion of each PCT budget devoted to each disease area' (The Kings Fund, 2006: 3). Furthermore, in 2007 and 2008 there were a number of examples of fiscally driven forms of restructuring and reorganization by PCTs, involving hospital unit closures and cuts in services, including in some instances loss of local accident and emergency (A&E), maternity, and paediatric services, leading thousands of affected people, who were reliant on their local hospital services, to demonstrate, sign petitions, write to their MPs, and lobby the PCTs responsible. With financially driven decisions of this kind, taken in the face of local community opposition, decisions that are not only reducing the choices of existing patients, but also represent a limitation of choice for future patients, political rhetoric or spin is generally employed to try to convince disenfranchised consumer-citizens that their health prospects and choices are actually being enhanced by hospital unit closures, mergers, and associated consolidations of service provision in pursuit of financial economies.

The promotion of a market in health care in the UK led in 2006 to NHS hospitals being given the green light to advertise for patients. The introduction of marketing was justified on the grounds that to make choices patients needed reliable information. The chief executive of the NHS Confederation, Dr Gill Morton, commented that 'publicizing information on everything from operation results to car parking was a vital part of giving patients choice', but the British Medical Association (BMA) and UNISON (the Public Service Union) expressed criticism of the idea of hospitals spending taxpayers' money advertising for patients when such resources might have been directed to increasing provision of front line healthcare. The policy was introduced without any meaningful consultation with taxpayer-patient-consumers who were given no opportunity to express choice as to whether they wanted precious NHS funds spent on advertising budgets rather than on front line patient care (BBC, 2006; Hawkes, 2008).

Choose and Book

Although 'Choose and Book' was formally launched in January 2006 it was not until April 2008 that the 'free choice' project came fully into effect, making it possible for 'patients referred by GPs for planned, non-emergency treatment … [to] choose to have that treatment in any hospital or clinic that can provide NHS standard care, at NHS prices' and to assist patient choice an NHS Choices website was established (NHS Direct). In addition to being able to mount advertising campaigns to compete for patients NHS hospitals were granted permission to pursue sponsorship deals providing that any companies involved were unable to gain 'commercial advantage' from any deal, thereby ruling out Nike sponsorship of a hospital health and fitness program, or Durex sponsoring a hospital sexual health campaign. Entering fully into the marketing ethos a Department of Health director of 'system management and new enterprise' stated 'The NHS brand is very powerful and we are not going to let any commercial activity damage that. It's too important to the public' (Hawkes, N., 2008). However, no limit was placed on the advertising expenditure hospitals might make to attract patients.

For the free choice project to work effectively in its own terms patients need to be in a position to make informed choices and for this they need to have appropriate, up to date, and understandable information on which to base their choices. The role of GPs is crucial in the choice project too, they need to devote time to research the appropriate information required by patients and assist them in making a choice, should they wish to do so. In particular, GPs need to be attentive to resource differences between patients.

But whether they are in a position to empower disadvantaged patients, in particular those who are poor or have low income, the old, and those with lower levels of educational attainment, or significant limiting family commitments, to make a considered and informed choice is questionable. Indeed, it has been argued that there is a significant risk that any gains in efficiency and responsiveness achieved through reforms associated with the choice agenda may well be 'at the expense of equity'(Winters, 2006: 11; see also Clarke, 2006: 436). In addition, as research has established, the ability to be able to exercise choice in respect of location for medical treatment and/or care is affected by availability of suitable transport and time and cost constraints. The affordability of the cost of travel between home and a non-local or distant hospital has an impact on the possibility of exercising patient choice and differentiates more affluent from poorer patients, with the former being less affected by time and cost constraints and more able to choose to travel further to receive their treatment (Propper et al., 2006). As John Clarke states, 'Choice mechanisms carry the risk of reproducing economic inequality (as people spend to 'trade up' within or beyond public services), or they may produce choices shaped by the unequal distribution of … social and cultural capital' (2006: 436).

The 'Choose and Book' referral system, the primary vehicle for the introduction of choice within the NHS in the UK, started slowly and initially had a very disappointing take-up rate. In a membership magazine published by the British Medical Association on 17 February 2006 it was reported that data collected from Strategic Health Authorities across England revealed that 'only 67,820 referrals have been made by GPs in England out of an estimated yearly total of 10 million', that is a take-up rate of 0.007% (*The Register*, 2006). While usage subsequently increased, particularly in the period covered by the national GP incentive payment scheme for Choose and Book – the Directed Enhanced Services (DES) scheme for choice and booking ran from 2005 until 31 March 2007 – it fell back again when the incentive scheme ended as GPs felt they were not being compensated for the extra burdensome workload involved and in any event they considered the benefits of Choose and Book to be limited (*Health Insider*, 2007). An assessment of the system conducted in the period May–August 2006 and involving 104 patients at a London hospital concluded that 'Choose and Book did not deliver choice as portrayed in UK government policy to this patient community' (Green et al., 2008). Further research conducted on the scheme by the BMA in 2009 revealed very mixed responses with some GPs very positive, proclaiming that they would be 'unwilling to revert to paper-based referrals', while others protested that it was unreliable and slow, that they had 'insufficient time to use it', were 'unable to find clinics on the system', and that it was effectively 'completely unworkable' (*Medical News Today*, 2009).

The assumption on which New Labour public sector 'modernization' policy was based was that creating quasi-markets within the public sector inevitably would serve to improve services, because resources would follow demand and those institutions that came to be regarded as 'unpopular' or 'failing' public sector providers would be effectively coerced by market forces to get their act together. However, there is a very real possibility that creating a market within the NHS will prove detrimental to patients and do little to enhance choice. The introduction of a healthcare market will expose hospital trusts to considerable financial uncertainty. The introduction of 'patient choice' and a system of payment for procedures conducted, or treatments carried out, will mean hospital trust income is necessarily going to be uncertain, particularly with the growing privatization of NHS provision. Following the establishment in 2003 of private-sector owned Independent Sector Treatment Centres (ISTCs) contracted to treat NHS patients, the transfer of funds from public to private sector was expected to increase. In 2006, Labour Prime Minister Tony Blair expressing support for an increase in private provision in the NHS anticipated that by the end of 2008 up to 40% of the work carried out by private hospitals would be for NHS patients and funded out of the NHS budget (Hall, 2006; Leys, 2006b). The transfer of funds from hospital budgets to the private sector, plus the costs arising from the imposition of private finance initiatives and the employment of the auditing personnel that are an inevitable corollary of the introduction of quasi-market mechanisms into the public sector, had been expected to increase financial difficulties in the NHS (Monbiot, 2000). As one convinced critic commented, 'the government's idea that marketising the NHS will improve it is not based on evidence, but on ideology' (Leys, 2006b).

Education

As with the health sector the attempted extension of consumer choice to education and schooling has given rise to problems and criticisms. Reports on the early experience of the introduction of parental choice in respect of schooling in particular areas of the UK was at best mixed and in one instance it was suggested that 'choice ... is largely illusory [and] that people would be much happier with a better local school and less "choice"' (Seaton, 2006: 8). Given schools have limits on the number of pupils they can accept the idea of attempting to allocate school places on the basis of expressions of parental choice is a recipe for discontent and dissatisfaction for those missing out at over-subscribed schools. It is not something that can be remedied by quickly re-ordering to increase 'supply' to meet an unanticipated high 'demand' for places. Children

and parents become winners and losers through a process that promises choice and raises expectations, but cannot avoid delivering disappointment and dissatisfaction to those whose wishes are not met. For
those with sufficient financial resources one response has been to 'shop
elsewhere' and purchase education from the independent sector, but
this constitutes a choice that has always been unavailable to the great
majority of parents and with the economic downturn that increased in
gravity in 2008 it became so for a number of middle-class families in the
UK who were forced to contemplate withdrawing their children from
private education as their economic resources declined in value (Tweedie,
2008).

Reflecting on significant differences between experiences in England
and Scotland, one critical observer notes that in the latter there is far
less diversity in secondary education and the 'great majority of parents
simply accept the local council's choice of school', which tends to be
based on allocation of places according to residence in a designated geographical area proximate to the school. The data on parents taking their
cases to appeal in 2004/5 reveal significant differences with only 0.6%
of all applicants pursuing this course in Scotland in comparison to 9.3%
in England lodging an appeal and 7% proceeding all the way through
the appeal hearing process, demonstrating that 'the level of dissatisfaction is much higher in England, the country with the more developed
school 'choice' system', and further, that 'the more choice you offer, the
greater the level of dissatisfaction' (Baker, 2007). In one area of England,
Brighton and Hove, school admissions policy was changed ostensibly to
increase the choice of all parents living in the area. Parents living nearest
the two most sought after schools were no longer guaranteed places for
their children after catchment areas were redrawn. Where expressions
of parental choice led to schools being over-subscribed an electronic bal-
lot or 'lottery' system was introduced to resolve any remaining selection
problems after other considerations had been taken into account, for
example exceptional circumstances such as special educational needs
and the 'sibling rule', that is whether a brother or sister already attends
a chosen school. The change in policy and introduction of a lottery system element led to demonstrations, allegations of gerrymandering, and
threats of High Court legal action and a judicial review (Laville and
Smithers, 2007). In 2007, the first year in which Brighton City Council
employed a random allocation method to determine places at over-
subscribed schools, 16% of parents failed to get their children into their
first choice school, by 2008 this figure had risen to 22%.

Reported data from other local authorities in the UK revealed a comparable trend, namely that in 2008 fewer parents were succeeding in being
offered their first choice of school for their children's education and in the

spring of 2009 a survey of 43 local authorities told a comparable tale with an estimated 20% of children failing to get into their first-choice school (Curtis and Lipsett, 2008; Frean, 2009). Government data confirmed that the raised expectations of a significant number of parents and children were failing to be met and that not only were fewer children able to attend their first choice school but the number who were unsuccessful in being offered a place at any of their preferred schools had also increased (Shepherd, 2009).

Choice: Limits and Costs

There are political benefits to be derived from the promotion of consumer choice-based systems, from allowing individuals to feel that they are exercising their will-to-consume, not least that in the public sector it may serve to legitimate the introduction of quasi-market mechanisms and simultaneously make patients, students and their families, and welfare clients feel in some part responsible for the service provision they are receiving in some areas of their lives because they have had an opportunity to express 'choice'. However, the tendency within neo-liberal policy to conflate range of consumer choice with degree of human freedom is unwarranted (McChesney, 1999). It is a mistake to equate human freedom with range of consumer choice as Marcuse observed in a series of critical reflections:

> The range of choice open to the individual is not the decisive factor in determining the degree of human freedom, but *what* can be chosen and what *is* chosen by the individual. The criterion for free choice can never be an absolute one, but neither is it entirely relative ... Free choice among a wide variety of goods and services does not signify freedom if these goods and services sustain social controls over a life of toil and fear ... And the spontaneous reproduction of superimposed needs by the individual does not establish autonomy; it only testifies to the efficacy of the controls.

> The people recognize themselves in their commodities; they find their soul in their automobile, hi-fi set, split-level home, kitchen equipment. The very mechanism which ties the individual to his society has changed and social control is anchored in the new needs which it has produced. (1968: 23–4, emphasis in original)

It is important to consider what can and cannot be chosen and what is chosen. In respect of the first point, what can be chosen, or what it is possible to choose, in particular areas of the public sector, such as health and education, consumer choice-based systems have been introduced with mixed results to date. However, there are a variety of other strategically important 'public sector services', representing a very substantial element of public expenditure, where notions of choice are rarely, if ever, entertained. For example, decisions are taken and choices are made about exceptionally large expenditures in significant areas of the public sector concerned with military, defense, and security provision, yet rarely, if ever, are the potential alternative options presented to democratic electorates as matters in respect of which they might genuinely exercise their sovereign right to choose how public resources are disbursed.

The issue of choice is very relevant here for there is an important matter of 'opportunity cost', as the 34th US President, Dwight D. Eisenhower, frankly acknowledged in a revealing speech given in 1953 to the American Society of Newspaper Editors. Eisenhower gave a series of examples of the respects in which policy choices in respect of public expenditure on military-defense procurement necessarily meant significant trade-offs with material implications for the quantity and quality of public services available to sovereign subjects, the citizens, in whose names such decisions were taken:

> the cost of one modern heavy bomber is ... a modern brick school in more than 30 cities ...[or] two electric power plants each serving a town of 60,000 population ... [or] two, fine fully equipped hospitals ... [and the cost of] a single destroyer [is] new homes that could have housed more than 8,000 people. (Quoted in Parker, 2005: 414)

How many hospitals and schools might be constructed for the cost of a renewed Trident nuclear weapons system? How many drugs currently not considered 'cost-effective' enough by NICE'S fiscal rationing regime might be available for clinicians to treat patients and improve their quality of life and in many cases extend their lives? What increases in the state pension might have been possible if an illegal war had not been waged in Iraq? What choices would the citizen-consumer electorate have made in respect of such matters had they been given the opportunity of engaging in a genuinely participatory democracy? Would it have been £25 billion to be spent on a regenerated nuclear deterrent, which contravenes Article VI of the 1968 treaty on the non-proliferation of nuclear weapons, to which an earlier UK government was a signatory, or the same sum invested in medical treatments, drugs, and health facilities and staffing that would genuinely protect and improve the survival and well-being of citizens? Currently this type of civic choice is off the agenda; it is *not* what can be chosen, even in democratic states that extol the virtues of choice and promote its extension to strategically delimited regions of the public sector.

Choice is often represented as an unquestionable good for consumers, the economy, and society as a whole, but there are circumstances where restricted or edited choice may prove to be advantageous for communities and individuals. While a consumer culture promoting the value of increasing choice prevails in the USA and the UK, and is proving increasingly influential around the world as others are led to consume in a similar way (Ritzer, 2005), there are some circumstances in which individuals are electing to limit choice, where choice is being deliberately restricted to achieve beneficial outcomes for consumers, communities, and the environment. For example, Japan has a number of consumer cooperatives with around one in six of the population as members. One of these, the Seikatsu Club Consumers' Cooperative Union (SSCU), has 25 branches and provides its 260,000 members with an edited or restricted range of around 600 goods, which it considers to be the best to meet consumer needs, rather than the wider range of around 15,000 goods available at supermarkets (Gabriel and Lang, 2006: 129). Since 1994 the SSCU has given priority to 'the selection of returnable bottles as packaging media for culinary seasonings, soft drinks, and ... [other products, including] soy sauce and jams', as well as other resource recycling initiatives (http://www.seikatsuclub.coop/english/3r_appeal.html 2/5/09). Such measures led to substantial annual reductions in packaging waste (approximately 7700 tons), as well as financial savings in refuse collection costs (about 690 million yen) and a reduction in emission of greenhouse gas (estimated at 2200 tons). The benefits of the neo-liberal era of 'endless consumer individualization' are increasingly being called into question and this raises the possibility, Gabriel and Lang suggest, that increasing ecological problems may lead to more collective, cooperative, and shared forms of consumption, although this would necessitate a radical change in contemporary consumer culture (2006: 129–30).

Rising rates of consumption and the promotion and expression of consumer choice have costs as well as benefits, with costs ranging from personal feelings of stress and anxiety, disappointment and frustration about choices made, opportunities spurned, directions not taken, products and services not selected, as well as the harmful effect of some chosen commodities and services on the health and well-being of consumers, to feelings of fatigue aroused by the recognition of a growing range of respects (e.g. education, health, pension provision) in which making choices has become, if not a necessity, certainly something that increasingly has to be taken seriously if welfare and material interests are to be protected, and other unintended and unwanted consequences of consumerism such as light, noise, water, air and soil pollution are to be alleviated, if not avoided (Soper, 2009: 1–2; de Geus, 2009: 121–2). To which problematic and/or unwanted consequences might be added evidence of significantly reduced levels of personal savings and a rapid escalation in levels of indebtedness following the rise of a consumer society promoting increasing choice of goods and services and a 'live now pay later' lifestyle (Schor, 1998; Offer, 2006).

Reflecting on the fact that rising levels of wealth and consumption of goods and services have been accompanied by a decline in recorded levels of contentment and happiness Schwartz comments that the '"success" of modernity turns out to be bittersweet, and everywhere we look it appears that a significant contributing factor is the *overabundance of choice*' (2005: 221, emphasis added). Happiness, mental well-being, and contentment are not it seems inevitably, if at all, enhanced by increasing the scope for expressions of choice in a corporate-driven consumer culture (Jackson, 2009). Rather the civilization that has succeeded in rapidly accelerating the rate and the scale of consumption appears also to have presided over an increase in forms of personal discontent and depression rather than an enhancement of feelings of well-being (DeAngelis, 2004; Schwartz, 2005; Offer, 2006).

Psychological distress, depression, and anxiety provoked by worries about comparative social standing, the endlessness of the circuits of consumption in which participation is necessary if 'the desire to have the best of everything – to maximize' (Schwartz, 2005: 221) is to be sustained and, no less important, displayed for others, and the rapidly upward spiraling of consumer credit indebtedness, are some of the more problematic outcomes of the accelerating proliferation of choices to which consumers are increasingly treated, exposed, and vulnerable, and to which there have been a range of anti-consumerist and anti-shopping responses (Klein, 2001; Schor, 2004; Levine, 2007). Other consequences that are attracting critical concern include the ways in which the growth in production of consumer goods and services and increase in levels of consumption and expression of consumer choice have led to increasing quantities of waste, a squandering of, in many instances, relatively scarce resources, and a range of other serious environmental problems, including concerns over climate change (Princen et al., 2002; Gardner et al., 2004; Renner, 2004; Jackson, 2008b).

There is accumulating evidence of the problematic consequences of a way of life that relentlessly pursues economic growth, strives to increasingly raise levels of consumption, and celebrates consumer choice as its core value. Appreciation of the damaging and irreversible environmental impact of current levels of consumption and a growing awareness of the speed with which any personal pleasure derived from the experience of consumption may be transformed into feelings of dissatisfaction, disappointment, and frustration suggest that late modern lifestyles need to change (Brown, 2006; Schwartz, 2005). The goal of continually working to extend choice and maximize private consumption has proven detrimental to the provision of public goods, collective forms of consumption, and the environment (Schor, 2004). The increased emphasis placed upon the consumer's freedom of choice and the provision of an ever-growing range of goods and services have been accompanied by a decline in the proportion of people declaring that they are happy or contented with their consumption-driven way of life, by an increase in symptoms of anxiety and depression, and most significant of all, by a growing body of scientific research which demonstrates the world is consuming goods and services at an unsustainable pace (Princen et al., 2002; Schwartz, 2004; Starke, 2004; Simms et al., 2006).

Notes
1. The problem of funding the public sector, to which Galbraith makes reference, was identified early in the twentieth century by Schumpeter (1954[1918]), addressed later by Bell (1976), and duly became the focus of a number of neo-liberal economic policy initiatives (Smart, 2003). However, while for the most part 'civilian' public expenditure has been subject to close regulation, being relatively restrained and at times subject to significant reductions, a frequent exception has been military and defense expenditure which has been 'meticulously excluded ... from all pleas for public economy' (Galbraith, 1969[1967]: 234; 1975: 312; see also Baran and Sweezy, 1970[1966]: 177, ch. 7; Shah, 2008c).
2. To give but one example, the rising quantity of consumer waste being produced and the problems associated with its disposal have led to calls for alternatives to landfill dumping to be introduced. Many existing landfill sites in the UK, USA, and Japan are approaching full capacity (http://news.bbc.co.uk/1/hi/business/3086405.stm;http://www.foe.co.uk/resource/press_releases/20020528000102.html;
    http://www.planetark.com/dailynewsstory.cfm?newsid=20190&newsdate=17-Mar-2003).

3

CULTIVATING CONSUMERS: ADVERTISING, MARKETING, AND BRANDING

In the USA in the late nineteenth century merchants feared that growing productive capacity would lead to overproduction and economic crisis. For some observers it represented a 'crisis of distribution', the problem being how to move the increasing quantity of goods being manufactured on to consumers, a crisis that was considered in substantial part to be bound up with the distribution of wealth and income (Leach, 1993). While many businessmen considered the market to be the appropriate mechanism for resolving the problem of wealth distribution, intervention was considered to be necessary to remedy the distribution problems arising from the rapidly increasing growth in productive capacity. Reference began to be made to the need to produce a 'new consumer consciousness, by transforming the imagination', the importance of diffusing 'desire' throughout the population, and of generating 'the ability to want and choose' through the development of advertising, 'new methods of marketing and ... the dissemination of strategies of enticement' (Leach, 1993: 37).

Manufacturers had been advertising in newspapers in England from the eighteenth century and by 1750 advertisements accounted for around half the content, hence the frequency with which 'Advertiser' was used in the name of newspapers (Flanders, 2006: 130). Initially, more prestigious trades refrained from advertising in newspapers on the grounds that they could exercise little control over the appearance of advertisements, their precise place in the newspaper, the advertisements they would be adjacent to, and so on. However, by 1757 the *Liverpool Chronicle* was able to report that 'it is become now fashionable for very eminent tradesman to publish their business, and the peculiar goods wherein they deal, in the News Papers, by way of Advertisement' (Flanders, 2006: 67). In addition, promotional articles, 'puffs', attributed to journalists, but in practice based on copy supplied by manufacturers, began to appear more frequently in newspapers. Various forms of 'street advertising' taking the form of posters, sandwich boards, and horse-drawn advertising carts became increasingly evident early in the nineteenth century, especially in London, and shopkeepers not prepared to just wait for trade to come to them continued to solicit for business by distributing circulars to draw in potential customers (Flanders, 2006). The later creation of attractive window and interior merchandising displays, introduction of 'loss leaders', extension of consumer credit, and various other stunts and gimmicks, also served to entice customers into stores and persuade them to purchase commodities they may well have not set out to buy (Leach, 1989, 1993; Flanders, 2006).

The abolition in 1853 of Advertisement Tax followed in 1855 by abolition of Stamp Duty on newspapers in the UK contributed significantly to newspaper circulation, the emergence of new titles, as well as to the growth of advertising. Advertising in the 1850s in the UK remained mainly of a 'classified kind', confined to particular parts of the paper and conforming to the publication's general news column layout and type size, with advertisements for 'pills and soaps' prominent, but in the following decades two other categories of consumer goods began to be 'heavily advertised', namely patent foods, with 'Bovril, Hovis, Nestle, Cadbury, Fry, and Kellogg ... [becoming] household names', and new products, 'inventions of a more serious kind, such as the sewing machine, the camera, the bicycle and the typewriter' (Williams, 1980: 176). It was towards the close of the nineteenth century, with the development of 'the new monopoly (corporate) capitalism', that Williams argues the system of modern advertising really began to take shape: operating on a new and bigger scale; promoting a wider range of products; constituting one of the means through which a significant degree of influence might be exerted over the market; and exemplified by the appointment of newspaper advertising managers, the transformation of agencies from simply buying and selling advertising space to 'serving and advising manufacturers', and the formation in 1917 of the Association of British Advertising Agents (1980: 178–9).

For the USA in the nineteenth century advertisements appeared in many forms, including 'broadsides' – advertisements for commercial products and services posted on walls, buildings and fences; 'advertising ephemera' such as trade cards, calendars, almanacs, postcards, flyers, and leaflets; 'house advertisements' that simultaneously promoted products and the advertising agency involved, for example the J. Walter Thompson Company established in 1864 'promoted its name and its work at a time when using an outside advertising agency was not routinely assumed to be part of doing business'; and billboards and signs (J.W. Hartman Center for Sales, Advertising and Marketing History). By the late nineteenth century manufacturers were developing strategies for mass distribution of consumer commodities, some early examples being the National Biscuit Company founded in 1898, whose campaign to promote Uneeda Biscuits – 'Lest You Forget, We Say It Yet, Uneeda Biscuit' – was the first million dollar US advertising campaign, one that many others sought to copy, but such obvious imitations as 'Uwanta beer, Itsagood soup, and Ureada Magazine' were not as successful (Schlereth, 1989: 355).

What lay behind all of the strategies that were increasingly being employed from the late eighteenth century was a notion that customers or consumers could be persuaded or encouraged in various ways to buy particular goods and services, indeed needed to be persuadable to an increasing degree if growing output was not to languish in warehouses and stores. In short, it was widely accepted that consumer demand was amenable to influence and management, that consumer desire could be cultivated, aroused, and directed through the use of advertising and marketing strategies and the spectacle of display and decoration, especially 'show windows, merchandising interiors, and ... colour and light displays', and that appropriate spatial arrangements and aesthetic presentation of goods inside shops and stores would promote increases in sales (Leach, 1989: 106, 119).

To represent customers and/or consumers as persuadable, suggestible, and open to influence in various ways, is by no means to imply that they were or are clueless, or that their desires are false, rather it is to argue that though consumers are 'active' they are not 'autonomous' (Wang, 2008), that while 'processes of choice and decision making ... [may be] willfully shaped by the person making the choices' they are also 'heavily conditioned at several levels by shared group dynamics and experiences' (Dawson, 2005: 55). It is in respect of the exertion of a variety of social and psychological influences that may serve to condition, shape, and stimulate consumer conduct that advertising and broader marketing strategies have been directed. The primary objective being to attempt to identify and influence the motivations that might lead people to choose to purchase and use a particular commodity, including any emotional aspects that might be associated with a particular product or service and related consumer activity. The ultimate objective behind such strategies being to nurture and direct, and/or where necessary cultivate and manage, consumer demand for the benefit of the client – the manufacturer, producer, and/or corporate brand – ensuring that consumers remain 'reasonably dissatisfied' with what they have, sufficiently 'stimulated to desire the new product enough to buy it', and motivated to replace any comparable product(s) they already possess (Dawson, 2005: 95; see also Miller and Rose, 1997: 32).

While it is necessary to reject the simplistic notion of the consumer as a programmable cultural dope it is also important to recognize the limitations of the 'consumerist vision' of the world, that view which portrays consumers exercising a significant degree of power and influence over economic life and depicts consumer culture as simply representing what it is consumers have demanded, what 'sovereign' consumers want and have freely elected to choose. Those upholding such a vision tend to respond to critics of consumerism by suggesting that they are being elitist, that they are guilty of portraying 'the consumer as dumb ox' when in reality, by virtue of the medium of the 'free market', it is consumers who are, in actuality, 'the ones with the power', and further that 'consumer driven culture … [is created by] 270 million Americans' (economist Stanley Lebergott cited in Frank, 2001: 70; see also 296–7). Such a conception of consumer culture fails to recognize that markets are not in any meaningful sense 'free' and that a range of factors contribute to the continuing development of consumerism as a way of life, to the formation of a variety of consumer identities, as well as to the shaping of the social, economic, and cultural contexts in which consuming practices occur (Ewen and Ewen, 1992). Consumers are active and they do exercise choice and make decisions, but they do so under a range of influences and not under conditions of their own making. Advertising and marketing are important influences, 'promising pleasures that mere goods could never deliver' and exploiting the dissatisfactions they engender to lead consumers into 'an interminable series [of economic and emotional exchanges] in which they discard an item which they once thought indispensable, in order to acquire something that satisfies a desire which they did not previously know they had' (Miller and Rose, 1997: 32).

Cultivating new consumers

In one section of the previous chapter attention was drawn to the significance corporations attach to the socialization of children and adolescents as consumers and the marketing strategies they employ to cultivate tastes and stimulate appetites for particular goods and services (McNeal,

1999; Shah, 2006; Which?, 2006; Williams, 2006). Consideration is given below to the tobacco industry and the significance it has accorded to the recruitment of young people as consumers of its products, as well as to examples of the advertising and marketing strategies employed in some other industries to cultivate consumer demand.

The tobacco industry knows from its market research that it is in their teenage years that the majority of smokers take up the habit, which makes young people a crucial market for companies. Researchers found that for young people smoking is 'as much about image as it is about product attributes' and that 'the tobacco industry regards the image consciousness of this group as a vulnerability they can exploit' (Devlin et al., 2003: 4). Access gained by The House of Commons Health Select Committee in 1999 to the internal documents of five main advertising agencies associated with the UK tobacco industry revealed that the industry have detailed material on reasons for 'smoking initiation', including data for children as young as eight years of age, as well as data on the values and aspirations of other young smokers, and that the recruitment of young people is regarded as integral to the future success of cigarette brands. The documents studied revealed that the industry 'is acutely aware of serving young smokers' emotional needs' and that brands and marketing strategies are deliberately associated with attributes of 'youth'. Strategies are developed specifically to 'recruit young smokers' and the industry actively searches 'for ways to bend and circumvent the voluntary regulations set in place to protect young people', using youth style magazines as an important component of their marketing (Devlin et al., 2003: 2).

Cigarettes and tobacco use

The cigarette is a globally popular consumer good, the commercial production of which can be traced back to the seventeenth century. With the development of machine operated production from the 1890s cigarettes were no longer as expensive to make and as companies began to recognize the profitable prospect of mass production, and the emerging potential for mass consumption, they proceeded to increase advertising, especially in the USA and Europe (Whiteside, 1971; White, 1988; Burns, 2007). In the USA in the period from 1900 to 1963 the introduction of new blends of tobacco, improvements in mass production and distribution, and the increasing use of mass media advertising to promote consumption, including campaigns specifically targeted at women, led to a significant increase in annual per capita consumption of cigarettes from 54 to 4345. For many men and women in the 1930s and 1940s, including many health professionals, smoking was the norm. As evidence about health risks arising from cigarette smoking began to emerge tobacco companies began to employ advertisements that referred positively to medical opinion, employing the image of the doctor and invoking clinical judgment to assure consumers of the safety of their particular brand (Gardner and Brandt, 2006). For example, in 1949 a Camel cigarette television advertisement affirmed that 'More Doctors smoke Camel than any other cigarette' (http://www.youtube.com/watch?v=gCMzjJjuxQI, accessed 12 August 2008) and in the 1950s when in the region of 67% of physicians were smoking, advertisements were claiming that cigarettes promoted 'good digestion or beat stress' and tobacco companies were advertising in respectable medical journals (University of Alabama Media Relations). In this period Chesterfields ran a television advertisement with the following message:

> A responsible consulting organization reports this study by a competent medical specialist and his staff on the effects of smoking Chesterfields. A group of people smoked only Chesterfields for six months, in their normal amount 10–40 a day. 45% of the group had smoked Chesterfields from one to thirty years, for an average of ten years each. At the beginning and end of the six month period each smoker was given a thorough examination, including X-rays. The examination covered sinuses, nose, ears and throat. After a thorough examination of every member of the group the medical specialist stated, 'It is my opinion that the ears, nose, throat and accessory organs of all participating subjects examined by me were not adversely affected in the six months period by smoking the cigarettes provided'. Remember this report and buy Chesterfields, Regular or King-Size, Premium quality Chesterfields, much milder. (http://www.youtube.com/watch?v=UyhvHB62ph8&feature= related, accessed 12 August 2008)

From the mid-1960s the accumulation of research indicating a link between smoking and cancer, increasing publication of relevant information on health risks associated with smoking, campaigns by non-smokers, increased rates of taxation on cigarettes, and restrictions on advertising, contributed to a steady reduction in smoking in the USA to a per capita figure of 2261 by 1998 (Figure 3.1).

Growing concern in the USA about a link between smoking and cancer had led to a number of significant developments, including the 1964 Surgeon General's Report on 'Smoking and Health' and from 1966 the Federal Communications Commission (FCC) became increasingly concerned about balance and fairness in respect of the marketing of cigarettes, arguing that the public interest demanded that free air time should

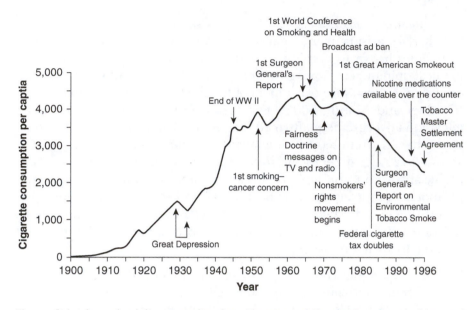

Figure 3.1 Annual adult per capita cigarette consumption and major smoking and health events – United States, 1990–1996

Source: Anonymous (1999) 'Tobacco use: United States, 1900–1999', *Oncology*, Vol. 13, No. 12, http://imaging.cmpmedica.com/cancernetwork/journals/oncology/images/o9912df1.gif

be given to counter 'the paid advertisements broadcast for a total of five to 10 minutes each broadcast day' promoting 'the virtues and values of smoking'. The FCC campaign was upheld by the US Court of Appeal in 1968. The court stated that 'the danger cigarettes may pose to health is, among others, a danger to life itself' and that the commission could use its fairness doctrine to require free time for anti-smoking commercials (http://www.druglibrary.org/schaffer/Library/studies/nc/nc2b_9.htm). From the mid-twentieth century there were a series of class-actions as well as individual private lawsuits brought against tobacco companies for damages and in the 1990s these increased significantly leading in 1998 to tobacco companies signing an agreement with 46 state governments and five US territories to settle lawsuits totaling US$206 billion. The Master Settlement Agreement led to the American Legacy Foundation being established, 'dedicated to building a world where young people reject tobacco and anyone can quit', and given a mandate to develop effective tobacco education programs based on scientific research (Anonymous, 1999; American Legacy Foundation).

Although advertising of cigarettes on television and radio was banned in the USA from 1971 the tobacco industry has continued to direct significant sums of money to advertising and promotion, for example in 2003 US$15.15 billion was reported to have been spent, representing an increase of US$2.7 billion over the 2002 budget, on a product regarded by the American Legacy Foundation as 'our nation's leading cause of preventable death'. In the UK there has been a comparable history, with health concerns about smoking being expressed initially by the Royal College of Physicians (1962), followed by a television ban on cigarette advertising (1965), inclusion of health warnings on cigarette packets (1971), and then following the Tobacco Advertising and Promotion Act 2002, the banning of remaining forms of cigarette and tobacco advertising. However, notwithstanding increasing scientific research demonstrating the harm to health worldwide arising from voluntary and involuntary smoking of tobacco, companies have continued to work to increase sales by generating new markets for their cigarettes, especially in Asia, and now not only are there more people smoking, but those who do smoke are tending to smoke more cigarettes. It is estimated that due to global population increase there will be two billion more smokers by 2030.

The World Health Organization, reflecting on the growth in cigarette consumption from 10 billion to 5500 billion in the period 1880–2000, reported that:

> The consumption of tobacco has reached the proportions of a global epidemic. Tobacco companies are cranking out cigarettes at the rate of five and a half trillion a year – nearly 1,000 cigarettes for every man, woman, and child on the planet. Cigarettes account for the largest share of manufactured tobacco products, 96 percent of total value sales. Asia, Australia and the Far East are by far the largest consumers (2,715 billion cigarettes), followed by the Americas (745 billion), Eastern Europe and Former Soviet Economies (631 billion) and Western Europe (606 billion). (World Health Organization, 2004)

In 1998, China alone accounted for around 30% of the world market, consuming 1643 billion cigarettes.

As markets for cigarettes declined in North America and Europe Philip Morris, the world's largest multinational cigarette company, spent heavily on advertising its products overseas, spending more than US$3 billion in total in 1996 making it the ninth largest advertiser in the world, bought newly privatized cigarette companies, and built distribution and sales networks to expand its overseas markets, especially in Asia, Eastern Europe, Russia and countries that were formerly part of the USSR, where the majority of smokers now live (Weissman and Hammond, 2000; World Health Organization, 2002). Philip Morris now sells more than three-quarters of its cigarettes outside the USA. However, it is not only cigarettes that they export but also the advertising and marketing strategies that worked successfully in America before they were prohibited – 'free cigarette giveaways, television advertising, promotional t-shirts and hats, sporting events and rock music concert sponsorships' – and successive US administrations have pitched in to help multinational cigarette companies to find markets and promote their products overseas:

> Under the guise of providing assistance to needy countries, the Federal Government's Food for Peace program shipped hundreds of millions of dollars worth of tobacco to developing countries until the end of the 1970s. In the 1980s, the Office of the U.S. Trade Representative (USTR), working hand-in-glove with U.S. cigarette companies, used the threat of trade sanctions to pry open key markets in Japan, Taiwan, South Korea, and Thailand. (Weissman and Hammond, 2000)

Moreover, wherever US brands of cigarettes are marketed, Weissman and Hammond note, smoking among teenagers and young girls especially tends to rise. For example, following the opening of markets in South Korea to US companies 'the smoking rate among male Korean teens rose from 18.4% to 29.8% in a single year [and] … among female teens [the rate] more than quintupled from 1.6% to 8.7%' (Weissman and Hammond, 2000). Similar fears were raised by public health groups in response to the insistence of the Clinton administration in the course of bilateral trade negotiations with China in 1999 that its markets be opened up to foreign tobacco imports. Given smoking rates were already very high among Chinese men it was argued that opening the market to US and other multinational tobacco companies would probably lead to a significant increase in tobacco-related deaths, especially given the prospect of 'a surge in smoking rates among Chinese women' few of whom were smokers at the time (Weissman and Hammond, 2000).

In 2007, it was reported that 'China … with 350 million smokers, most of them men, has the highest per-capita density of tobacco users on earth' and that the industry, largely controlled by the central government, constitutes the second-largest source of tax revenue (Schmidt, 2007). Attracted by the prospect of lower labor and manufacturing costs the American company Philip Morris has entered into an agreement with the China National Tobacco company, which 'supplies 1.7 trillion cigarettes to Chinese consumers annually', to manufacture Marlboros there, allowing the Chinese company to benefit by selling its own brands through the Philip Morris international distribution system (Schmidt, 2007). Reflecting on this development Greg Connolly, whose research encompasses projects on the prevention and control of tobacco and tobacco related diseases, as well as work on the structure and marketing practices of the tobacco industry, comments that while the 'companies benefit from the partnership [it is] at the expense of global public health' (cited in Schmidt, 2007). It is through links of this nature and the acquisition of national monopolies that global tobacco corporations have been able to expand markets for their products.

The World Health Organization (2004) describes cigarettes as 'possibly the most marketed product in the world', estimating that in 'the USA alone over $10 billion is spent a year on marketing cigarettes' and that global cigarette marketing expenditures run to 'tens of billions of USA dollars a year'. With the banning of cigarette advertising on television and radio and increasing limitations placed on other forms of cigarette promotion in the USA and Europe companies have shifted their attention to developing countries and have taken advantage of the marketing opportunities they continue to provide, for example, through the promotion of cigarette smoking via television and radio advertising and a variety of other possibilities, including sports matches and tournaments, arts festivals, pop music and fashion events, and so on. In addition, in both the developed and developing world product placement in films and television programs continues to provide opportunities for hidden advertising as does indirect advertising, often termed brand-stretching or brand-sharing, where non-tobacco goods are marketed bearing a cigarette company name or brand logo (World Health Organization, 2004).

In respect of the cigarette and tobacco industry the neo-liberal notion of free markets and consumer choice bears little, if any, relation to reality. The cigarette market is not 'free' but subject to oligopoly and there is continuing 'consolidation' with US, UK, and Japanese multinational corporations now exercising market dominance. Moreover, political administrations in the USA, in particular, have played an important role in making it possible for American tobacco interests to be able to operate profitably in overseas markets where they have succeeded in cultivating consumers for a product the scientifically verified addictive properties of which render any notion of 'consumer choice' meaningless. Tobacco companies have repeatedly justified significant advertising expenditure and associated promotional activity as having little if any effect on persuading people to smoke, claiming that the primary purpose is to promote brand switching. But research conducted in the USA in 1987, commissioned by Imperial Tobacco and RJR-Macdonald of Canada, revealed that while the industry spent in the region of US$9 per person per day on advertising and promotion in an average year, only 10% of smokers switch brands. This finding led Joel Cohen, the author of the report, to comment that 'such expenditure – purely for brand switching – would seem to be difficult to justify economically' and that there was no justification for the view promoted by the industry that cigarette advertising only appealed to and had an effect on existing smokers (1987: 3–4). Cohen proceeded to argue that:

> Nonsmokers, and particularly adolescents, cannot be made immune to advertising effects ... [the industry's argument] is as if a magic curtain could be put in place to shield children, teenagers and others from the impact of these appeals. No convincing theoretical argument or empirical evidence has yet been introduced by the cigarette industry to demonstrate that otherwise effective advertising is mysteriously ineffective for adolescents who have yet to become smokers. (1987: 8–9)

The report notes that the tobacco industry adopts a notion of 'the rational consumer acting on the basis of personal preference and exercising freedom of choice', but goes on to point out that the industry's own research demonstrates that such a view is completely inadequate. There are various reasons why people may smoke but one category predominates in the research findings and that is 'physiological factors', or as a Philip Morris internal document from 1972 states, 'the primary reason is to obtain the physiological response. All other reasons ... are secondary' (cited in Cohen, 1987: 40). Cohen notes how industry research had revealed the addictive qualities of nicotine and its role in creating 'habitual response patterns and maintaining them despite the desire of smokers to quit', long before the 1988 Surgeon General's Report on 'The Health Consequences of Smoking: Nicotine Addiction'. Confirmation is provided by additional industry research documents referring to the 40% of smokers who have tried to quit the habit in the previous year, only to fail, as 'a vulnerable group'. To further emphasize how inappropriate a notion of consumer choice is in this context Cohen draws attention to proposed advertising copy for a brand of cigarettes, Vantage Lights, which reads 'You had to make a choice when it came to smoking'. When this statement was placed before a consumer focus group of smokers they reacted very negatively commenting that 'they did not make a choice when they began smoking, they began for fun and enjoyment without regard for the fact that it would be difficult to stop if they should want to. Now when they would like to stop smoking they find that there is no choice ... habits are too deeply ingrained for smoking to be considered a choice' (Cohen, 1987: 40–1).

Fast food and alcohol consumption

Broadly comparable arguments have been outlined in respect of some other forms of consumption, including the development of tastes for unhealthy foods, particularly fast foods high in fat, sugar, and salt (Martindale, 2003; Ofcom, 2004) and the relationship between exposure to alcohol advertising and promotion and alcohol usage, especially among adolescents (Alcohol Concern, 2004). The contributions from the drink industry and critics concerned about the influence of alcohol advertising broadly resemble arguments presented in relation to cigarettes and tobacco. Alcohol Concern's view is that the drink industry would not be spending the substantial sums that it does – in 2001 in the UK£181.3 million was spent on alcohol advertising – unless it expected to generate increased sales and profits. The view from the drink industry is that consumers are 'independent rational decision makers with needs and desires that can be met through the goods/services they choose to purchase' and that rather than serving to increase market size and/or volumes consumed, alcohol advertising merely constitutes a 'weapon in the war between brands for market share' (Alcohol Concern, 2004: 2). However, research drawing on local North American studies and data from 20 Organization for Economic Cooperation and Development (OECD) countries, indicates otherwise by showing that significant increases in the advertising of alcohol has led to substantial increases in consumption levels (Alcohol Concern, 2004: 3).

A very different, but no less relevant example, and one which also challenges the consumerist vision, is provided by marketing strategies introduced to generate new markets in the Asia-Pacific region for another consumer commodity, the commercial deodorant, a product which was first developed in the late nineteenth century.

Deodorant marketing

In 2008, it was reported that sales of deodorants in the more developed consumer regions, including the USA and Western Europe, had reached saturation point and that two sources of future market growth remained available to producers. These have been identified as, on the one hand, innovations in the use of natural materials and the development of more gender-specific products, with distinctive packaging, and employing enhanced advertising, and, on the other hand, targeting the expanding populations and rising levels of disposable income becoming available to some consumers in Latin America and Asia-Pacific regions.

In respect of the former it is argued that 'demographic factors such as gender and age are emerging as key factors for deodorant manufacturers across the world' (Mortished, 2008: 5). Manufacturers have recognized the success of campaigns to increase emphasis on personal grooming, hygiene, and appearance among male consumers and have introduced gender-specific products in order to take advantage of the potential growth opportunities represented by male consumers. The drive to increase sales has also led to a focus on young adult and teenage consumers. But the most significant aspect of the report is the reference made to the challenge of developing a market for deodorants in regions of the world where there is an apparent lack of self-consciousness about body odor and seemingly no consumer need waiting to be met. There is intense competition between a few major corporations in the global deodorant market, the likes of Unilever, Procter & Gamble, Henkel/Dial, Church & Dwight, Beiersdorf AG, and Colgate-Palmolive Company (Global Industry Analysts Inc., 2008). Reflecting on potential markets one Unilever executive is reported to have commented that 'Asia is a market we have never really cracked. They don't think they smell'. He is quoted as describing the region as a 'billion pound opportunity, the last empty space on the map'. According to Unilever only 7% of Asians use a deodorant and consumption in India and China is reported to be 'virtually nil' (Mortished, 2008).

Comparing Asia with the UK the Unilever representative is reported to have remarked that 'Before the Second World War we didn't use deodorant … and [that] *it took upfront advertising to educate a generation of Britons about body odor*. "The sense of paranoia created the market"' (Mortished, 2008: 5, emphasis added). In short, a deliberate commercial strategy was developed to persuade, embarrass, and/or shame consumers into engaging in a re-appraisal of their bodies, and how they might appear and be experienced by others, in order that they might subsequently be induced to purchase a product for which they previously felt no need or desire. Now it is potential Asian consumers who are being targeted and while it might be argued that '[n]obody can blame a transnational deodorant maker for fantasizing about refreshing the 2.6 billion armpits of China, of which 70 percent belong to rural residents – never minding the fact that Chinese people, especially poor country folks, don't use deodorants' (Wang, 2008: 272) – it demonstrates the inappropriateness of the notion of 'consumer sovereignty' and some of the mundane respects in which 'consumer choice' is subject to deliberate corporate cultivation and conditioning.

Also worthy of note here is a very questionable assumption on which the commercial campaign to promote deodorant sales in Asia is based, notably that there might be a universal requirement for such a commodity and that a significant demand for deodorant products might be generated. The commercial corporations involved seem to lack any awareness of traditional Asian hygiene practices, for example the long-standing use of alum crystals to remove body odor, and appear to be unaware of significant physiological differences, notably that East-Asians have markedly fewer apocrine sweat glands, the main cause of body odor, compared to people from other ethnicities.

However, in the particular case of Japan, it has been suggested that while people have never been fond of strong perfumes and are inclined to consider distinctive smelling scents and other comparable products, such as aftershaves, as equally offensive as more natural smells, there are increasing signs that body odor is becoming a matter of concern, especially for Japanese women discomfited by the smell of middle-aged men, and that this is leading to a variety of new consumer products, including impregnated shirts that are said to cut down or eliminate body odor altogether. Reflecting on this development a Japanese analyst, Dr Shoji Nakamura, who works for cosmetic corporation Shiseido, suggested that a growing awareness of and sensitivity to different bodily odors among Japanese people, and among young women in particular, may well be a consequence of a cultural shift in the way in which people have begun to live, specifically that a change from multi-occupation dwellings, where living at close quarters people become accustomed to many different smells, to more people living alone, has led to people becoming more sensitive to the smell of others (Hindell, 2000; see also Low, 2005). Additional factors that might be explored through further research in this regard would be the relationship between ethnicity, diet, and body odor, including the possible impact of dietary changes on body odors, as well as various cultural conceptions of the relationship, exemplified by the reaction attributed to Japanese people on first coming into contact with Europeans, who were considered to have unpleasant body odor because of a diet that included animal fat, hence the description of them as *bata kusai* – 'stinking of butter' – a derogatory term that is still employed for things considered unpleasantly or excessively 'Western' (Malcolm, 2001: 182; see also Drobnick, 2006).

The discussion of research presented above on issues associated with the cultivation of demand for products such as cigarettes, fast food and alcohol, and deodorants, puts into perspective the autonomy attributed to the consumer which is a feature of the 'consumerist vision' and for that matter some social science narratives on modern consumerism (Campbell, 1987). While consumers are certainly active their demands are, in varying degrees, subject to influence, open to persuasion and suggestion, and amenable to cultivation, management and direction (Ewen, 2001). When consumer choice is expressed it is in reality the product of wants, desires, and fantasies which have been subject to complex processes of conditioning to which a number of intermediaries in the fields of product design, advertising, marketing, and branding will have contributed in a variety of ways and with varying degrees of significance.

Advertising Expenditure

Before turning to a consideration of some of the critical views expressed by particular analysts on the subject of the part played by advertising and marketing in the cultivation, management, and expression of consumer demand, it is worth briefly taking stock of the increasing scale of resources that have been directed to advertising products and services. Advertising agencies are now significant businesses with leading international agencies reporting substantial worldwide annual revenues. In 2007, the world's top

Table 3.1   Top 10 global marketers by revenue, 2007

Company	Country	Revenue ($US)
Proctor & Gamble Co.	USA	9.358 billion
Unilever	UK	5.295 billion
L'Oreal	France	3.426 billion
General Motors Corp	USA	3.345 billion
Toyota Motors Corp	Japan	3.202 billion
Ford Motor Co.	USA	2.902 billion
Johnson & Johnson	USA	2.361 billion
Nestle	Switzerland	2.181 billion
Coca-Cola Co.	USA	2.177 billion
Honda Motors Co.	Japan	2.047 billion

Note: Companies based in the USA accounted for 48 of the top 100 global marketers and 43.3% of the total measured worldwide advertising expenditure was in the USA, with 35% in Europe and 15% in the Asia-Pacific region.

Source: Advertising Age (2008b: 3–7). Reprinted with permission, adage.com/datacenter.

five agencies ranked by revenue were Omnicom Group (US$12.7 billion), WPP Group (US$12.4 billion), Interpublic Group of Cos. (US$6.5 billion), Publicis Groupe (US$6.4 billion) and Dentsu (US$2.9 billion). Out of the top 50 agency companies ranked according to revenue 27 were based in the USA (*Advertising Age*, 2008a; see also Sklair, 2002: 181). In the same year the top 10 'global marketers', the corporations with the highest measured worldwide advertising expenditure, were as given in Table 3.1.

Advertising expenditure in America is estimated to have increased from around US$50 million in 1867, to US$360 million in 1890, and to just under US$2 billion by 1919. By 1945, advertising expenditure across all media was reported to have risen to just under US$3 billion, but in the years immediately following the end of World War II expenditure grew rapidly, reaching US$10.3 billion by 1957, almost doubling in size by the early 1970s to US$19.5 billion, and then increasing more than tenfold to US$215.3 billion by the end of the century, before rising to US$271 billion by 2005 (Baran and Sweezy, 1970: 122–3; Klein, 2001; Galbi, 2005). In the UK advertising expenditure also increased steadily in the early years of the century rising from £17.2 billion in 2003 to £19.4 billion in 2007, however, the fastest developing advertising market in this period was in China where between 1997 and 2006 advertising expenditure was reported to have increased more than 13-fold (Advertising Association, 2008; World Advertising Trends, 2007).

Modern forms of advertising began to appear in China in 1926 when The China Commercial Advertising Agency was established by C.P. Ling, but it was disrupted by World War II, revived in 1945, and then subjected to socialist reform from 1959. Following the Cultural Revolution in the mid-1960s 'advertising almost completely disappeared from the Chinese media until 1978' (Swanson, 1990: 21). With the introduction of economic reforms from the late 1970s advertising was rehabilitated, one Communist Party newspaper affirming that advertising constituted 'a means of promoting trade, earning foreign exchange, and opening the eyes of the masses' (cited in Swanson, 1990: 22). In 1979, advertising industry revenue in China amounted only to 10 million yuan. However, by 2003 it had increased to over 100 billion yuan and by 2007 it had grown into a 174.1 billion yuan industry. Over the period 1979–2007 employment in the industry increased rapidly from around 1000 to 1.11 million people (*Modern Advertising*, 2007).

From the late 1970s the gradualist process of economic reform initiated by the Chinese government transformed agricultural production and then other industries, including the broadcasting media. A deal struck between CBS and the Chinese authorities in 1982 to allow '320 minutes of air time for commercials on Chinese TV in exchange for sixty hours of US television programmes' is described by Sklair (2002: 267) as opening 'the floodgates for the rapid expansion of the Chinese advertising industry, which rocketed from ten (state-run) agencies in 1980 to 7,000 (mostly not state-run) in 1988'. In 1983, the Association of Chinese Advertising was established and a process of decentralization of broadcasting administration began. A period of rapid media expansion and liberalization followed which contributed to the rapid growth of terrestrial television stations and print media. Between 1984 and 1990 'the number of terrestrial television stations increased from 93 to 509' and by the end of 1995, a year after the passing of the Advertising Law of the People's Republic of China, there was a total of 2740 stations comprising terrestrial broadcasters, cable stations, and university television channels, each of which, along with a growing print media, looked increasingly to advertising revenue to compensate for declining state funding (Keane and Spurgeon, 2004: 2; *Modern Advertising*, 2007). Following China's accession to the World Trade Organization in 2001 the advertising industry was further transformed by being opened up to international competition and 'market reform'. By 2002, there were 2901 television stations, 710 radio stations, 2235 newspapers, and 252 cable channels in China, all of which were principally advertiser funded, and total advertising expenditure was reported to have grown to an estimated US$18.6 billion (Keane and Spurgeon, 2004). In 2004, it was reported that television, newspaper, and magazine advertising expenditure had increased by 32% over the previous year to reach US$34.3 billion (*China Daily*, 2004).

Global advertising expenditure in major media continued to increase in the early years of the twenty-first century and was estimated to have risen from US$345.7 billion in 2003 to US$369.7 billion in 2004 (ZenithOptimedia, 2004). Moreover, despite the credit squeeze that affected major Western economies in 2007, global advertising expenditure continued to grow, the increase being attributed in part to a series of internationally significant events which took place in the course of 2008, notably the UEFA Euro Football tournament, the Beijing Olympics, and the US Presidential election. Each of these events was considered to have played an important part in generating an increase in global advertising expenditure, but the continuing growth of developing markets was identified as the major contributor (ZenithOptimedia, 2007: 2008a). World advertising expenditure estimated to be US$453.5 billion in 2006 and US$485 billion in 2007 increased to US$491.6 billion by December 2008 (ZenithOptimedia, 2007: 2008b). But global advertising expenditure was anticipated to decline in 2009 following further evidence of deterioration in the prospects for the global economy (ZenithOptimedia, 2008b).

Promotion of Consumer Demand

The modern consumer, an abstract figure possessing needs, wants, and desires that are expressed in and through choices made in the impersonal setting of the marketplace, is argued to exist in a world that is subject to 'an organized system of commercial information and persuasion' (Williams, 1980: 179), a world in which decisions about the purchase of goods and services are conditioned by the generation and circulation of seductive advertising images and deployment of sophisticated marketing techniques (Ewen and Ewen, 1992; Ewen, 2001; Dawson, 2005).

From the late nineteenth century analytic attention has been directed to the development and impact of advertising, marketing, and salesmanship on consumption. In the 1920s the American social and economic analyst Thorstein Veblen (2006[1923]) drew attention to the growth of corporate marketing and salesmanship and the subtle methods employed to redesign product lines and influence the decisions of prospective consumers. Veblen anticipated that as manufacturing costs fell the financial resources available for marketing budgets would be destined to increase. In the late twentieth century, in the context of a global neo-liberalization of trade, many large corporations have effectively withdrawn altogether from manufacturing, electing to have 'products made for them by contractors, many of them overseas', while they invest their financial resources in global advertising, marketing, and brand promotion campaigns designed to attract, if not produce, consumers (Klein, 2001: 4).

In an increasingly competitive economic environment modern corporations have turned more and more to advertising, marketing, and salesmanship to promote consumption and as they have done so the distinction between 'workmanship [production proper] and salesmanship [advertising, marketing, and branding, that is productive work directed to the cultivation of consumers] has progressively been blurred' (Veblen, 2006: 300). Reflecting on the process of erosion to which a categorical distinction between production costs proper and sales and marketing costs has been subject, Veblen commented that 'the fabrication of customers can now be carried on as a routine operation … under the surveillance of technically trained persons who might fairly be called *publicity engineers*' (2006: 306, emphasis added). As expenditure on marketing and salesmanship has grown increasing specialization has led to rising employment opportunities for 'publicity engineers'. The brief for those working in advertising, marketing, branding, and design has been to promote increasing global consumption of goods and services, to stimulate consumption by working not only on people's pursuit of pleasure, but also on their 'fear of losing prestige' if they do not keep pace with escalating levels of consumption, thereby contributing to the process that turns 'articles of superfluous consumption into items of morally necessary use' (Veblen, 2006: 310, 395).

The issue identified by Veblen of the increasing significance of publicity and marketing and associated redirection of resources from manufacturing to 'the sales effort' has become even more relevant with the passage of time as a number of analysts have noted (Galbraith, 1963, 1969; Baran and Sweezy, 1970; Klein, 2001; Dawson, 2005). Taking stock of the growth of affluence in American society in the mid-twentieth century Galbraith took issue with economic orthodoxy and the 'conventional wisdom' it sought to disseminate by drawing attention to the respects in which 'production, not only passively through emulation, but actively through advertising and related activities, creates the wants it seeks to satisfy' (1963: 134). Rather than viewing the demands and choices of consumers as imperatives to which producers needs must respond, Galbraith draws attention to the ways in which production, what gets produced, and the wants and desires (or demands and choices) of consumers, achieve articulation through 'modern advertising and salesmanship':

> A broad empirical relationship exists between what is spent on production of consumers' goods and what is spent in synthesizing the desires for that production. A new consumer product must be introduced with a suitable advertising campaign to arouse an interest in it. The path for an expansion of output must be paved by a suitable expansion in the advertising budget. *Outlays for the manufacturing of a product are not more important in the strategy of modern business enterprise than outlays for the manufacturing of demand for the product.* (1963: 133–4, emphasis added)

Galbraith proceeds to note how as consumption increases with affluence, so through processes of suggestion and emulation, and corporate advertising, marketing and salesmanship, consumer wants, desires, expectations, aspirations, and ambitions continue to grow. Moreover, he suggests that the further consumers are from 'physical need' as a consequence of 'increasing affluence', the more susceptible or vulnerable they are to 'persuasion or management' as to the goods and services they choose to purchase (Galbraith, 1969: 207). The specific objective of corporate strategies of persuasion or management is to get consumers to purchase their particular products and services, but the more general aim of advertising and marketing, Galbraith contends, is to 'shift the locus of decision in the purchase of goods from the consumer where it is beyond control to the firm where it is subject to control' (1969: 210). The aim being to cultivate 'loyalty' and generate 'brand recognition' so that the firm or corporation can anticipate that 'if they make it we will buy it', not just once, but over and over again.

It is often argued that increases in productive capacity have led to increasing consumer choice, but while in respect of some products the range of goods has increased, in respect of other aspects of consumer activity choice has diminished (Gabriel and Lang, 2006). For example, consider the impact of consolidation in the food retail market where the growth of supermarket monopolies has driven many independent retailers out of business, thereby diminishing a significant aspect of choice for the majority of consumers, namely removing the option of choosing to buy food from independent specialist retailers. As one report states, 'Supermarkets claim that they provide choice to consumers, but in reality they often erode *real* choices for people' (Friends of the Earth, 2005: 2). Moreover, with the growth of monopolies increasing resources have been devoted to advertising and marketing which have become 'the principal means for establishing and maintaining' differences between the products of competitors:

> differentiation is sought chiefly by means of advertising, trademarks, brand names, distinctive packaging and product variation; if successful, it leads to a condition in which the differentiated products cease, in the view of consumers, to serve as close substitutes for each other. (Baran and Sweezy, 1970: 121)

Advertising, Marketing, and Branding

Corporate advertising before the 1950s tended to be focused on product promotion and was pitched at a consumer market that, in the absence of any detailed knowledge and understanding of 'who their customers were and how they perceived, thought, and acted', was treated as undifferentiated, as a mass market, which it largely was until the late 1940s and early 1950s (Dawson, 2005: 108). Recognition of the need to go beyond merely promoting products, to what had been presumed to be a mass market of undifferentiated consumers, and to target particular categories of consumer, specific market segments, and ultimately market niches, is traced by Dawson to the rapid dissipation of the money, savings, and purchasing power Americans had accrued in the course of World War II, when employment was buoyant, wages were relatively high, and there was a 'more equitable distribution of a much greater national income', and the subsequent (re-)emergence of corporate concerns about stagnant markets (2005: 38, 40). Dawson notes that wartime demands and the need for military production had restricted the availability of consumer goods and led to a significant increase in personal savings, but that these were rapidly eroded in the post-war consumer boom, declining from US$37 billion in 1945 to a mere US$5 billion by 1947, and that as the positive economic effects associated with the war-time period declined so corporations realized that they could no longer count on a 'monolithic mass market' and that 'they needed new methods of targeting consumers more precisely' (2005: 40, 41).

With the post-World War II return to restrictions on the incomes of working-class consumers and the consequent relative deterioration in consumer spending power, the matter of how to generate a sufficient growth in demand to meet rapidly rising productive capacity led to a heightened corporate awareness of the limitations and increasing ineffectiveness of existing mass marketing schemes and, in due course, to what has been termed a 'marketing revolution' (Dawson, 2005). The 'marketing revolution' led to a significant shift of emphasis in corporate advertising and promotion from the product and 'sales approach' to the consumer and 'marketing approach', and with this shift advertising came to be regarded as one aspect of modern marketing strategy. It led to a movement away from a predominantly 'product-centered strategy of advertising creation' to the generation of 'user-centered messages intended to persuade precisely targeted audiences through themes of "self-fulfillment, escape and private fantasy"' (Dawson, 2005: 109).

Rather than regarding themselves as 'goods purveyors to whom product users came for their own inscrutable reasons', from the 1950s corporate executives increasingly considered that they needed to 'actively seek to find out and managerially manipulate the needs and desires, both actual and potential, of their customers' (Dawson, 2005: 33). A first step was to identify potential consumers, to distinguish those who might be susceptible to persuasion to purchase from those who might be less receptive or lacking in the necessary resources, in order that marketing budgets and associated advertising and promotional campaigns might be directed towards the more likely targets. Targeting is an important part of marketing strategy and it has become increasingly effective as data about consumers (demographic profiles, lifestyles, socioeconomic status, spending patterns and interests, etc.) has become more plentiful, readily available, and rapidly analyzable. But identifying and targeting the market or market segment is merely one part of a complex process that involves motivation research, product management, and sales communication (Dawson, 2005).

While within the discourse of economics the conventional wisdom has been that the consumer is 'sovereign' and engages freely in expressing choice in the marketplace, corporate marketing agencies must work with a different notion, one that considers consumers as open or vulnerable to influence, suggestion, persuasion, and enticement, otherwise there would be little point in trying to find out what motivates consumers to purchase and use particular products and services, or attempting to affect where they shop and what they buy. Motivation research has thrown up a range of alternative tactics that marketing agencies can employ to try 'to influence targeted *potential* buyers to become *actual* buyers' (Dawson, 2005: 56). The various tactics employed to promote products and trigger sales identified by Dawson include the following:

(1) Psychological tactics – the attempted creation of a connection between a product and strong emotional feelings.
(2) Information control tactics – involving strategic deployment and selective presentation of product information.
(3) Promotional tactics – use of provocative or striking messages and price claims to attract attention and interest.
(4) Existential tactics – trying to convey the impression that given the nature of 'the structures and flows of individuals' everyday existence' purchase of a particular product is virtually unavoidable. (2005: 61–4)

Marketing, as Dawson cautions, is not monolithic, but marketers do have at their disposal a good deal of information about consumers and the decisions they make in respect of how and where they shop, what they buy, and even the use(s) they make of goods, which makes possible various forms of interaction with consumers and opens up the possibility of employing 'stealth and superior knowledge' to manipulate 'the motivations of prospective buyers' (2005: 60, 53, 56).

Advertising and marketing aim to alert consumers to products, to induce positive feelings about innovations in design and performance in respect of familiar products (the corollary of which is fueling discontent and dissatisfaction with pre-innovation products), and to arouse desire for new products, the common objective being to raise interest and increase the prospect of a purchase being made. In addition, as part of the process of attempting to generate sales and profits in a context where there are an increasing number of competing products, a good many of which consumers may find virtually indistinguishable, corporations have turned to marketing, and in particular to branding, to position or place their products in the minds of consumers and, when and where possible, to create buyer attachment to a specific product, or loyalty to and affinity with a particular brand. In anticipation of potential consumer indifference towards products and/or problems that might arise from difficulties experienced by consumers attempting to differentiate between comparable products (for example, the similar tasting Coca-Cola and Pepsi-Cola), problems which may be exacerbated by the increasing proliferation of consumer goods on the market, commercial corporations have sought to create brand identity, to attempt to associate unique positive qualities and attributes with their particular brand, qualities and attributes that it is hoped will resonate with consumers and quite literally create a difference by making their brand of product stand out from the rest (Dawson, 2005).

What counts with a brand is the perception consumers have of it, the image that comes to mind when the brand name or logo appears, as well as lifestyle, status, attitude, and emotional associations and attachments which may be aroused by it (Klein, 2001; Walker, 2008; Wang, 2008). It is not so much the commodity and its utility that consumers now relate to as the brand, or branded product. The way consumers relate to commodities is subject to a range of signifiers, including shop-window displays, advertising, and marketing campaigns, and increasingly brand name and/or logo, with all the connotations involved (Baudrillard, 1998). As the advertising executive, Angus Ogilvy, remarked:

> A brand is a complex symbol. It is the intangible sum of a product's attributes, its name, packaging, and price, its history, reputation and the way it is advertised. A brand is also defined by consumers' impressions of the people who use it, as well as their own experience. (http://www.ogilvy.com.cn/about_ogilvy_china/main.html, accessed 3 September 2008)

Advertising and marketing communicate messages and images about a branded product to potential consumers, hoping to create positive feelings, emotions, and associations which may predispose consumers to consider that particular company's product/brand more favorably than those of competitors. Significant financial resources are now directed to brand marketing campaigns, the aim of which is generally to attribute a particular set of appealing qualities and emotional associations to a specific branded product. However, as well as product branding corporations may also be the focus of branding campaigns (Wang, 2008). Nike and Adidas represent successful examples of corporate branding – other examples might include McDonald's, Microsoft, Diesel, Audi, and Virgin. Nike, the sportswear corporation, provides a good example of the increasing shift of emphasis from manufacturing to advertising, marketing, and branding and the scale of resources now devoted to brand promotion. Indeed, its 'vertically integrated … on-the-cheap outsourced

production structure' and 'product-free brand' have become models for
other more traditional companies (Klein, 2001: 198). In 2006, it was
reported that Nike had set aside US$1.7 billion for brand promo-
tion in the course of the year, including US$476 million for celebrity
endorsements by the likes of Tiger Woods (US$20 million), Lebron
James (US$13 million), Maria Sharapova (US$6 million) and the
Brazilian football team (US$12 million) (Rovell, 2006).

The effectiveness of a brand is determined by the extent to which its
trade mark or logo is instantly recognizable; the degree to which it promotes in the minds of potential consumers a range of positive associations
and emotions; and the respects in which, in comparison to competing
brands, it is trusted, preferred, and attracts loyalty from consumers who
return to it over and over again, notwithstanding that it might cost more,
or be less accessible. Over time successful campaigns effectively create
brand equity, they build brand capital. Reflecting on the increasing
pervasiveness of branding Klein remarks that:

> Savvy ad agencies have all moved away from the idea that they
> are flogging a product made by someone else, and have come
> to think of themselves instead as brand factories, hammering
> out what is of true value: the idea, the lifestyle, the attitude.
> Brand builders are the new primary producers in our so-called
> knowledge economy. (2001: 196)

In a critical analysis of the social and economic order of mid-twentieth
century America advertising was described as '[t]he very offspring of
monopoly capitalism ... as much an integral part of the system as the
giant corporation itself' (Baran and Sweezy, 1970: 126). It was the effect
of advertising on 'the magnitude of aggregate effective demand', rather
than its impact on the distribution of consumer choices between different
commodities, that was considered to be of greatest economic significance
(Baran and Sweezy, 1970: 128). The most important, indeed dominant,
function of advertising was outlined in the following terms:

> Waging, on behalf of the producers and sellers of consumer
> goods, a relentless war against saving and in favour of con-
> sumption ... the principal means of carrying out this task are
> to induce changes in fashion, create new wants, set new stand-
> ards of status, enforce new norms of propriety. The unques-
> tioned success of advertising in achieving these aims has greatly
> strengthened its role as a force counteracting monopoly capi-
> talism's tendency to stagnation and at the same time marked
> it as the chief architect of the famous 'American way of life'.
> (Baran and Sweezy, 1970: 132)

With the emergence of neo-liberal capitalism in the 1970s, marketing operations and advertising campaigns became even more vital for generating sufficient consumer demand for the growing range of new consumer goods, models, and styles that were being produced at an ever-increasing rate. Modern advertising has continued to be one of the most important means for 'ensuring the market', for creating and expanding markets, and it remains the case that 'modern capitalism could not function without it' (Williams, 1980: 186). This assessment of the importance of advertising is shared by a number of other analysts who have focused on 'the sales effort' (Baran and Sweezy, 1970), its evolution from 'hawking product' to 'creating a corporate mythology powerful enough to infuse meaning into … raw objects' (Klein, 2001: 21–2), and the continuing global proliferation of consumer targeted advertising and branding campaigns and associated growth in 'product management, sales communication, and macro-marketing operations' (Dawson, 2005: 24).

Advertising is now to be found virtually everywhere and constitutes a powerful and influential medium for marketing specific products. But its broader cultural impact, promoting the values of materialism, individualism, and private property, is of even greater importance. Appealing images of family life, love, friendship, and pleasure presented in advertising copy convey the impression that a good and happy life can be secured only through consumption of goods and services available through the market, that happiness and satisfaction are but a purchase away (Jhally, 2000).

Goods are valued and desired for more than their utility, tastes in food are not limited purely to nutritional and economic value alone, and clothing and other consumer goods are not regarded simply in terms of their functional attributes. It is in respect of the cultivation of attention and interest, the nurturing of a positive attitude or orientation, and the promised offering of emotional meaning and symbolic value in respect of a product (or service) that advertising is of particular significance, for by delivering a continual stream of stimulating messages and appealing images it promotes 'the unquestioned desirability, indeed the imperative necessity, of owning the newest product that comes on the market' (Baran and Sweezy, 1970: 132). The 'newness' ascribed to a product may reflect genuine innovation or improvements in performance and function(s), but equally it may amount to no more than a matter of 'difference' fabricated, or novelty simulated, through the creative ingenuity of design, advertising, and marketing agencies. In the great majority of cases product promotion or the cultivation of consumer interest in and demand for 'the newest product' necessarily requires the simultaneously implied designation of existing comparable products as 'old', out of date, unfashionable, lacking in style and/or function(s), effectively rendering them obsolete and warranting their 'retirement', consignment to landfill, or, it is to be hoped, recycling, whenever and wherever possible.

4
DESIGNING OBSOLESCENCE, PROMOTING CONSUMER DEMAND

The logic of growth within a capitalist market economy necessitates continual pursuit of increases in productivity and perpetual innovations in design and manufacture of an endless stream of products, an essential corollary of which is the need to ensure consumer demand for the proliferating variety of 'new' goods is continually generated by utilizing a variety of techniques and strategies to cultivate appropriate levels of interest and desire. As one critical analyst of the promotion of consumer culture has noted:

> In response to the exigencies of the productive system of the twentieth century, excessiveness replaced thrift as a social value. It became imperative to invest the laborer with a financial power and a psychic desire to consume. (Ewen, 2001: 25)

Increasingly, from the mid-twentieth century, corporations turned to marketing and product management to nurture and expand markets for the growing range of new goods being produced, directing particular attention to innovative ways of rendering older products out of date, unfashionable, obsolete, and in need of replacement.

The impression of a product's 'newness' may be achieved and conveyed in a number of ways, for example through 'aesthetic' modifications, such as relatively superficial changes in appearance, perhaps involving repackaging or a modest modification of the exterior, or by introducing more substantial differences in styling and design, and, more significantly, by virtue of the introduction of 'physical' or 'technological' modifications, which promote improvements in performance, or the addition of innovative features, which have implications for a product's range of functions and use. The principal aim is to convey the impression that the production of newer versions or later models renders existing products aesthetically or technologically obsolete. It is more than a matter of things not being made to last, although that is part of the story. It also involves the generation of an understanding that in a modern consumer society things are not *meant* to last, because each tomorrow will deliver new models and new goods, and the presumption is that the 'new' will necessarily be better and more desirable.

Planned Obsolescence

Planned or organized obsolescence assumes two principal forms, 'aesthetic' and 'physical', both of which serve the corporate objective of promoting repeat consumer purchases of products (Packard, 1963; Dawson, 2005; Slade, 2006). In the case of aesthetic modifications, confined to packaging, appearance, style, and design, the 'new' product generally performs the same functions as existing comparable products, but the availability and marketing of the new model, charged with symbolic value by virtue of its status as the latest product, effectively renders all the earlier models in use 'old', or unfashionable in appearance, and, looking out of date, they appear, and are designated as, in need of retirement, disposal, and replacement, even though they may still be fit for the purpose(s) for which they were originally designed, produced, and purchased.

Physical or technological modifications also promote the prospect of increasing the frequency of repeat purchases by engineering obsolescence. Two possibilities need to be distinguished, namely (1) the development of new products bearing new functions and/or containing technical innovations and additional specifications, which lead existing products to be regarded as obsolete and virtually worthless by virtue of their significantly inferior range of functions and performance, and more contentiously (2) the production of goods deliberately designed to function for a limited period, or to have limited life spans, effectively goods manufactured with built-in or engineered 'death dates', goods which are not made to last. By deliberately manufacturing products with a limited term design-life – 'product death-dating' – corporations have sought to prevent market saturation and maintain the prospect of economically viable volume production (Packard, 1963: 58; Dawson, 2005: 88–9; Slade, 2006: 164–7).

The phrase 'planned obsolescence' is often associated with a leading American industrial designer, Brooks Stevens, whose creative skills were employed in designing clothes dryers, refrigerators, irons, as well as a number of cars including the Jeep Station Wagon, but the practice had in fact been around since the mid-1920s and the term was originally used in the early 1930s by a Manhattan real-estate broker Jack London who produced a pamphlet with the title *Ending the Depression through Planned Obsolescence* (Slade, 2006: 73, 152–3). It was in the course of delivering an address to an advertising conference in 1954 that Stevens first made the controversial suggestion that planned obsolescence constituted the mission of industrial design. Elaborating on his understanding of the notion of planned obsolescence Stevens commented that it meant instilling in the buyer 'the desire to own something a little newer, a little better, [and] a little sooner than is necessary' (cited in Slade, 2006: 153). It is evident that for Stevens obsolescence was primarily a 'psychological' rather than a technical or functional matter, although innovations in both of these respects frequently play a part in mobilizing consumer demand for new products. As Galbraith observed, a combination of product innovation and advertising 'plays a vital role in stimulating the psychic obsolescence of goods and their replacement', with advertising serving to persuade the consumer that the new form of the product makes earlier versions appear deficient and that in respect of the latter 'possession and use … [will] reflect discredit on the person so owning and using it' (1975: 167). It is the image and aesthetic qualities ascribed to the new product and the popular appeal accorded to it through advertising campaigns, more than improved technical or functional aspects, that Galbraith argues are ultimately 'decisive for success' (1975: 167).

Cars and Mobile Phones

Galbraith refers to product promotion in the car industry as a good example of the way in which advertising, independently of the promotion of specific makes or models, has worked to persuade consumers that contemporary designs, shapes, and details are desirable and that 'those of the past are obsolete, eccentric or otherwise unworthy' (1975: 156). In his study of obsolescence in America Giles Slade (2006) describes how market competition between Ford and General Motors in the 1930s led to frequent style changes and associated advertising campaigns designed to encourage consumers to buy the new models regularly rolling off the production lines.

The introduction of regular model changes to maintain growth in car sales is argued to have been the idea of the president of General Motors, Alfred P. Sloan, who, recognizing that the market at the time was approaching saturation point as nearly everyone who could afford a car had already purchased one, reasoned that 'unless automakers gave a motorist a reason to buy a new car, even when he already had one, automakers would have no one left to sell to' (Loab, 1995: 79). The solution promoted by Sloan was an annual model change, involving innovations in design and, where and when possible, performance, which would promote disenchantment with the models consumers already owned and convince them the new model in the showroom was worth purchasing. Sloan sought to 'decrease durability and increase obsolescence' by introducing regular changes in design, style, and color, the intention being to influence the consumer to 'exchange his car a year or more old for a new car of the latest design' (Slade, 2006: 43, 44).

Subsequently, Sloan has been credited with introducing the practice of planned obsolescence to stimulate consumer demand not just into the car manufacturing business, but more broadly into American industry and consumer culture in general:

> After the mid-1920s, middle class consumers were encouraged to buy a new car every year, and the annual automobile shows made viewing the new models into a cultural spectacle of progress ... the idea that models would be phased out and replaced with new ones each year, changed not only the auto industry but also the way Americans thought about consumption. (Sheumaker and Wajda, 2007: 54)

Other industries worldwide now operate in a broadly comparable manner, aiming to increase product turnover by designing 'artificially short life-spans for commodities' and introducing aesthetic and design innovations that promote forms of 'stylistic obsolescence' which will serve to promote an optimal frequency of repetitive consumption (Dawson, 2005: 88, 90). The twenty-first century mobile phone industry provides a comparable example to the early twentieth century car industry in the sense that, in addition to being the target of well established marketing strategies, phone users are actively encouraged by letter, text, and calls, on a 12–18 month frequency, to 'upgrade' by exchanging their existing phone for a later model, one generally offering a new design and more functions and services. In the USA and the UK most mobile phones have a 9 to 12 months market life cycle and a consumer replacement cycle under two years. New designs of mobile phone have been emerging on a regular basis as models are 'tweaked' or 'freshened' so that several 'new' versions can be readily produced each year. Where more significant modifications of hardware and software and added functions are involved the product development cycle is generally in the region of two years.

The following advertisement ironically acknowledges how the mobile phone industry is continually engineering obsolescence and inducing product retirement, while simultaneously appearing to sympathize with the consumer's predicament of knowing that any 'upgrade' model they choose is destined to become outdated within a few months of agreeing to a new contract:

> Ashamed of your outdated old mobile? SWAP.it!
>
> 'Your phone's only got Bluetooth and a dozen polyphonic ring-tones? Well look at this, mine's got 3G, wi-fi, pie-in-the-sky, fifty mega-pixel camera and fully enabled toast capabilities. And I only needed to re-mortgage the flat to buy it.' Sound all too familiar? We sympathize. It's ridiculously hard and expensive to keep up with the latest mobile trends these days – that contract phone that looked so appealing nine months ago is probably already outdated by a newer, faster, more glorious model. So if you haven't got the latest Golden Fallace 3000, the Carphone Warehouse is here to help, with their new SWAP.it service. (http://www.shopping place.co.uk/blog/ashamed-of-your-outdated-old-mobile-swap-it, accessed 20 August 2008)

Waste, Disposability, and Obsolescence

In a series of popular books, written in the 1950s and 1960s, Vance Packard focused on advertising and marketing, status seeking through consumer activity, and the growth of private consumption and waste. In *The Waste Makers* published in 1960 Packard directed attention to the strategies that were increasingly being employed to induce citizens 'to consume more each year' and what he termed 'the wastefulness being promoted', including the ways in which natural resources were being depleted by 'industrial firms ... grinding up more than half of the natural resources processed each year on this planet for the benefit of six per cent of the planet's people' (1963: 18–19, 22).

In particular, Packard focused on the marketing strategies that were being employed to increase consumption in line with growth in productive capacity, including persuading consumers into 'buying more of each product', an objective that manufacturers sought to achieve in a variety of ways. For example, deodorant manufacturers introduced gender differentiated products; carpet makers encouraged consumers to aspire to wall-to-wall floor covering; cosmetics, clothing, and home accessories companies introduced a wider range of colors and placed emphasis on color coordination; opticians promoted the idea that people needed more than one pair of spectacles, and that glasses should be considered a 'fashion accessory'; companies producing electrical goods for the home promoted the idea of 'two refrigerators in every home', as well as 'two washers and two driers'; and house builders started to suggest that 'every family needs two homes' (Packard, 1963: 37–9). In addition, one car per family was no longer deemed sufficient for modern life and those families so 'deprived' were described by a Chevrolet company representative as 'victims of "one-car captivity"' (Packard, 1963: 40).

As well as being enticed to buy more of each product, encouraged to aspire to own more than one house, car, refrigerator, radio, television, phone, or whatever, marketing strategies have been employed to induce consumers to expect further innovations, to look forward to increases in power, performance, and function(s), and to anticipate the continual proliferation of products differentiated in terms of design, styling, and/ or appearance. Insofar as the reproduction of the prevailing system of economic production is increasingly dependent on 'technological ... or organized obsolescence' (Baudrillard, 1998: 46), consumers are encouraged to consider durability as no longer a virtue and to regard disposability, rather than attachment, as the appropriate relationship to cultivate with existing products in an increasingly 'throwaway' consumer society. In such a society today's goods are destined to be rapidly replaced as consumer markets strive to create 'instant obsolescence ... shortening the distance between the novelty and the rubbish bin', offering products 'for immediate consumption [and preferably] for one-off use, rapid disposal and replacement' (Bauman, 2004a: 118). Things are not made to last. Consumer goods have to have a limited life if the will and/or the need to (re)purchase are to be sustained and reproduced. If the quality of the product is too high, if it is designed too well, not only will it probably have raised production costs, but more significantly it is likely to extend 'the time that end users' needs are satisfied by the product, slashing into or – if quality levels were truly sky-high – killing repeat purchases' (Dawson, 2005: 86).

Music Reproduction: Vinyl, CDs, and iPods

The music reproduction industry offers a number of examples of the generation of forms of physical obsolescence where technical innovations have served to make existing products and formats obsolete. Writing in the 1960s Packard describes how the development of stereophonic equipment for the consumer market, which was destined to make existing music reproduction products obsolete, was deliberately held back until 'the demand for additional new-model hi-fi sets was slowing'. It was anticipated that the introduction of the new stereophonic product would 'induce owners of existing hi-fi sets to feel their product was now inadequate' and lead them to replace it (Packard, 1963: 59). The music reproduction industry has continued to provide examples of forms of technologically induced obsolescence as new equipment and a series of new formats have been successfully developed and marketed.

In his discussion of the economic significance of '"reformatting" the attributes of commodities to force people to purchase new means of satisfying existing needs and wants' Michael Dawson (2005: 89) refers to observations made by *The New York Times* music critic Allan Kozinn. In a series of considered reflections on the respective merits of vinyl long-playing records (LPs) and compact discs (CDs) as cultural commodities and music reproduction formats, Kozinn expresses his concerns about the commercial engineering of obsolescence that led to the format change from the LP to the CD. Kozinn's suspicions are that it was not 'consumer apathy' that led to the 'unnatural' and 'rather suspicious' demise of the LP, or the superior sound reproduction quality, or even the potentially greater convenience of the new CD format, it was, quite simply, commercial interest. Five years after the introduction of the format, less than one in seven American homes had a CD player and even by 1993, the 10th anniversary of the CD, Kozinn notes that less than half of American households had CD players.

An interview conducted with Norio Ohga, at the time the president of the Sony Corporation and one of the individuals who had worked to encourage the development of the new format, served to confirm Kozinn's concerns about the process of product innovation that led to the displacement of the LP by the CD. Ohga explained that LP market saturation and signs that the cassette market was also slowing led Sony to believe there was a potential commercial market for a 'new carrier', a new format, and encouraged their development of the compact disc. As Ohga comments:

> We reached an agreement with Philips on the details of the format, and we demonstrated it at a meeting of the International Music Committee, in Athens. At that time, there was no support from any other record company. In fact, they almost threw us out of Athens. They all thought that the LP was fine. But we introduced CD, and within five years, we had kicked the LP out of the industry. (Cited in Kozinn, 1993)

Subsequently, the CD itself has been threatened with obsolescence. Introduced in the USA in the 1980s sales figures have begun to decline with 62.5 million fewer being sold between 2001 and 2002, representing a drop of 9% to 649.5 million, and in 2007 *The Wall Street Journal* reported a 20% drop in CD sales, while digital downloading sales of songs grew by 54% and it was estimated that close to a billion songs were being traded on pirate digital networks (Smith, 2007). Consumers remain as interested as ever in acquiring music but there are now a range of new options, the most popular being the iPod player with the capacity to store anywhere between 240 songs (iPod Shuffle) and 20,000 or 40,000 songs the (iPod Classic 80 GB and 160 GB versions). The Apple iTunes site, promises 'Instant sonic gratification' without entering a store or having to wait for a CD to arrive in the mail. Online music is growing rapidly and as Internet delivery and new technologies increase in popularity, not to mention the impact of 'technological convergence', which is leading to an erosion of functional differences between mobile phones, music players, and digital cameras, the CD may, like the audio-cassette before it, be rendered obsolete.

Apple's iPod

Noting the number of costly format wars that have taken place, for example back in the 1980s between VHS and Betamax recorders and more recently between Blu-ray and HD DVD players, as well as the succession of audio technologies that have emerged, made it to market, sold to consumers, and then been rendered obsolete by yet more ingenious, innovative, even more portable and powerful devices for collecting, storing, and playing music, Giles Slade (2007) designates Apple 'champion of audio obsolescence'. Slade argues that by adopting a unique digital non-MP3 format Apple's iPod creates problems of compatibility and leads to situations in which different types of music file cannot be transferred to it, effectively limiting downloads to iTunes website. The reverse also holds, so music collected on iPod cannot be transferred to, or used on, other players, leading Slade to caution that when after just 13 months or so of heavy use the consumer finds the lithium-ion battery may have lost 'more than half of its functionality' and the player is fading out, even after more frequent recharging, the options are relatively limited. The new battery route is fraught with problems, not least because it is sealed inside the iPod, takes several weeks to fix, costs US$65 to replace when a brand new 1-gig iPod shuffle costs only US$79, and 'worst of all – because the new battery comes in a refurbished and wiped-clean iPod – you'll lose all your songs' (Slade, 2007).

With the iPod imminent disposability is effectively a designed feature, because in addition to battery deterioration, 'speedy obsolescence' is promoted by the continual development of new models. The iPod transformed Apple from a largely marginal computer company into a manufacturer of digital music players, and simultaneously provided the company with what has become a powerful and popular brand, one which has been enhanced by the addition of a new product, the iPhone. Following the development of the iPhone a new generation of iPods emerged in 2007 with one new model the 'Touch' utilizing design features and user interface concepts from the new phone product. However, any consumer pleasure that may be derived from purchase of the latest model is fleeting, rapidly diminished, and ultimately surpassed by the emergence of even newer models promising to deliver more. As Steve Jobs, co-founder and CEO of Apple Inc., is reported to have stated, 'If you ... want the latest and greatest ... you have to buy a new iPod at least once a year' (cited in Slade, 2007). Although Apple recycles obsolete iPods free of charge, their policy of planned product obsolescence contributes to the volume of electronic waste (e-waste) that is being produced and is difficult to reconcile with their claim to have 'a really strong environmental policy' (Slade, 2007).[1]

The potential environmental impact of continual electronic product innovation generating obsolescence and contributing to increasing e-waste leads Slade to argue that:

> the disposability of the iPod and the fight among manufacturers over DVD formats seem irresponsible if not criminally negligent. iPods are crammed with lead, mercury, and flame retardant, and the 70 million already sold represent a sizable amount of toxic chemicals that seep through landfills and contaminate groundwater. Electronic waste accounts for 2 percent of America's trash in landfills but 70 percent of its toxic garbage. In 2003 alone, 3 million tons of e-waste were generated in the United States. (Slade, 2007)

A number of other examples of continuing electronic product innovation and associated developments likely to contribute to e-waste are discussed by Slade (2007), including the continuing growth in mobile phone sales with their 18 month lifespan – over 3.3 billion were reportedly in use worldwide in 2008 – and the introduction by Microsoft in 2007 of Vista the new operating system with memory and graphics requirements that have rendered many existing PCs and laptops obsolete. An additional comparable example arises from the decision of governments around the world, starting in 2006, to move from analog terrestrial broadcasting to digital signal transmission. This is leading consumers either to purchase set-top converter boxes for existing televisions or to buy new digital televisions and dispose of existing sets with all the attendant e-waste problems. In 2009, '300 million analog TVs in the United States' became obsolete with the switch to digital; by 2012 in the UK it is planned that the analogue switch off process will have been completed and that all households will have some form of digital television receiver (Slade, 2007).

The volume of e-waste being produced has increased significantly with estimates ranging from '20–50 million tonnes ... worldwide every year' (Greenpeace, 2005: 4; United Nations Environment Programme, 2006). As the average lifespan of electronic products decreases and the quantities sold worldwide increase, the problem of e-waste is destined to grow. It has been estimated that in the period 1997–2005 the average life of computers in developed countries fell from six to two years and that the lifecycle of mobile phones was 'less than two years'. Moreover, in the calendar year 2004 global sales of computers increased by 11.6%, an additional 183 million over the previous year, and mobile phones by 30%, an additional 674 million over 2003 (Greenpeace, 2005: 4). Given continuing innovations and developments in the manufacture of electronic products and expectations of further growth in sales with the emergence of potential new markets in China and India in particular, the environmental impact of e-waste is likely to remain a significant problem.

Fashion and style: marketing obsolescence

Obsolescence is not confined to the functional and technical qualities of goods alone, it also extends to appearance, design, and look, in respect of which, as a number of analysts have noted, advertising and marketing exercise a persuasive influence on consumer preferences (Packard, 1963; Galbraith, 1969, 1975; Ewen and Ewen, 1992; Baudrillard, 1998; Klein, 2001; Ewen, 2001; Dawson, 2005). In late 1950s America, Packard noted that advertisers were making increasing references to 'the desirability of creating "psychological obsolescence"', manufacturers were seeking to emulate the automobile industry's policy of trying to 'make everyone ashamed to drive a car more than two or three years', and merchandisers were being advised to become 'merchants of discontent' (1960: 24). A combination of advertising and marketing campaigns to promote style and fashion conscious consumers, alongside the manufacture of new models and styles of products, would promote dissatisfaction with existing product ranges, which would appear 'old and outmoded', and stimulate purchase of the latest designs (Packard, 1960: 143–5). In France in 1970 in a related analysis of the myths and structures of consumption in late modern societies Baudrillard re-affirmed the cultural and economic significance of advertising, noting how in the prevailing system of production a substantial budget is devoted to 'the sole aim not of adding to the use-value of objects, but of *subtracting value from them*, of detracting from their time-value by subordinating them to their fashion-value and to ever earlier replacement' (1998[1970]: 46), in short, devoted to the promotion of aesthetic obsolescence.

The importance of perceived aesthetic features and qualities of goods is well recognized by advertisers and within corporate marketing and product management. Consumer goods not only have utility and function(s), but also acquire or have attributed to them, aesthetic or sign value, to which consumers react and respond. If appearance is not quite everything, it certainly is of great importance for every thing that is produced for the consumer market, as the level of attention and scale of resources devoted to presentation, styling, and packaging in production and marketing effectively demonstrate. Style, as Dawson notes, is used to 'stimulate attention and condition targets', to strike an emotional cord with potential consumers, to promote an 'I want it' and often an 'I must have it' emotive response:

> By consciously controlling the style conveyed by the product attributes they treat as marketing stimuli, corporate marketers profitably exploit the fact that people have aesthetic reactions to objects. (2005: 90)

Style is not everything, but it matters, it conveys an instant impression, arouses interest, may prompt an inquiry and lead to a sale, and in that respect external appearance, packaging, shape, textures, material, color, and aesthetic appeal are of paramount importance. Placing an emphasis on the novelty, difference, or fashionable character of the styling of a product promoted as contemporary, as new, as 'now' in advertising and marketing, serves another vital purpose, notably making existing comparable products, quite literally, look obsolete. Planned aesthetic or stylistic obsolescence is integral to a significant number of industries, including clothing, where 'designers and manufacturers rely on a carefully managed fashion cycle of revolving colors, cuts, patterns, logos and hem lengths to boost their sales by outmoding last year's apparel' (Dawson, 2005: 90). Cosmetics manufacturers operate in a similar manner, as do the big brand companies in the sports goods business, the likes of Nike and Adidas, who strive to continually develop new lines of sports clothing and footwear, and so increasingly do producers of other household consumer goods, the durability of which is deliberately compromised by the introduction of 'planned style changes [that] are ... effective in making "the mean replacement time ... earlier than the failure time of the product"' (Dawson, 2005: 90). The pace of the fashion cycle in clothing in particular has accelerated and as style changes have become increasingly more rapid observers have commented on the emergence of 'fast fashion' and have expressed concern about the environmental problems arising from the tons of 'old' clothing being thrown out to make way for the 'new', a great deal of it being shipped off to poorer countries where the prevalence of man-made materials means they may never biodegrade and soil productivity is impaired (BBC, 2004, 2009c).

Changes in fashions and styles, especially in respect of clothing and appearance, have a long history in the West, arguably extending back to the fourteenth and fifteenth centuries (Braudel, 1981). However, it was only really from the mid-nineteenth century that developments in communications such as 'telephones, the wireless, a transatlantic cable', increases in personal mobility and travel, which 'made swifter transmission of ideas and designs possible', and the production of ready-to-wear goods in particular, provided the preconditions for a fashion market to develop in the USA and Europe (Leach, 1993: 93). The marketing of fashion(s) has subsequently grown in significance and scope and the pace or rate of change in styles and fashions has accelerated significantly. As Leach observes, 'in the context of the American mass market, fashion demanded constant change, incessant newness … Since the specialness of any single fashion tended to go stale or vanish quickly as many consumers struggled to buy it, merchants had to supply the market at a feverish rate to maintain the fiction or glamour of uniqueness' (1993: 92).

Magazines and newspapers play a significant part in marketing fashion, offering attractive images, articles, and advertising copy of styles and 'looks' that are represented as fashionable. Readers are exhorted to 'update' their personal appearance, their 'look', their possessions, and the interior of their homes, by buying this season's deliberately differently styled clothing, accessories, décor, and furnishings, the subtext being not so much an invitation as an injunction to the reader to recognize the extent to which they, their possessions and their homes are destined to be out of date and in need of a makeover, which only repetitive consumption can remedy. Fashion and style images and texts contribute to aesthetic or stylistic obsolescence by promoting a proliferating variety of new designs through multimedia dissemination, mobilizing consumer demand by generating awareness of new products, and promoting interest in new styles and fashions, serving simultaneously to diminish the appeal of things already owned, worn, and used, and to induce consumers to shop and shop again. As the industrial designer Brooks Stevens remarked in an interview in 1958:

> Our whole economy is based on planned obsolescence … We make good products, we induce people to buy them, and then next year we deliberately introduce something that will make these products old fashioned, out of date, obsolete. We do that

for the soundest reason: to make money ... It isn't organized
waste. It's a sound contribution to the American economy.
(Cited in Packard, 1963: 58; see also Slade, 2006: 153)

Planned aesthetic or stylistic obsolescence has become an even more
significant feature of late modern economic life as increasing competition has led to a growth in innovations in styling and packaging, which
either lead to modifications of existing products, or to new wrappings
and containers – 'elaborate packages ... [constituting] essential platforms
for marketers' planned behavior-modification campaigns' (Dawson,
2005: 91), both of which serve to color perception and lead pre-existing
commodities to appear as out-of-date, old fashioned, or obsolete.

Romancing the Consumer

A significant counter-argument to the views of analysts who have placed
emphasis on the part played by marketing and product management in
the generation of consumer demand and promotion of consumer activity is developed in a treatise on modern consumerism outlined by Colin
Campbell (1989). The acknowledged template for Campbell's thesis
is Max Weber's social and economic analysis of the contribution the
protestant ethic made to the formation of a culture conducive to the
development of capitalist economic life. Campbell's analytic interest is in
the possibility of an association between consumption and romanticism,
between the emergence and development of a culture of modern consumerism and a romantic ethos, one which it is suggested can be traced
back to the mid-eighteenth century and the emergence of an intellectual,
artistic, and literary counter-Enlightenment movement. The core thesis
outlined is that:

> The Romantic Movement assisted crucially at the birth of mod-
> ern consumerism; it is also maintained that romanticism has
> continued in the two centuries or so since that time to work
> in such a way as to overcome the forces of traditionalism and
> provide a renewed impetus to the dynamic of consumerism.
> (Campbell, 1989: 206)

Presented as a challenge to what is described as 'the productionist economic bias which pervades most of social science' (Campbell, 1989: 7: 13),
the counter-argument has a number of distinctive elements. It is suggested that we lack a 'satisfactory account of consumer behaviour' and
that in its absence there is a failure to understand precisely what drives

modern consumption and explains the apparent insatiability of modern consumers, their seemingly inexhaustible and 'endless pursuit of wants' (Campbell, 1989: 36, 37). Given the assumptions on which the study proceeds it is understandable that issues associated with consumption should predominate, but it is surprising that no consideration is given to the various ways in which consumption is articulated with production. There is a recognition that the substitution of an analytic bias towards consumption for a perceived bias towards production will not lead to a satisfactory analysis, but in the final instance while the question of the relationship between modern production and modern consumption is briefly posed, its answer is deferred to a 'subsequent work'.

Consumption and production are closely articulated and the relationship between them is complex and varied, as has been noted above (see Chapter 1). However, the analytic starting point for Campbell is not the articulation of production and consumption, but how, given his assessment of the limitations of explanations that are considered to prioritize production, to account for the consumer revolution, the increase in consumption that was a corollary of industrialization, 'that dynamic generation of new wants that is so characteristic of modern consumerism' (1989: 202). Rejecting a range of explanations that favor emulation of the conspicuous consumption of the rich, an increase in productive capacity, and associated cultivation of a mass consumer market through the development of new techniques in marketing and distribution accompanied by the 'rise of advertising', Campbell argues that the 'standard account' is unable to offer an adequate explanation of either the historic emergence of a 'new propensity to consume or indeed of modern consumerism more generally' (1989: 23). Expanding on the limitations of existing explanations he comments that all we have is an identification of relevant factors – emulation, fashion, market manipulation – 'but there is no worked out understanding of the relationship between these, or any statement of the precise manner in which they might be considered to have interacted so as to have brought about such a transformation' (1989: 23). To achieve a more effective account he argues that not only is a more adequate conceptualization of modern consumerism required, but also an analytic appreciation of the importance of a hedonistic or pleasure-orientated dimension to human conduct, one that does not reduce the 'origin of wants' to the pursuit of utility (Campbell, 1989: 202–3).

While there may be some respects in which it is warranted to regard aspects of consumer activity as guided by notions of utility, function, and rational pursuit of satisfaction, Campbell suggests this far from exhausts what is distinctive about consumption and that it is important to acknowledge the significance of what is presented as a 'romantic' ingredient or dimension to consumer activity, which primarily means pursuit of the experience of pleasure. In developing his argument

Campbell distinguishes between 'satisfaction-seeking' and 'pleasure-seeking' consumer activity (1989: 60). The distinction presented is between a 'state of being' in which needs, described as forms of deprivation – the lack of 'something necessary to maintain a given condition of existence' – are represented as driving the pursuit of satisfaction through consumer activity, and a 'quality of experience', pleasure, which represents a desired 'favorable reaction' that is sought in and through consumer sensations (Campbell, 1989: 60–1). Needs are said to require very particular forms of satisfaction – hunger requires food, thirst necessitates something to drink – whereas pleasure can be derived from a variety of eminently inter-changeable or substitutable experiences.

Where the satisfaction of needs remains uncertain, where the threat and experience of deprivation continues to haunt the human condition, Campbell argues that there will be relatively little awareness of a distinction, or of a possibility of choice, between 'maximizing satisfaction' and 'maximizing pleasure', and that the very act of satisfying a basic or fundamental need (e.g. hunger) may itself promote pleasure. However, with the emergence of affluence, enjoyed in the first instance by the privileged, the wealthy and powerful, fundamental needs are regularly and routinely met and in consequence it is suggested that, rather than being aroused, consumer sensations associated with need satisfaction are dulled, rarely experienced as pleasurable, and that this promotes 'the pursuit of pleasure for its own sake, rather than its mere appreciation as an adjunct of action pursued for other purposes' (Campbell, 1989: 65).

Traditional and modern hedonism

It is argued that it was with the regular production of surplus supply of food that the intensity of pleasure deriving from satisfaction of need began to wane and traditional forms of hedonism emerged. Campbell describes how from classical antiquity accounts can be found of the practices employed by those with wealth and power to regenerate 'the cycle of need-satisfaction experience' that would promote pleasure and he cites as one example the alimentary practices used by the Romans to extend the pleasures derived from eating, as well as the cultivation of arts or techniques to master, manipulate, and enhance 'sensations associated with appetites' (1989: 65–6). But such experiences of pleasure are limited by the very nature of human appetitive needs, by 'the small number of human senses and the restricted range of sensations which they can distinguish', and this, it is suggested led to the identification of other potentially compensatory sources of pleasurable experience (Campbell, 1989: 66). These include aural and visual forms of entertainment, which it is argued 'rapidly pall', participation in intensive, uncertain, risky, and dangerous activities, which may produce an anticipatory and/or retrospective sense of pleasure, and aesthetic forms such as music, poetry, and drama, which 'offer a greater variety and complexity of stimuli than is possible with "traditional" entertainments' (Campbell, 1989: 67).

The significant difference between 'traditional' and 'modern' hedonism identified by Campbell is that the former is concerned with 'pleasures', a particular range of human activities that includes eating, drinking, sexual activity, and playful pastimes, effectively prioritizing specific sensations experienced as yielding pleasure, activities deemed to be synonymous with pleasure, whereas modern hedonism values 'pleasure' as a quality present as potential in all sensations, a quality inherent in all aspects of life awaiting realization or experience (1989: 69). Campbell adds that with modern hedonism the emphasis has shifted from sensations to emotions and that what has been important is the development of self-awareness and emotional self-control on the part of modern individuals. Modern individuals have the ability to imaginatively generate pleasurable experiences independently of any external stimuli by employing:

> their imaginative and creative powers to construct mental images which they consume for the intrinsic pleasure they provide, a practice best described as day-dreaming or fantasizing. (Campbell, 1989: 77)

It is in relation to the development of 'modern, autonomous, imaginative hedonism' that Campbell (1989: 88) believes answers can be found to questions about the origin and seeming insatiability of modern consumer wants, as well as the tendency to tire of existing products and services. In contrast to accounts that favor instinct or 'inherited inclinations', invoke the influence of external agencies, or turn to a notion of social emulation to account for consumer conduct Campbell argues that:

> individuals do not so much seek satisfaction from products, as pleasure from the self-illusory experiences which they construct from their associated meanings. The essential activity of consumption is thus not the actual selection, purchase, or use of products, but the *imaginative pleasure-seeking to which the product image lends itself* ... Viewed in this way, the emphasis upon novelty as well as that upon insatiability both become comprehensible. (1989: 89, emphasis added)

In summary, consumers dispose of existing products in the hope, or belief, that imaginary or idealized pleasurable experiences or fantasies can be realized through purchase and use of a new model, consumer product, or service, generally only to confront the sobering reality of disappointment and disillusionment. Campbell suggests this provides an explanation of why once eagerly awaited products lose their appeal for consumers, and why it is that consumer desire appears insatiable.

The consumer experience

Undoubtedly, as Campbell contends, fantasy, day-dreaming, and the imputation of meanings, images, and novelty are all potentially a part of the consumer experience, but so also are emulation and status seeking through consumer activity, through the possession and display of fashionable and socially desirable consumer goods, as is the cultivation, stimulation, management, and manipulation of consumer demands through product management, design, and marketing. It is not a matter of either/or; it is not a case of either invoking a notion of the consumer exercising choice, acting freely and expressing demands in a 'voluntaristic, self-directed, and creative' manner in the marketplace, or presenting consumers as cultural dopes led unwittingly to consume whatever is laid before them by advertising and marketing agencies (Campbell, 1989: 203). Consumers are hedonistic, to a degree, and placing emphasis on the importance of pursuit of pleasurable experiences in and through consumer related activities, such as shopping, following fashions, window shopping and so on, is warranted (Campbell, 1989: 92). But presenting the emergence and dissipation of 'wants' as entirely a consequence of the agency of the consumer – 'a consumer creates (and abandons) "wants"' – is to neglect the panoply of powerful influences to which consumers are exposed (Campbell, 1989: 203). Likewise, emphasizing how crucial 'imaginative enjoyment of products and services is', without giving due consideration to the several agencies operating to stimulate, influence, guide, and direct consumer imagination, does not advance the prospect of achieving a more effective understanding of the complex reality of consumer behavior (Campbell, 1989: 92).

The few references made by Campbell to advertising are confined to criticisms of analyses of the consumer revolution and consumer activity, which are represented as being over-reliant on a notion of the manipulability of consumer conduct. For example, it is suggested that in the work of McKendrick et al. (1983) emulation is invoked as the motivating factor stimulating consumer conduct and that it is advertising and sales campaigns that ultimately are deemed responsible for 'the manipulation of social emulation' by making products widely known and fashionably desirable (Campbell, 1989: 20–1). In the work of Galbraith (1963) it is suggested, the wants of consumers are held to be 'deliberately manufactured ... through such agencies as advertising and salesmanship' (Campbell, 1989: 42–3). A notion of manipulation is also considered to be implied in criticisms (non-attributed) of 'non-informative' advertising for seeking to promote consumption of products and services through the dissemination of attractive, enticing, and desirable images and symbolic meanings devoid of any information about the intrinsic utility of the commodities and services involved. Campbell is correct to point out that in addition to cognition and conceptions of utility, emotion and feeling are at least just as likely, arguably are more likely, to be a part of consumer behavior and that 'images and symbolic meanings are as much a "real" part of the product as its constituent ingredients' (1989: 48). Nowhere is this more apparent than in respect of the brand, an increasingly important and prominent part of consumer culture, but this constitutes a potentially problematic example for Campbell's argument.

Branding

A brand is recognizable as a commercial name, a sign, or logo, associated signifying colors, and increasingly a slogan or statement which may have lifestyle connotations and pretensions. Brands are built through a creative commercially driven process in which resources are directed towards the construction of an image or 'personality'. An image that it is anticipated consumers will find attractive and appealing, a process that provides a brand's products with distinctive attributes which serve to differentiate them from those of competitors. A vital part of the process is to establish emotional ties between brand and consumer, to promote in consumers a feeling of brand loyalty, and to generate a sense of identity with the brand among consumers that will lead them to base purchasing decisions less on price than on a felt sense of brand affinity (Dawson, 2005). The brand is about 'lifestyle' and 'experience'; it has an almost 'spiritual' dimension (Klein, 2001). Brands are fantasy-like, 'collective hallucinations'; their logos now adorn the bodies of most consumers and this contributes to the 'creeping ad expansion' that Naomi Klein (2001: 36–8) notes has become an increasing feature of city landscapes around the world. Branding is a deliberate process in which symbolic resources and iconic figures are deployed to promote the brand and build a synergy between it and potential consumers in order to engender 'logo-loyalty' (Soper, 2008: 202). Individual consumers are not in control of the symbolic resources and iconic figures employed to excite their interest in a particular brand or conjure up an emotional response from them. Once again the implication here is not that any brand will necessarily achieve its aim, but that consumers are subject to the persuasive forces associated with branding and the techniques employed to position a particular product and differentiate it from comparable products by conveying distinctive, if not unique, attributes, qualities, images, and meanings, with the aim and hope that these will become synonymous with the brand in the minds of consumers (Klein, 2001; Dawson, 2005).

Campbell does not discuss branding or marketing and where advertising is addressed it is primarily to take issue with particular conceptions of its significance and to qualify assumptions about its impact. For example, advertising is described, and appropriately so, as constituting 'one part of the total set of influences at work on consumers'; its message is held to be interpreted differently according to 'who receives it'; and it is argued that in any event it will not simply be accepted unthinkingly, but met, 'if only to a degree, in a discriminatory and purposeful manner' (Campbell, 1989: 47). While there is an acknowledgement that advertising agencies seek to associate meanings, images, fantasies, illusions, and day-dreams with products to 'awaken desire', and to achieve that end deploy motivation research to discover 'the dreams, desires and wishes of consumers', ultimately their influence is underestimated (Campbell, 1989: 47, see also 91).

Consumers, it is true, are not completely malleable, but we are amenable to persuasion, to enticements. In the consumer milieu a range of industry influences are in play which attempt to stimulate, direct, manage, and, where possible, achieve a degree of control over consumers and the ways in which they exercise choice in the marketplace. It is the ways in which influences and forms of persuasion stimulate and articulate with consumer dreams, desires, and wishes, the extent to which images, messages, symbols, and other seductive forms invoked in marketing campaigns successfully arouse awareness, entice interest, provoke desire, and promote the prospect of purchases producing pleasurable experiences, that condition consumption. As analysts of the role of advertising and promotional communication in the growth of the market economy in the course of the twentieth century have noted:

> What chiefly distinguishes our contemporary society from earlier ones is not only the sheer volume of goods and services available to consumers in a market economy, but also *the sheer intensity of the promotional effort whereby marketers seek to link consumer needs to the characteristics of the products they sell*. (Leiss et al., 2005: 5, emphasis added)

Window displays and window-shopping: designs on consumer desire

In taking issue with what are represented as 'deterministic theories of consumer behavior' Campbell places emphasis on the growth of 'modern, autonomous, imaginative hedonism' (1989: 88). The popular practice of window-shopping is discussed to illustrate the pleasurable experiences derived by consumers from 'imaginative use of objects' displayed, for example the imaginary trying on of clothing, or imagining how displayed furniture might look in one's own home (Campbell, 1989: 92). Consumers certainly do window shop and seem to derive pleasure from so doing, and it is likely that some consumers do indeed engage in the imaginary practices identified. It is also likely that some of the enjoyment some consumers derive from window shopping is 'aesthetic, involving an appreciation of the art of the designers and window-dressers involved' (Campbell, 1989: 92). But the contributions of the designers, window-dressers, and display artists goes beyond the 'aesthetic', the purpose and intended point or impact of window displays that promote window-shopping is ultimately 'economic', to entice consumers to enter retail premises and purchase goods.

Plate-glass windows became a feature of better quality shops in major American cities from the late nineteenth century where it is argued that they 'closed off smell and touch' as they 'amplified' the consumer's visual relationship with goods (Leach, 1993: 62–3). The development and use of plate-glass windows increased the possibility of merchandise display and transformed 'the way people related to goods' (Leach, 1993: 61; see also Flanders, 2006: 110, 117). Elaborating on the impact of this retail innovation Leach adds that:

> Glass was a symbol of the merchant's unilateral power in a capitalist society to refuse goods to anyone in need, to close off access without being condemned as cruel and immoral ... At the same time, the pictures behind the glass enticed the viewer. The result was a mingling of refusal and desire that must have greatly intensified desire ... Perhaps more than any other medium, glass democratized desire even as it de-democratized access to goods. (1993: 63)

With the increasing installation of glass-plated windows on shop fronts, merchandising display and decoration grew in importance as merchants sought to 'stimulate desire for all goods' (Leach, 1993: 65). By 1915, half of the world's supply of polished plate-glass was being consumed in the USA, but by 1925 the quantity being used had almost doubled as more and more American merchandisers and retailers sought 'an effective, high density visual environment to *encourage consumers to replace old styles rapidly with new ones*' (Leach, 1993: 305, emphasis added). With the production of ready-to-wear clothing early in the twentieth century mannequins or wax dummies began to be introduced in window displays, providing merchants with an even greater ability to 'manipulate goods in their windows' (Leach, 1993: 65). Some of the early displays of

women's underwear aroused considerable controversy, including criticisms that they were 'immoral', and the large crowds attracted seemed
at times on the verge of rioting, prompting police intervention. Worries
were also expressed by some perceptive exponents of the arts of display that
'show windows' might 'induce people to spend their money on things they
cannot afford' (cited in Leach, 1993: 68).

Shop 'show windows' constitute part of a range of techniques, events, and
media that were developed to cultivate a commercial aesthetic of desire.
Along with 'electrical signs, fashion shows, advertisements and billboards'
they were designed to conjure up a consumer vision of 'the good life and
of paradise', the primary objective being to entice consumers into shops
and promote the sale of goods in substantial volume (Leach, 1993: 9).
The value of 'show windows' was recognized early on by the American
Gordon Selfridge who introduced them to Marshall Field's department
store in the 1890s and, ever conscious of the importance of continually
cultivating customers, inaugurated its 'Children's Day' in 1902, remarking
that 'children are the future customers of this store and impressions made
now will be lasting' (Leach, 1993: 68–9, 86–7). It was in advertising and
promotion that Selfridge's main contribution was to be found, according
to Flanders, who attributes to him the view that 'window displays were
not simply to convey information about stock to passers-by ... but
to create desire' (2006: 117). A few years after resigning from Marshall
Field's, Selfridge moved to London where in 1909 he opened the department store that bears his name, introducing innovative window displays
containing 'unified, thematically coherent images', deploying a substantial
advertising budget to purchase '104 full-page advertisements [which] ran
for a week in 18 national newspapers' to launch the business, and exagger-
atingly proclaiming the venture successful in attracting '1 million visitors in
its first week' (Flanders, 2006: 119–21).

Reflecting further on the impact the introduction of plate-glass shop windows, display techniques, and associated innovations had on consumerism,
Leach comments that:

> By 1910, American merchants, in their efforts to create the
> new commercial aesthetic, took command over color, glass and
> light, fashioning a link so strong between them and consump-
> tion, that, today, the link seems natural. (1993: 9)

The connection does indeed seem to have become 'natural', so much
so that while Campbell considers it appropriate to acknowledge the
window-shopping consumer's aesthetic appreciation of the efforts of
designers and window-dressers, the matter of the potential influence
or impact on consumers, public space, and the culture of city life of the
emergence, development, and proliferation of shop window displays, and

Figure 4.1

Source: Gareth Cattermole and Getty Images. Reproduced with permission.

http://www.nitrolicious.com/blog/wp-gallery/0407/km_topshop_online/kate_moss_topshop.jpg retrieved 4 September 2009.

related promotional forms, such as advertising hoardings, or billboards, and neon signs, is left unaddressed (Klein, 2001).

Shop window displays remain prominent features of contemporary consumer culture, but as with advertising and marketing, capturing attention and arousing interest have become more challenging as consumers have grown accustomed to the employment of familiar designs, layouts, and display techniques. In this context it is worth reflecting on the innovative celebrity window display associated with the widely publicized appearance, albeit brief, of English fashion model Kate Moss as a live mannequin in the window of high-street clothing retailer Topshop in May 2007. Moss was present to launch a line of clothing under her name and the publicity given to her planned appearance in the shop window aroused significant interest among consumers and predictably drew the attention of the media whose coverage provided the anticipated free advertising copy (see Figure 4.1).

Several thousand consumers were estimated to be waiting outside the Oxford Street branch of Topshop as Sir Philip Green escorted Kate Moss into the building. Media reports claimed that consumers started queuing eight hours before the Kate Moss collection was available to the public and that by the time the model arrived at the store and appeared in the window display 'the scenes were more reminiscent of the premiere of a West End movie than the debut of an affordable clothes range' (telegraph.co.uk, 2007).[2] As other marketing and promotional media have developed the advertising value of the conventional shop window display has diminished and this has led to a number of other innovations, such as the interactive shop window at Tommy Hilfiger Denim in Oxford Street employing touch-screen technology, which allows passers-by to add their own images to the Hilfiger Hall of Fame, and Orange's interactive shop window in Carnaby Street, which allows users to 'check the news, watch music videos and movie trailers, play computer games and access content through the Orange internet portal'. Such examples of digital window displays are considered to represent 'a sign of things to come' (Mallaghan, 2008).

In the competitive environment of the high street retailers must do all that they can to draw the attention of potential consumers to their products and introducing well-publicized innovations in shop window displays is one way to (re)generate consumer interest. The Kate Moss window display served its purpose by drawing crowds and attracting publicity to both the store and the celebrity endorsed fashion brand. The principal appeal was that the clothes were associated with the Kate Moss brand, prospective consumers remarking that 'I don't mind what I get, as long as it's Kate Moss' and 'I'm here because I love Kate Moss … I love her sense of style' (telegraph.co.uk, 2007). Later that year Topshop reported that the Moss brand and clothing designs had boosted 'sales by more than 10 per cent' (Mail Online 2007). Such anecdotes constitute a reminder of the influence that iconic celebrity figures and the brands with which they are associated may exercise over consumers and simultaneously suggest that a notion of emulation remains of relevance for making sense of at least some aspects of consumer conduct. As the dream merchants at Nike and Adidas and a variety other corporations would be able to confirm, there are a significant number of consumers who like to imagine emulating their sporting heroes, are eager to 'Be Like Mike' as the Gatorade advertisement featuring Michael Jordan exhorted consumers in the 1990s, and corporations employ their branding strategies and marketing skills to promote that end as they vie for the attention, interest, and purchasing power of consumers whose fantasies they do everything to encourage (Rovell, 2005; Smart, 2005). Suggestible consumers, and most of us are open to suggestion and influence to a degree, are already favorably predisposed towards celebrity figures and the idea of emulating their style, including signifying to others that they/we are doing so by bearing their designer brand and/or sporting their logo. So, for example, young female consumers have taken to the idea that they can be like Kate Moss by embracing her style and those with sporting inclinations and pretensions can fantasize that given the right clothing, footwear, and sports equipment they too, after a fashion, will be able to 'Just do it', like Tiger Woods, Rafael Nadal, Roger Federer, Maria Sharapova, or LeBron James, or that playing in the fashion of David Beckham, Novak Djokovic, Ana Ivanovic, or Kevin Garnett will not be impossible with the right stuff because 'Impossible is nothing'.

The consumer cycle described by Campbell ('desire–acquisition–use–disillusionment–renewed–desire' [1987: 90]) – does not occur in a vacuum, it is subject to an array of social, cultural, and economic forces. While from the consumer's perspective the process may appear to commence with desire and, after a completed cycle, recommence with desire renewed, consumer desire is given form and direction, aroused and intensified, and targeted by a range of influential factors, including product management and design, retailing and marketing strategies, as well as media representations of appealing consumer life-styles promoted as worthy of emulation. The desire–acquisition–use–disillusionment–renewed–desire cycle revolves around, indeed is driven by, awareness of the proliferating range of new goods being produced, commodities that constitute its object, means of expression, and source of provisional or temporary fulfillment. Consumer desire is stimulated by attractive retail presentation and display of products, mobilized by enticing images presented through marketing campaigns, and excited by media promotion and celebration of materially acquisitive lifestyles.

Consumerism's force field

Consumer activity is located in a force field of influences that includes:

(1) people's historically formed and culturally variable wants, tastes, desires, wishes, and fantasies, as well as the pleasures they may crave;
(2) the products and services available at any one time for consumption, plus those that are imminent or anticipated;
(3) the wealth and other financial resources, including credit, available to people that makes participation in the purchasing of goods and services possible and determines scale, extent, and frequency;
(4) factors that bear on consumer confidence such as employment status and security, as well as perception of future economic prospects;
(5) the standard of living and lifestyles of friends, acquaintances, and the media profiled consumption extravagances and excesses of iconic celebrity figures, which in varying degrees people may aspire to and seek to emulate.

Additionally, but by no means of least significance, there is the growing repertoire of marketing techniques that in one way or another are brought to bear on virtually all of the above, with the intention of making people aware of the existence of products and brands, but more importantly attempting to increase existing predispositions to consume by arousing desire, stimulating fantasy, and promoting the idea of a pleasurable experience being but a purchase away. Given consumer activity is indeed exposed to such an extensive range of influences, the notion that consumer demand is cultivated, nurtured, and shaped, in short subject to various forms of mobilization and management, becomes uncontroversial (Ewen and Ewen, 1992; Ewen, 2001; Klein, 2001; Dawson, 2005; Leiss et al., 2005).

To view consumer demand as cultivated and managed is not to promote the idea that consumers simply respond positively to whatever corporate marketing strategy is employed. Consumers do actively exercise degrees of choice and make decisions about what goods and services to purchase, but they do so under conditions which are subject to a range of influences, prominent among which are those that emanate from manufacturers of products and the work of cultural intermediaries in product design and marketing. The logic of economic growth necessitates continual production of, what are represented as and appear as, 'new' goods, a status which may derive from physical or technological innovations in design, function, and/or performance, as well as aesthetic developments in respect of appearance, styling, and packaging. Marketing and product management seek to influence consumers in respect of the things they desire, wish to own, and most importantly choose to purchase, and the frequency with which they do so. The aim is to ensure that consumers do not get (too) attached to a specific fashion or product for any length of time and to this end innovations in design and style, new performance features, and new products are perpetually being promoted through enticing advertising images and persuasive marketing techniques, the intention being to continually (re)generate consumer desires and stimulate interest in purchasing the new commodities becoming available. Appropriately marketed as the latest, fashionable, more contemporary looking, or 'better' designed, the new products, represented as possessing different features, additional functions, and other potentially appealing attributes, almost inevitably make existing comparable commodities, the ones already owned, appear tired, old, obsolescent, and in need of replacement, which they are, over and over again, by persuaded individuals, most of us, for whom life is increasingly all-consuming.

Notes
1. Apple's environmental policy is outlined in 'A Greener Apple' (http://www.apple.com/ hotnews/agreenerapple/). (retrieved 1 July 2009)

2. In 2009, in the midst of the global economic recession Topshop entered the American market. Although it was described as 'the worst possible time to open a fashion store' shoppers were reported to have queued for up to five hours in anticipation of the opening of Topshop in Manhattan. Once again the consumer appeal of celebrity was employed to launch the brand, but rather than appearing in a window display, for this event Kate Moss appeared alongside the owner Sir Philip Green 'standing on a podium decorated with crowns and the Union flag' in the SoHo superstore (Clark, 2009).

5

GLOBALIZATION AND MODERN CONSUMER CULTURE

Significant increases in the material standards of living of a substantial proportion of the world's population occurred in the course of the second half of the twentieth century. The perennial gale of 'creative destruction' Schumpeter (1975[1942]: 82) identified as a necessary feature of capitalist economic life continually brought into being new consumers, goods, methods of production, technologies, and forms of organization. The number of products and services produced and consumed around the world has continued to grow as more of the world's population has aspired to the materially acquisitive lifestyles that predominate in 'overdeveloped' and 'over-consuming' countries (Renner, 2004). Over the period in question worldwide consumer expenditure increased by a factor of six to US$24 trillion, but of this sum 86% was accounted for by the wealthiest 20% of the world's population while the poorest 20% accounted for a mere 1.3%. Moreover, in Africa, during the final quarter of the twentieth century, average household consumption actually fell by 20% (United Nations Development Programme, 1998).

In the early years of the twenty-first century global per capita consumption continued to grow and was reported to be increasing at a rate between 8 and 12 times faster than population (Princen et al., 2002: 4). Between 1993 and 2004 'real personal consumption expenditures per capita' increased by one-third in the USA alone and by the end of this period the lifestyles that in the twentieth century had been largely limited to the rich nations of North America, Europe, and Japan had been adopted by around 1.7 billion people worldwide (Schor, 2005). This global 'consumer class' currently represents over 25% of the world's population and it is continuing to grow as a significant proportion of the populations in China and India emulate American and European consumer lifestyles. The number of such consumers in China and India is now greater than in Western Europe, although currently the average Chinese or Indian consumes significantly less than the average Western European or North American (Gardner et al., 2004: 6).

Economic Growth

The increase in global consumption is a corollary of the pursuit of economic growth and is an objective aggressively promoted by commercial corporations around the world and enthusiastically endorsed by governments of virtually all political persuasions. Economic policy narratives have consistently tended to place emphasis on the necessity of pursuing economic growth, achieving year-on-year increases in production, in the value of the goods and services produced by commercial corporations and the economies of nation states, a necessary result of which is that rates of consumption, in turn, have to rise to absorb growth in production. The strong implication conveyed by such narratives is that 'growth is good' and that 'more' is necessarily better. However, the idea that economic growth is necessarily beneficial is questionable. Economic growth may have the potential to produce material and moral benefits insofar as the production of more goods and services may lead to an increase in material standards of living, promote an increase in opportunities, enhance tolerance, improve social mobility, and perhaps even raise the prospect of greater commitment to democracy (Friedman, 2006). However, much depends on what is produced, the terms and conditions under which things are produced, how commodities and services are socially distributed, and, increasingly, what impact production and consumption have on the environment (Princen et al., 2002; Starke, 2004, 2008, 2009; Jackson, 2009).

The neo-liberal pursuit of economic growth through economic deregulation to promote entrepreneurship and free up market forces, along with an associated imposition of market philosophy on the public sector, coupled with the introduction of tax breaks for corporations and the wealthy, has not led to greater savings, investment, and enhanced economic activity of benefit to all – the great myth of supply-side or 'trickle down' economics. Rather, neo-liberal 'free-market' economic policy, the cultivation of a 'consumerist culture', and the transformation of citizen-subjects into desiring consumers, has led to a form of unregulated global capitalism – 'turbo-capitalism' (Luttwak, 1999), 'savage' or 'wild' capitalism (Bruner, 2002; Davis and Monk, 2007), 'disaster capitalism' (Klein, 2007) – that has precipitated a rapid growth in inequality and luxurious forms of consumption alongside rising poverty rates, and in addition has been recognized to be increasingly threatening the very eco-system on which we all ultimately depend (Harvey, 2005; Shankar et al., 2006).

At the heart of the neo-liberal promotion of the 'virtues' of deregulation and free-market forces as the means to increase economic growth, prosperity, and freedom is the institution of 'a consumerist vision of the world' (Bourdieu, 2003: 30), the most persuasive and globally pervasive version of which was born in the USA in the late nineteenth century from where it has for 'well over a century ... extended its global power through aggressive marketing of consumer products' (Wilk, 2001: 255). A critical consequence of which has been 'the global replication of the American pattern of intensively commercialized and commodified life-styles' (Dawson, 2005: 127), in short, other nations consuming 'more and more like Americans' (Ritzer, 2005: 38: see also 41–3).

Global consumerism: made in America

Global consumer culture was made, initially at least, in America. In the late-nineteenth century a culture of acquisition and consumption that equated happiness with materialism, with the pursuit and possession of things, began to acquire firm roots in America. It was a culture that relentlessly promoted 'the cult of the new'; a culture made possible by what was considered to be 'the benign genius of the "free" market' which seemed to have the potential to provide an 'infinitely growing supply of goods and services' to all Americans, holding out the prospect of a 'democratization of desire', of everyone sharing in the consumer dream (Leach, 1993: 3–6). A mass production economy, mass consumer institutions, and aggressive marketing of mass produced goods emerged first in America. Various institutions contributed to the promotion of consumption, to the generation of consumer culture, in particular commercial corporations, banks, department stores, business and design schools, intermediaries in advertising, marketing, design and display, and government agencies, each of which served in different ways to nurture and direct people's aspirations 'toward consumer longings, consumer goods, and consumer pleasures' (Leach, 1993: 10). As the American domestic market expanded to become the largest in history so American businesses began to look beyond national boundaries and to actively pursue global markets (Leach, 1993; Stearns, 2001).

The late twentieth-century neo-liberal economic configuration, with its rhetoric of 'free markets', consumer sovereignty and consumer choice, policies promoting privatization, and promises of social, economic, and political benefits trickling down the social hierarchy, became synonymous with the USA (Beck, 2000: 112). The pursuit of globally free markets and the necessary corollary, promotion of a globally extensive culture of consumerism, has been described as 'an American project' (Gray, 1999: 100) and, in turn, criticized for 'universalizing the particular interests and the particular tradition of the economically and politically dominant powers (principally the United States)' (Bourdieu, 2003: 75). The deployment of policies ostensibly designed to promote the development of a neo-liberal, global free-market 'utopia' has had, at best, mixed results, producing a number of 'dystopian' consequences, including significant increases in inequality and a growing disparity in wealth distribution, an erosion and undermining of public services and social provision, and the generation of a 'political economy of insecurity' following the deregulation of significant aspects of economic life, associated demands for greater flexibility on the part of workers, and the off-shoring of jobs to locations around the world where labor costs and health and safety standards are lower (Bourdieu, 1998; Beck, 2000; Giroux, 2003).

Since the early 1970s, despite continuing economic growth, associated increases in the overall wealth of the country, and the global economic dominance of American corporate brands – in 2007 they represented over half of the top 100 brands (Kiley, 2007) – a significant number of American citizens, if not the majority, have had to come to terms with income stagnation, or worse, decline, and a steadily diminishing share of national wealth. During the period 1978–1995 'average weekly earnings of … 80 percent of rank-and-file working Americans, adjusted for inflation, fell by 18 per cent', while chief executive officers (CEOs) in the period 1979–1989 enjoyed real annual pay increases of 19% (Gray, 1999: 114). The ratio between the pay of the average CEO and that of the average worker in America rose from 44.8 in 1973 to 172.5 in 1995 and to 262 in 2005 (Castells, 1998: 130; Mishel, 2006). Over this period 'the richer families increased their average annual income the fastest, while the poorer ones saw their income decline the most' (Castells, 1998: 132). In addition, on top of sharp increases in income inequality, wealth inequality almost doubled. By 2003, the concentration of wealth, as measured by the Gini coefficient, had reached 0.82 and was noted to be 'pretty close to the maximum level of inequality you can have' which is 1.0 (Wolff, 2003).[1] The USA, where in 1998 the top 1% owned 38% of all wealth, is recognized to be 'much more unequal than any other advanced industrial country', its closest competitor in terms of inequality being the UK, where at the time the top 1% owned around 23% of all wealth (Paxton, 2002; Wolff, 2003).

Promotion of the free-market 'utopia' has proven costly, especially for those suffering from the hardships of 'inequality, polarization, poverty, and misery' in an increasingly dual America (Castells, 1998: 133–4). Yet despite growing inequality there have been very significant increases in private

forms of consumption since the 1970s, leading analysts to make reference
to rapidly growing 'personal consumption expenditures' (Toosi, 2002: 13)
and the 'triumph of rampant, individual and individualizing consumerism'
(Bauman, 2007b: 145; see also Beck, 2000: 75), as well as the increasing
identification of personal fulfillment with 'individualized hyperconsumption' (Castells, 1998: 160). As a proportion of US GDP consumer expenditure rose from 64.8% in 1970 to 66.7% in 1990, then to 67.8% by 2000 and
70% by 2006 and over this period 'durable goods, non-durable goods and
services ... all enjoyed growth' (Toosi, 2002; 13; Hoover Institution, 2006).
Consistent increases in consumer spending above the rate of growth in
GDP were made possible by a drop in saving levels, rising stock market and
housing values, and significantly a growth in credit – 'total (non-mortgage)
consumer credit outstanding increased from US$119 billion at year-end
1968 to US$1456 billion in June 2000 (in current dollars, not seasonally
adjusted)' and stood at US$2470 billion by the middle of 2007 (Durkin,
2000: 1; Harvey, 2003; Schroeder, 2007). However, as the 'credit crunch'
that began with the meltdown in 2007 of the US sub-prime mortgage market started to affect global stock markets, housing values, employment,
interest rates, and consumer confidence, concerns began to be expressed
about the *economic* sustainability of prevailing patterns of American hyper-
consumption and, in turn, global consumption, and such concerns grew in
the course of 2008 as the financial crisis deepened significantly. However,
even more troubling and certain has been the accumulation of a wealth of
scientific evidence indicating that prevailing patterns of global consumption are
ecologically unsustainable (Princen et al., 2002; Starke, 2004).

America – the global consumer brand

The popularity and influence of American consumer culture and the products and services it has developed, including all manner of goods ranging
from clothing styles and brands, to tastes in food and beverages, to films
and television programs, as well as the development and deployment of
software and hardware innovations in information technology, has been
truly global in scope. Coca-Cola, Ford, Levi, Gap, Nike, McDonald's, KFC,
Pizza Hut, Starbucks, Heinz, Wrigley's, Marlboro, Hollywood, Disney,
MTV, IBM, Microsoft, Apple, Motorola, Kodak, Google, e-Bay, Amazon,
American Express, Gillette, and Budweiser, represent merely some of the
American brands that have achieved a global profile and impact. The
proliferation, adoption, and local adaptation of innovative and popular
consumer products, services, and styles around the world, including for
example, jeans and other types of casual clothing, rock'n' roll and other
forms of popular music (e.g. rap, hip-hop, garage, grunge, etc.), fast food
dining, and drive-ins, to which might be added influential popular

cultural figures, American celebrities from the worlds of entertainment and sport, many of whom have become global icons, for example, the likes of Michael Jordan, Tiger Woods, and Madonna, further exemplify the globalization of American consumer culture.

The international popularity of American films and television programs and the respects in which they glamorize and simultaneously promote a consumerist way of life, the global proliferation of US military bases (estimated at eight hundred) and personnel, and the scale of tourism and travel around the world by American citizens, have been identified as important contributory factors in the global diffusion of American consumer culture (Stearns, 2001). The global appeal of American consumer products, services, and lifestyles is exemplified by the economic success of American film, television, music, fashion, and food corporations, the popularity of their commodities, and the numerous local imitations they have given rise to, ranging from the Indian film industry's Bollywood emulation of Hollywood, to products designed to counter American economic and cultural imperialism, two appropriate examples of the latter being Coca-Cola like beverages intended to appeal to Muslims, notably Zamzam Cola, the Iranian drink, and Mecca Cola, launched in France, bearing the slogan 'no more drinking stupid, drink with commitment' (Murphy, 2003). But, as the survey of the top 100 global brands conducted by Interbrand in 2008 demonstrates, American brands continue to dominate global rankings accounting for 52% overall and, more significantly, occupying 8 of the top 10 places and 30 of the top 50 places. Coca-Cola, IBM, and Microsoft were one, two, and three, respectively, with McDonald's, Disney, and Google at 8, 9, and 10, Hewlett-Packard 12, Gillette 14, American Express 15, Marlboro 18, Pepsi 26, Nike 29, with Dell at 32, Budweiser 33, and Ford at 49 (Interbrand, 2008: 85).

America has constituted *the* global brand insofar as American corporations have proven to be able to cultivate popularity and develop markets for their branded products and services around the world, a significant contributory factor in this success being the benefits that accrued from economies of scale deriving from a vibrant and sizeable locally generated consumer market. American-based corporations have been able to build on their local market strength as they have set about exporting their brands and 'the American way of consuming them' to people around the world who have become 'enamored of the American way of consuming' (Ritzer, 2005: 38, 39). As American corporations embraced trade liberalization and 'outsourced' and 'off-shored' production, continuing growth in American rates of consumption led to increasing 'dependency of the rest of the world on the US consumer market' (Harvey, 2003: 225; see also Klein, 2001). This became especially significant for those developing countries whose rising rates of economic growth from the closing decades of the century were heavily dependent on export-led production of consumer goods, a dependency that proved highly problematic as the

Table 5.1 Outstanding US consumer debt as percentage of disposable income ($US billion)

Year	Consumer debt	Consumer disposable income	Debt as percent of disposable income
1975	736.3	1187.4	62.0
1980	1397.1	2009.0	69.5
1985	2272.5	3109.3	73.0
1990	3592.9	4285.8	83.8
1995	4858.1	5408.2	89.8
2000	6960.6	7194.0	96.8
2005	11496.6	9039.5	127.2

Note: Disposable income is the income after paying taxes.
Source: Board of Governors of the Federal Reserve System, Flows of Funds Accounts of the United States, Historical Series and Annual Flows and Outstandings, Fourth Quarter 2005 (9 March 2006). Available at http://www.federalreserve.gov/releases/Z1/Current/ (cited in Foster, 2006).

'almost entirely debt-financed' consumption of American consumers and their European counterparts began to be affected by the onset of a global economic recession in 2008 (Harvey, 2003: 225; Macartney, 2009).

Consumer expenditure constituted 69% of US GDP and accounted for 80% of American jobs in 2002, but such consumer expenditure was debt-led and largely credit-based or credit-dependent (Schwenninger, 2003). As Table 5.1 illustrates, between 1975 and 2005 outstanding consumer debt increased from 62% to 127.2% of disposable income (Foster, 2006).

Explanations of increasing household indebtedness have included references to over-borrowing by uninhibited consumer hedonists, too-readily available loans and credit from a deregulated banking sector employing new (and riskier) financial instruments in pursuit of increasing profitability, and persuasive marketing campaigns which have enticed consumers to spend beyond their means (Montgomerie, 2007). However, towards the end of 2007 consumer spending in America was still increasing and was calculated to be approaching US$9.5 trillion a year, approximately 20% more than European consumers were spending, and considerably in excess of both the US$1 trillion a year that Chinese consumers were considered to be spending and the US$650 billion being spent by Indian consumers (Roach, 2007; Roubini, 2008).

American consumption: limits and limitations

Insofar as American economic policy has increasingly been based upon 'debt-led consumption growth … financed by capital from abroad' (Schwenninger, 2002) the key question occupying analysts has been that of its sustainability. The financial difficulties that began with the sub-prime mortgage crisis in 2007 led to a drop in house prices and the value of equity in property, restrictions on credit and access to mortgages, a reduction in the means available to finance consumer expenditure, and a consequent erosion of consumer confidence. As one observer at the time speculated:

> Consumers will have to resort to spending and saving the old-fashioned way, relying on income rather than assets, even as mounting layoffs will make income growth increasingly sluggish. For the rest of the world, this will come as a rude awakening. America's recession is likely to shift from homebuilding activity, its least global sector, to consumer demand, its most global. (Roach, 2007)

As the economy entered a recession late in 2008 fears about an end to US consumption-led economic growth increased. Signs of the unsustainable character of America's consumption-driven economy had been growing for some time. For a number of years 'current' US consumption had been funded by a combination of factors, including depletion of non-renewable natural resources, debt, sale of domestic assets to foreign agencies, currency inflation, and significantly reduced funding of social entitlement programs. After World War II the level of individual, corporate, and government debt stood at 158% of national income, but by 2007 it had risen steeply to 366%. Levels of debt carried by individuals increased significantly as consumers increasingly drew on equity to purchase goods and services, the value of equity held in homes declining from 81.5% in 1950 down to 47.5% in 2007 (Table 5.2).

However, as well as running up debts that have to be met in the future, essential social entitlement programs in the USA have been deprived of 'current' necessary levels of funding by successive political administrations that have sought to make a virtue of relatively low levels of taxation. Increases in consumer expenditure have effectively been funded through

Table 5.2   Unsustainable costs of US consumption, 1950–2007

Measure	1950	1980	2007
Accumulated US debt as percentage of US national income	158	194	366
US home equity as percentage of real estate value	81.5	68.5	47.5
Incremental annual US debt as percentage of US national income	6.2	18	33.2
Total US debt as percentage of US net worth	31.7	35.7	61.2
Foreign ownership as percentage of US domestic assets	–	3.1	17.6

Source: US Federal Reserve (cited in Clugston, 2008).

levels of taxation on income set at rates lower than required to fully meet
public expenditure on health and welfare provision (e.g. Social Security,
Medicare and Medicaid programs). The problems arising from 'current'
shortfalls in public sector funding of 'social entitlement' programs effectively have been deferred to an unspecified future for another political
administration to deal with. However, the financial cost is growing at a rate
of US$2.5 trillion a year and, estimated to be in the region of US$77 trillion,
is in excess of 'total national net worth ... [of] approximately $73 trillion'
and increasingly acknowledged to be unsustainable (Clugston, 2008).

   The crisis in financial markets, which increased significantly in intensity in 2008, and led to the nationalization of two pivotal US mortgage
lenders (Freddie Mac and Fannie Mae) and the world's largest insurer
AIG, the collapse of an American investment bank (Lehman Brothers),
and the takeover of another (Merrill Lynch), lent weight to the diag-
nosis of the unsustainable scale of American debt-led consumption
and support to those who identified the rapidly growing economies
and developing consumer markets of China and India as of increasing
global significance (Harvey, 2003; Ehrenreich, 2008). A number of
indices, including growth in manufacturing, services, and importantly
infrastructural investment, have been identified by some analysts as signifying the prospect of a 'power shift' towards Asia, especially towards
China and India, whose economies, including consumer markets, have
been expanding at a rapid rate (Harvey, 2003). However, the global
consequences of the economic crisis, the catalyst for which was the collapse of Lehman Brother's bank, which filed for bankruptcy in the USA
in mid-September 2008, demonstrated that a rude awakening would
not be confined to the American economy and its consumers, but would
also encompass the economies of countries, especially those in Asia, that
had been export beneficiaries of America's consumption-driven import-
ing of manufactured goods and outsourced services. By the beginning
of 2009, it was evident that the growth rates of the economies of China
and India were slowing, the former having declined quite significantly
from 13% in 2007 to 9% in 2008, the latter declining from a reported
9.3% in 2007 to 7.3% in 2008 (International Monetary Fund, 2009;
Macartney, 2009). As *The Economist* noted in a lead article on the Asian
economies:

> America's consumer boom and widening trade deficit, which pow-
> ered much of Asia's growth over the past decade, has come to an
> end. America's return to thrift is unlikely to prove a cyclical blip.
> For years to come, Americans will have to save more and import
> less. Asia's export-led growth therefore seems to have reached its
> limits ... It needs a new engine of growth: in future it must rely
> more on domestic demand, especially consumption. (2009)

Globalization, Homogenization, Localization

Globalization is a complex term employed to refer to a variety of processes and a range of factors that are not only economic, but also cultural, social, political, technological, and ideological in form and which, in various complex ways, have been transforming the lives of people and communities around the world from at least the fifteenth century if the epicenter is Europe (Robertson, 1990) and even earlier if the epicenter is Asia (Frank, 1998). The concept has spawned an over-extended family of related terms designed to provide a purchase on the respects in which globalization may, or may not, be promoting particular outcomes. The most significant broad outcomes attributed to processes of globalization are 'homogenization', that is the creation of similarities and/or forms of convergence through a reduction or an erosion of cultural differences, and 'heterogenization', that is the establishment of new forms of difference as local consumers and communities draw selectively on, adapt to, and/or accommodate global forces and flows in their way of life (Robertson, 2001).

The globalization of a consumer culture, which first emerged in America, is not synonymous with homogenization, standardization, or convergence, it does not necessarily mean that cultural differences are destined to be eroded, or are bound to disappear. To the contrary, markets might have become global but that should not be interpreted to mean that 'converging commonality' is the inevitable outcome (Levitt, 1983: 92). However, the global diffusion of American economic institutions, corporations, and practices, along with consumer cultural forms and brands – goods, services, and styles – undoubtedly has led to local cultures being transformed in various ways, to accommodations and adaptations between local and global forms, to changes in tastes, an increase in the quantity and range of goods and services being consumed, and a commensurate increase in lifestyle choices available to those included in a growing global consumer class. The globalization of American consumer cultural forms and lifestyles has led to costs as well as benefits, to concerns about the potentially detrimental impact on local forms of life (customs, practices, and tastes) and local environments, as well as recognition of potentially positive developments associated with new products, forms of organization, business practices, and related innovations.

To further explore aspects of the globalization of consumer culture consideration will be given to specific accommodations and adaptations to local tastes and conditions made by globally prominent American brands, as well as examples of local concerns aroused by unanticipated developments and unwanted consequences associated with the global diffusion of American corporate consumer commodities and services.

McDonald's beyond America: brand accommodation and adaptation

American corporations have achieved global prominence by successfully taking note of local cultural features, by modifying, customizing, and developing their product ranges and practices, where and when necessary, to adapt to and accommodate local cultures. In 2007, there were over 31,000 McDonald's fast food franchises operating in 119 countries serving 47 million customers every day (McDonald's, 2008). While some features of McDonald's restaurants around the world are to a degree standardized, including in many, but not all places, the prominence of the Golden Arches logo, restaurant layouts, color schemes, and product ranges, accommodations are made to local tastes and concerns. In Israel McDonald's has kosher and non-kosher restaurants, the former are not open on the Sabbath or on religious holidays and there are no dairy products on their menus and all food is prepared in accordance with kosher law. Accommodating the beliefs of Hindus and Muslims McDonald's in India has no beef or pork, or associated by-products on its menu, a significant proportion of which, around 50%, is vegetarian, including versions of popular local dishes. A further example is provided by McDonald's in Japan where the introduction of shrimp burgers and tofu burgers, as well as versions of popular local dishes, such as 'two types of *karei raisu* ("curry rice," white rice served with a thick curry-flavored gravy): beef and chicken' and '*omiotsuke* ("miso soup")', have been considered to exemplify the 'Japanification of McDonald's' (Andoh, 1993).

In 2008, there were 960 McDonald's with 60,000 staff in China, and it represented the corporation's fastest growing market. To put this in perspective KFC, which opened its first restaurant in Beijing in 1987, had 2200 outlets in 456 cities in China by 2008 and was said to be expanding at the rate of one a day and to be better placed than McDonald's because 'Chinese people love chicken more than beef' (Wang, 2008: 67; *China Daily*, 2008). As with other Asian countries the menu in McDonald's China has been modified to include foods designed to accommodate local tastes, one example being steamed corn cup which has proven very popular and has been introduced in other related marketplaces such as Hong Kong and Singapore. KFC has gone further than McDonald's by introducing a wider range of menu items appealing to the palates of Chinese consumers, for example congee, or rice porridge, and 'Old Peking Style Chicken Roll' (Jargon, 2008; Wang, 2008).

The first McDonald's in China was opened in Shenzhen in 1990 and the first drive-through opened in 2007, five years after the first drive-through opened by KFC, but reflecting the accelerating pace at which the country was changing, at least in the cities, from a predominantly bicycle culture to a rapidly growing car culture. In addition to the appeal of McDonald's as provider of a taste of American culture, with the Big Mac constituting an evocative 'symbol of Americana' and exemplifying 'the promise of modernization' (Yan, 2001), the corporation's reputation for reliability and its self-promotion in terms of 'quality food, good service, cleanliness, and good value' resonates strongly in China where there have been significant and understandable concerns about food safety following a number of scares (Zhou, 2004, 2006a, 2000b). To ensure its reputation for brand quality McDonald's has sought to maintain management control and has been cautious about franchising in China (Shen, 2007). As Watson notes:

> The equation between McDonald's and reliability is especially strong in China, where competitors not only dress their staff in McDonald's-style uniforms, but also engage in what are perhaps best described as public exhibitions of cleanliness. In Beijing, local fast food chains regularly employ one or more workers to mop floors and polish windows – all day long every day. The cleaners usually restrict their efforts to the entryway, where their performance can best be observed by prospective customers. Beijing residents often watch for such signs before they choose a place to eat. McDonald's is one of the few chains that carries this preoccupation with cleanliness into the kitchens, which are also on display. (2003: 147)

Rather than consider the globalization of McDonald's and other goods and services as leading to increasing homogeneity, it is more appropriate to conceptualize the associated economic and cultural consequences in terms of adaptations and accommodations made by global corporations to local customs, tastes, and practices and, in turn, the various ways in which the same local forms are simultaneously modified and transformed through processes of engagement with and selective adoption of global influences and factors, what has been termed 'glocalization', or the emergence of forms of 'difference-within-sameness' (Robertson, 2001: 462). Notwithstanding its American heritage and global profile and presence, McDonald's has to some extent become a 'local' institution in parts of Asia by adapting to and accommodating the tastes of indigenous communities, successfully becoming assimilated through a process in which both local cultures and aspects of global corporate practice are to a degree transformed. For example, a significant contribution to cultural change, including local hygiene practices, table manners, and other aspects of conduct in restaurants, has been attributed to McDonald's by analysts who have studied the complex forms of articulation between local cultures and global corporate influences in Hong Kong, Beijing, Taipei, Seoul, and Tokyo (Watson, 2006). But while new forms of 'difference' may have emerged, at the same time there are aspects of the experience of being in McDonald's restaurants in Israel, India, Japan, and China that would resonate with consumers in McDonald's in other locations around the world, including America, signifying elements of commonality.

Consumer product reorientation: US cookies in China

Oreos are a brand of chocolate cookie first introduced in America in 1912 by the National Biscuit Company (Nabisco), now a part of Kraft Foods. In 2005, it was described as the best selling cookie of the twentieth century with reported sales since its development totaling more than 490 billion (Toops, 2005). In 2008, Kraft Foods announced plans to grow 10 key brands in 10 overseas markets. The expressed intention was to focus promotion on a limited number of selected brands, including Oreo cookies and a range of chocolate bars, targeting specific overseas markets, notably China, Russia, Brazil, Southeast Asia, and Australia, as well as Germany, France, Italy, Spain, and the UK.

Oreo cookies were first introduced into China in 1996 but the US biscuits were not particularly popular and sales were relatively unimpressive. In 2005, after sales had been flat for five years, a Kraft marketing executive established a research team to study the responses of consumers to the product in China. What emerged was that Chinese consumers, who were not in any event big cookie eaters, considered the product too sweet and expensive. This led the company to develop a number of reduced-sugar versions of the US biscuit and, after product testing with Chinese consumers, select the one that seemed to best meet local tastes and, with fewer biscuits in each packet, meet concerns about expense by lowering the price. Growing signs that Chinese consumers were also developing a taste for milk led Kraft to introduce a campaign to 'educate Chinese consumers about the American tradition of pairing milk with cookies' for which three hundred university students were trained as Oreo brand ambassadors. Some of the students 'rode around Beijing on bicycles outfitted with wheel covers resembling Oreos' giving cookies away to 'more than 300,000 consumers', while others 'held Oreo-themed basketball games to reinforce the idea of dunking cookies in milk' (Jargon, 2008). However, in the face of competition from rival Nestle whose sales of chocolate covered wafer biscuits in China were growing faster than Oreo cookies, Kraft chose in 2006 to completely redesign their product for the local market.

The reformulated Chinese Oreo, consisting of 'four layers of crispy wafer filled with vanilla and chocolate cream, coated in chocolate', proved to be a great success, displacing a local biscuit brand HaoChiDian to become in 2006 the best selling biscuit in China (Jargon, 2008). From an initial strategy, trying to introduce a standardized US product into a very different overseas market, Kraft moved to an acceptance of the need to be appreciative of local tastes, the necessity of being open to innovation, and the importance of redesigning the product, alongside the employment of appropriately targeted marketing campaigns, to successfully generate a growth in consumer interest and an increase in product sales. Effectively Kraft abandoned their US product, the familiar cookie, and traded on the power of the Oreo brand, which they transferred to an alternative product, one which their research suggested would appeal to Chinese palates, and by so doing they succeeded in securing 23.4% of the US$1.3 billion Chinese biscuit market and simultaneously demonstrated that pursuit of global markets may require a policy of 'localization' (Jargon, 2008; Wang, 2008).

Coca-Cola's world: costs and controversies

Coca-Cola was introduced as a product, as a 'soda fountain drink', in America in the late 1880s and in the 1920s the company began to construct a global franchise network, which by the beginning of the twenty-first century embraced 200 countries and 450 brands of soft drink (Pendergrast, 2000; Hays, 2004). The company chronicle of Coca-Cola's development as a global business states that the company's power and prestige were made explicit in 1988 when 'three independent worldwide surveys conducted by Landor & Associates confirmed Coca-Cola as the best-known, most-admired trademark in the world' (Coca-Cola Heritage, n.d.). In 2007, the largest markets for Coca-Cola were Mexico, the USA, Brazil, and China, with the latter being identified by the company as an important focus for investment, research, and product development for its potential to become, in due course, the company's largest market.

Mexico

In the first four months of 2006 Coca-Cola's profits were reported to have increased by 10% thanks largely to significant market growth in Latin America and China, with the biggest increase being recorded in Mexico, where annual per capita consumption of Coca-Cola grew to 573 8-ounce (c. 220 ml) glasses in 2007 (*New York Times*, 2006; Coca-Cola Per Capita

Consumption, n.d.). Coca-Cola has been sold in Mexico since 1897 and now represents the company's largest market ahead of the USA. However, it is also a focus of environmental concern because of its use of a key resource, water, which is growing increasingly scarce. The manufacture of Coca-Cola requires substantial quantities of water, with estimates of the ratio of water consumed in the manufacturing process to beverage produced being between 3:1 and 4:1 (Bell, 2006; Tilly and Kennedy, 2007). Under the North American Free Trade Agreement (1994), through which the USA, Canada, and Mexico became a single integrated market, Coca-Cola was able to secure groundwater sources which had been designated a commodity that all parties are obliged 'to sell ... to the highest bidder under threat of being sued by private companies that want it' (Nash, 2007: 632, 633). After Vicente Fox, a former chief executive officer of Coca-Cola (Mexico), became President of Mexico (2000–2006) the Coca-Cola company was given permission by the federal water agency 'to tap deep groundwater resources', which are not metered and for which the 'municipality does not receive reimbursement' (Nash, 2007: 631). In negotiations held since 2000 with the Mexican government over water supplies Coca-Cola has secured 19 concessions 'for the extraction of water from aquifers and from 15 different rivers, some of which belong to indigenous peoples' and it has also been granted eight concessions to deposit ' its industrial waste into public waters' (Bell, 2006).

Bottled water

More than 10% of Mexico's population of 106 million do not have running water in their homes, yet the Coca-Cola company has been extracting and bottling groundwater from the Chiapan town of San Cristobal de las Casas and selling it 'throughout the world and to the people from whom it was expropriated' (Nash, 2007: 621–2). In 2004, the Coke plant used '107,332,391 liters of water – about as much as 200,000 homes would use' (Bell, 2006). The global consumption of bottled water in 2004 was more than 154 billion liters and in the period 1999–2004 consumption of the product doubled in Mexico to 18 billion liters making it the second highest consumer behind the USA on 26 billion liters, with China and Brazil not too far behind on 12 billion liters each (Franklin, 2006: 62). Third world countries, where 'potable water', that is water of a sufficient quality fit for drinking, is becoming increasingly scarce as population continues to grow, represent the fastest growing market for bottled water, a commodity that is argued to be '10,000 times more costly if one takes into account the energy expended in bottling, commercialization, and recycling' (Nash, 2007: 632; see also Ferrier, 2001). As well as the unregulated use of a valuable and, in a growing number of places around the world, increasingly scarce resource, bottled water production also has an impact on the environment. In 2001, the quantity of plastic used during the course of the year in the production of 89 billion liters of bottled water was estimated to be in the region of 1.5 million tons and environmental effects noted included toxic waste produced as part of manufacturing, recycling, and incineration, as well as emission of greenhouse gases associated with the global problem of climate change arising from the fact that 25% of the water bottled worldwide was being consumed outside the country of origin (Ferrier, 2001).

There is a rapidly growing global market for bottled water and Coca-Cola is one of the 'big four' corporations in the business, along with Nestle, Danone, and Pepsi. The market for bottled water seems destined to grow further given that demand for fresh water is rising faster than available supplies, one estimate being that by 2025 around two-thirds of the world's population will be living with some degree of concern or stress in respect of water and that up to one-third of the world's population may have no access at all to fresh water (Barlow and Clarke, 2002; see also Gleick et al., 2009). Bottled water began to be produced in America early in the nineteenth century. It was initially favored for its alleged curative properties for stomach ailments, but subsequently was recognized as a more reliable source of safe drinking water. By the end of the century the product was regarded 'as a desirable amenity rather than a luxury', but with improvements in the standard of tap water following chlorination the bottled water industry 'virtually ceased to exist' (Chapelle, 2005: 4).

For much of the twentieth century the industry, as Chapelle notes, 'limped along', but from 1960 to the end of the century the value of US consumption of bottled water grew from under US$50 million to in excess of US$5 billion. The increase in consumption was not down to any significant deterioration in water quality and tap water was still healthy to drink. However, media reports of the practice of dumping industrial waste and untreated sewage in rivers had led to growing concerns about water pollution, and occasional discoloring and odors led to further worries, on top of which questions began to be raised about taste. In addition, from the 1970s consumption of bottled water 'became trendy', was associated with 'style', and came to represent a form of 'conspicuous consumption', particularly among young urban professionals seeking a low-calorie beverage (Chapelle, 2005: 5). Reflecting on the growth in the bottled water industry during this period Chapelle identifies a successful US$5 million national advertising campaign for Perrier as an important catalyst:

> The distinctive green-glass Perrier bottle was cool, it was sophisticated, it was European, it was expensive. It was all the things the yuppies wanted in a lifestyle-defining product.

In the end, it was a rout. Sales of Perrier skyrocketed, and the rest of the American bottled water industry slipstreamed easily behind. Since 1980 sales of bottled water have increased steadily in the United States. (2005: 17)

In countries with good quality water on tap, bottled water was regarded as something of a luxury consumer item, but the major companies involved rapidly identified other potentially lucrative global markets. Companies such as Coca-Cola and Nestle recognized the scope for growing markets in non-industrialized countries where fresh drinkable water was either not readily available or was non-existent. It is precisely in locations such as these where the most significant increases in consumption of bottled water have taken place. For example:

Of the top 15 per capita consumers of bottled water, Lebanon, the United Arab Emirates and Mexico have the fastest growth rates, with consumption per person increasing by 44–59% between 1999 and 2004 ... Although in countries such as India and China consumption rates are not as high they have risen dramatically, tripling in India and doubling in China over the past 5 years. (Edwards, 2007: 2)

India

Coca-Cola was the leading brand of soft drink in India when it was removed from the country in 1977 for refusing to reveal its 'secret formula' and reduce its equity stake as required under the Foreign Exchange Regulation Act. The company returned in 1993 and immediately acquired leading local Indian brands, including the most popular and trusted Thums Up, along with Limca, Maaza, Citra and Gold Spot, plus all associated manufacturing, bottling, and distribution assets and resources (Kaye and Argenti, 2004). In 2000, Coca-Cola introduced Kinley, a brand of bottled water, and a year later developed a 'brand localization strategy' to improve its market position in India where it lagged behind rival Pepsi. In 2007, per capita consumption of Coca-Cola in India remained a modest seven 8-ounce glasses, placing it close to the bottom of the countries listed in the company's return. However, with a population of 1.1 billion and a growing consumer class, India, along with China, has been identified by the company as one of the markets with the greatest growth potential.

A significant quantity of the Coca-Cola Kinley brand of bottled water comes from MVR Mineral Water, a contract bottler whose estimate of groundwater extracted per day is 132,000 liters, of which 100,000 liters are used for bottling, with the remainder being used in the production process, or discharged as waste. A country that faces a significant water shortage, with around one-third of its villages lacking adequate supplies, has discovered that significant costs arising from bottled water and beverage production are being externalized on to the very local communities whose water security has been compromised by the activities of the global corporation (Kamat, 2002; Cockburn, 2005).

One particular Coca-Cola plant in India has been a focus of considerable critical comment and community opposition. The Coca-Cola bottling plant concerned, situated in Kerala's water belt, where there are large underground water resources, was granted a license from the local council and after sinking six bore wells began operations. In a relatively short period, less than six months, local villagers witnessed the level of water in their wells dropping sharply, in some cases running completely dry, and to make matters worse the quality of the water that was still accessible had deteriorated significantly. As Cockburn reports:

> The water they did draw was awful. It gave some people diarrhea and bouts of dizziness. To wash in it was to get skin rashes, a burning feel on the skin. It left their hair greasy and sticky. The women found that rice and dal did not get cooked but became hard. A thousand families have been directly affected, and well water affected up to three or four kilometers from the plant. (2005)

Following peaceful protest by local people the plant was closed down in April 2002 and the local council rescinded Coca-Cola's license in August 2003, shortly after which the water in local wells was declared unfit for human consumption. In the village of Plachimada close to where the plant was situated drinkable water is now a 4 km round trip away and with no accessible water local farmers have been driven out of business. Possibly after critically recalling the series of warm-fuzzy-feel-good advertising messages for which Coca-Cola has been responsible and by means of which the corporation has attempted to persuade us to purchase its product(s) – with slogans ranging from 'Sparkling – harmless as water, crisp as frost' (1908), 'Things go better with coke' (1963) and 'I'd like to buy the world a coke' (1971), to 'Life is Good' and 'Life tastes good' (2001) – Cockburn remarks of Coca-Cola's impact on the people of Plachimada that:

> The whole process would play well on The Simpsons. It has a ghastly comicality to it. When the plant was running at full tilt 85 truck loads rolled out of the plant gates, each load consisting of 550 to 600 cases, 24 bottles to the case, all containing Plachimada's prime asset, water, now enhanced in cash value by Cola's infusions of its syrups.
>
> Also trundling through the gates came 36 lorries a day, each with six 50-gallon drums of sludge from the plant's filtering and bottle cleaning processes ... Coca Cola was "giving back" to

Plachimada, the give-back taking the form of the toxic sludge, along with profuse daily donations of foul wastewater. (2005)

In addition to drawing down the community's scarce water supplies the company inflicted toxic waste on the environment by dumping its sludge, which it claimed represented free fertilizer. Subsequent analysis of the waste materials and nearby wells, into which it had seeped, revealed dangerous levels of cadmium and lead (Cockburn, 2005; Kamdar, 2007). In 2005, in Plachimada the community commemorated the 'thousand day anniversary vigil against Coca-Cola' demanding that the bottling plant be closed permanently and in 2006 the state government of Kerala banned the production and sale of both Coca-Cola and Pepsi-Cola on the grounds of the health hazards they represented (Coalition Against Coke Contracts, 2006).

A comparable sequence of events occurred in another Indian community in Kala Dera, where Coca-Cola commenced bottling operations in 2000. Within a year of the plant opening the local community, for whom agriculture is the main source of livelihood, began to see a rapid drop in the level of groundwater. Continuing loss of groundwater has affected the well-being and income of local farmers, women have been forced to walk an extra 5–6 km to obtain water for their household needs, and extraction and pollution associated with the plant's operation has led to a deterioration in water quality and availability, prompting the local community and 30 other villages to campaign for the plant to be closed. In 2007, a report by The Energy and Resources Institute (TERI) recommended that the company find alternative sources of water, relocate, or close down the plant, but late 2008 it was still operating and continuing to extract water (Adve, 2004; Srivastava, 2008).

In addition to legitimate concerns aroused by evidence of Coca-Cola's impact on local community water resources, the company also stands accused of using paramilitaries in Columbia to engage in anti-union violence, intimidating unionists and their families in Turkey, and engaging in 'union-busting activities in Pakistan, Guatemala, Nicaragua, Russia and elsewhere' (War on Want, 2006b).[2]

China

Coca-Cola was available in China from the early 1920s, with bottles being imported from the Philippines. In 1927, two bottling plants were established in Shanghai and Tianjin, but with the establishment of the People's Republic of China in 1949 all foreign companies were forced to leave and the company's manufacturing plants were nationalized. Bottles and cans of Coca-Cola were allowed back into China from Hong Kong in 1979 following the re-establishment of relations between the USA and China and in the following year a manufacturing plant was opened in Beijing with others quickly following in Guangzhou, Guangdong Province and Xiamen, Fujian Province. Since the mid-1980s the company has rapidly expanded activities in China and by 2001 it had 24 bottling facilities in 21 cities in addition to two concentrate plants. Local brands have also been developed through joint equity ventures, for example in 1996 Coca-Cola introduced Tian Yu Di (Heaven and Earth) brand, a range of non-carbonated beverages, teas, and bottled water and in the following year another local brand Xingmu (Smart), a range of carbonated fruit drinks that has proven very popular. The way in which the company has developed indigenous brands has been described as an exemplification of its 'flexible localization approach' in China (Teel, 2000: 16).

Coca-Cola has carefully adapted its products and business approach to the local Chinese market, employing what has been termed a 'think local, act local' strategy, encouraging local managers to produce new drinks and promote local initiatives. The process has been complex and constitutes a two-way exchange:

> Coca-Cola's international production and marketing expertise have both contributed and adapted to the unique local conditions and characteristics of the Chinese marketplace. The interchange is mutually reinforcing: just as Coca-Cola's presence in China has helped transform the Chinese economy, China's local conditions have required that the company adopt a "flexible localization" approach. (Teel, 2000: i)

While directing substantial funds to local advertising and marketing, US$26.1 million in 2001, the company has placed control in the hands of local managers. It is a policy that seems to have proven successful as a survey conducted in 2002 by the National Statistics Bureau and CCTV (China Central TV, the major television station) confirmed Coca-Cola as the best rated and most recognized soft drink in China for the seventh year in succession.

In an analysis of the development of advertising media and commercial culture in China Jing Wang (2008) has sought to clarify the notion of 'local' by exploring how in practice transnational corporations, such as Coca-Cola, McDonald's, and others have adapted to Chinese institutions, practices and tastes. As limitations on the effectiveness of standardized practices across multiple markets became increasingly apparent so corporations embraced the notion of 'localization'. As Sandy Douglas, President of the North American Division of Coca-Cola, stated in 2001 'Today successful companies meet consumers on their home ground – to talk, gain insight, tailor products, and build upon the brand', a strategy that is economically expressed in the corporate mantra 'Think local, act local' (Yang, 2001). Increasingly it is not location of manufacture, or corporate ownership that most matters, rather it is the identity or the meaning ascribed to a brand, to a product, and the perceived relationship and relevance of the brand to consumers. The primary aim of marketing, advertising, and branding is to connect with consumers by creating a sense that the brand is integrated into local lives.

The issue here is not one of 'cultural authenticity', the products emotionally branded as 'local' need not be local, as the success of the campaign to promote the Libo brand as a genuinely local Shanghai beer demonstrates. The campaign promoting Libo, the manufacturer of which 'has stakes in Singapore, Thailand, and the Netherlands, as well as Shanghai', effectively constituted an appealing sense of 'localness', in short constructed 'the local' (Wang, 2008: 323 n13). Although it is a global brand Coca-Cola in China has employed a localization strategy that has led to appropriately evocative, locally meaningful symbolic images being relayed in successful advertising campaigns. One particularly successful television advertisement set in Harbin in North East China provided a windmill based visual motif, Chinese music soundtrack, small children in bright jackets, a profusion of red colors, peasants happily welcoming fresh snow, and of course the obligatory final shot of 'a Coke bottle colored in the subtle shade of Chinese red' (Wang, 2008: 53). The commercial is considered to exemplify the 'think locally' corporate strategy which has been designed to optimize markets within the global economy, but drawing attention to the 'campaign's communication strategy and creative execution' Wang argues that in respect of camera angles and composition structure a Western aesthetic predominates and that the kind of narrative continuity and ordering that Chinese television viewers would be familiar with is completely absent. What would be very familiar to consumers around the world is 'the brand personality underlying the visuals … the same old Coca-Cola that we have known from the days of the Hilltop commercial and "Mean Joe Green" up to the more recent polar bear series' (Wang, 2008: 54).

The implication is that, notwithstanding the localization strategy, there is a significant underlying degree of continuity running through Coca-Cola's advertisements from the 1971 'I'd like to buy the world a Coke' Hilltop commercial and the 1979 'Have a Coke and a Smile' commercial featuring the defensive lineman from the Pittsburgh Steelers professional football team, through to the 1990s and the 'Always Coca-Cola' campaigns featuring, not the real thing, but animated polar bears and the slogan 'Always Cool'. There is a calculating corporate recognition that evoking and/or projecting a sense of the local, or being perceived to be attentive to local concerns, interests, and tastes, will be beneficial to sales and profitability. As Wang notes of the Harbin commercial:

> This commercial drives home a pedagogical lesson for those celebrating the emerging 'local' sensibilities of McDonald's,

Coke, and other transnational corporations. Precisely because there is a burgeoning Western market for 'difference' (that is, the exotic sells), accentuating local content has more to do with these corporations' new marketing strategy than their promotion of local cultural specificities. (2008: 54)

In practice there are a number of 'local' consumer markets in China, differentiated primarily according to social class: (1) a very small *nouveau riche*; (2) an aspiring but still relatively small middle class containing various categories of white collar workers (these first two categories representing less than 20% of the population); (3) a sizeable internally differentiated stratum of blue collar workers; and finally (4) agricultural workers and peasants (with the latter two categories accounting for the remaining 80% of the population). As well as social class based forms of consumer market segmentation consideration needs to be given to forms of generational segmentation, as well as significant differences between rural and urban communities. It is the urban communities that have been readily integrated into the global economy, the major coastal cities, places like Shanghai, Beijing, Guangzhou, and Shenzhen that were the first to experience market oriented reforms, along with other urban communities, wealthy provincial centers, and affluent county towns (Kalish, 2005: 11; Wang, 2008: 3).

Coca-Cola's local impact has been considerable. For example, in 1998 its activities added 1.5 billion RMB to taxation revenues, created 410,000 additional employment opportunities, and injected in the region of 8.16 billion RMB into the Chinese economy (Teel, 2000: ii–iii). Other local contributions have included enterprise reform, stimulating entrepreneurship, building supply networks, workforce training, developing domestic brands, and supporting education through a variety of initiatives, including 'Coca-Cola First Generation University Scholarships ... earmarked for underprivileged students ... [and donation of] 20 million RMB to the Chinese Project Hope to establish 50 elementary schools and 100 Hope libraries for China's remote areas' (Teel, 2000: v).

Through these contributions and other comparable high profile campaigns, including sponsoring the Chinese national football team in its World Cup qualifying campaign in 2001, the company has 'integrated its brand name successfully into the fabric of everyday life in China' (Wang, 2008: 133).

Consumer culture, globalization and sport

The popular appeal of sport increased significantly during the course of the twentieth century, becoming truly worldwide in scope and intensity with the growth of international sporting bodies, competitions, tournaments, migratory flows of competitors, and associated globally extensive forms of media representation, especially in the form of terrestrial, and subsequently, satellite television and the Internet (Maguire, 1999). Sport became increasingly closely articulated with the corporate world over this period of time, but it was not just a case of business values intruding into sport, of sport being turned into a business, and sport events and participants becoming commodities. It was also a matter of distinctive qualities possessed by the institution of sport and its participants, notably popular cultural appeal and an unrivalled aura of authenticity, being recognized to be of potentially unique value in the increasingly competitive process of capital accumulation in a fully-fledged consumer society, of unique value that is to the enhancement of corporate brands, global marketing, and the promotion and sale of products brought into association with popular sport events and iconic celebrity sporting figures (Klein, 2001; Amis and Cornwall, 2005; Smart, 2005, 2007).

Both the institution of sport and popular sporting figures have proved to be reliable sources of appropriately appealing promotional symbols and iconic images, by means of which it has become possible to successfully cultivate local markets for global brands. As the twentieth century unfolded commercial corporations were increasingly recognizing that there are few, if any, cultural forms that have the potential of modern sport to engender local manifestations of consumer cosmopolitanism. The formation of a global sporting network, to which the growth of media coverage and corporate sponsorship have made such a decisive contribution, provides an array of consumer culture signifiers which transcend differences of politics, culture, and religion and engender positive feelings of shared experience, if not a sense of common meaning, through the rituals of professional competition on display (Aris, 1990). Reflecting on the consumer marketing appeal of sport events and figures in the late 1980s, the deputy managing director of International Sport and Leisure, the most influential sports marketing agency of its era, commented that 'There are only four things that travel across borders: sport, music, violence and sex. And it's difficult to find sponsors for violence and sex' (cited in Aris, 1990: 169). The association of corporate brands, products, and services with global sport events and iconic globally popular sporting figures has proven to be a very effective marketing strategy, one which has, for the most part, significantly enhanced consumer appeal and generated increased sales and profits worldwide.

Coca-Cola's 'Africanization'

Coca-Cola's attempt to further integrate its brand into Chinese everyday life through sponsorship of the national football team exemplifies the way in which sports events and sporting figures have been used by global corporations to promote their brands and products in local markets. Notwithstanding all of its difficulties, including poverty, health problems, conflicts and civil wars, Africa represents another significant market for Coca-Cola, with the average African consuming twice as much of the company's product range each month as their Asian equivalents. In South Africa Coca-Cola is the leading brand, the brand that is 'most admired' and of which people are most aware, and this has been attributed to its advertising, marketing, and branding strategy and high local profile, which is enhanced by effective local community involvement in a range of events and activities, including in particular sponsorship of sports events, sports development, scholarships and education projects, as well as promotion of entrepreneurial activity. Reflecting on Coca-Cola's 'Africanization', Irwin (2001) states that 'the ultimate American product, manages to assimilate itself into utterly foreign cultures by utilizing local advertising campaigns that brilliantly link its products to people's aspirations and passions'.

In South Africa in the late 1990s a local advertising agency successfully promoted the beverage to townships and villages by running campaigns that very effectively and appealingly connected Coca-Cola with football, the sport which remains not only the country's but also the continent's obsession. In 2005, the company and football's world governing body FIFA announced at a press conference in South Africa (the location for the 2010 World Cup tournament) an extension of a longstanding commercial sponsorship arrangement, as well as the 'first global "FIFA World Cup™ Trophy Tour by Coca-Cola"', which in the period leading up to the 2006 tournament in Germany visited 31 cities in 28 nations. In addition, a new global marketing platform was introduced, 'We All Speak Football', which was described as bringing to life 'the optimistic vision of brand Coca-Cola to draw people together and set aside their differences, as a way of making the world a little bit better' (Coca-Cola, 2005). Coca-Cola has had some form of commercial sponsoring relation with FIFA since 1950, when it first began advertising in World Cup stadiums and it has an even longer association with the Olympic Games, stretching back as far as the 1928 Amsterdam games (Smart, 2007; Olympic Sponsorship).

Popular global sports events such as the FIFA World Cup, Olympic Games, and Formula 1, as well as cricket and rugby World Cups, tennis Grand Slam and Masters tournaments, and other significant sports events, such as major golf tournaments and athletics meetings, which also attract substantial television audiences from around the world, represent unrivalled opportunities for global corporations to integrate their brands into the everyday lives of the multiplicity of local communities that passionately follow sport and constitute potentially lucrative consumer markets. For example, McDonald's has been an official sponsor of the Olympic Games since 1976 and the FIFA World Cup since 1994. The company has sponsored a variety of other sports events, including football (UEFA Euro 2004 and 2008), and LPGA golf. In addition to its long association with the Olympic Games and FIFA World Cup, Coca-Cola has been a sponsor of the Rugby World Cup since 1995.

The IOC summer Olympic Games and FIFA's World Cup, staged every four years with a two-year interval between each organization's event, have been described by Visa's chief marketing officer as the 'only two "marquee property" events on the planet', events which global corporations can be confident will enhance the status and reputation of their brands with consumers around the world, providing they can secure Olympic Partner Programme or FIFA partnership status (*The Economist*, 2008). In confirmation of the commercial value and consumer appeal of corporate association with such global sports events, the chief executive of WPP, one of the world's largest communications services groups, taking stock of the marketing prospects associated with the Olympic Games of 2008, remarked that 'No multinational company bent on expanding into China or national company seeking to grow inside or outside China will miss out on the branding opportunity presented by the Olympics in Beijing' (quoted in Lane, 2008). It is the extent of the global audience exposure a sponsoring corporate brand is likely to receive through television coverage of the Olympic Games or the FIFA World Cup, wherever they happen to be held, that explains the commercial attractiveness of these two events to global corporations pursuing consumer markets around the world.

For example, consider the television viewing data for the Olympic Games in Athens (2004) and the FIFA World Cup in Germany (2006). The IOC reported that sponsorship targets were exceeded in Athens and that over US$1400 million was generated from broadcasting rights fees revenue. Over '300 television channels provided 35,000 hours of dedicated Olympic Games coverage over 17 days, delivering images from Athens 2004 to an unduplicated audience of 3.9 billion people in 220 countries and territories … Each television viewer worldwide watched an average of 12 hours of Olympic Games coverage on television over the 17 days of the Olympic Games' (IOC Athens, 2004). Some satellite and cable channels provided 24-hour per day coverage of the Olympics, including highlights, and 3G technology allowed some broadcasters to provide streaming video and highlight clips through mobile phones, and in some markets streaming video was available via the Internet and dedicated Olympic web sites (IOC Athens, 2004). It was estimated that around 80% of the world's population with access to electricity supply had watched the games at some point, with 60% watching every day, and that the total cumulative audience was in the region of 40 billion. For Coca-Cola, McDonald's, Samsung, Kodak, Visa, and the other TOP partners the global consumer brand exposure would have been unrivalled, the nearest equivalent being the worldwide appeal of FIFA's World Cup tournament. Matches from the World Cup in Germany in 2006 were broadcast to 214 countries on 376 channels. There were 43,600 'dedicated' programs broadcast and a total of 73,072 hours coverage, an increase on both the 2002 and 1998 tournaments. The cumulative television audience was estimated to be 26.29 billion (24.2 billion in-home viewers, 2.09 billion out-of-home) with the final between Italy and France attracting the largest cumulative audience of 715.1 million viewers (FIFA, 2006). For the principal sponsoring partners, Coca-Cola, Adidas, Emirates, Hyundai, Sony, and Visa, the event provided an effective and prestigious marketing platform through which to reach millions of consumers in more than 200 countries around the world.

Americanization and Globalization

Globalization has contributed to a 'consolidation of oligopolistic, monopoly, and transnational power within a few centralized multinational corporations … [for example] the world of soft-drinks competition is reduced to Coca-Cola versus Pepsi', as manufacturers find themselves overwhelmed by the entry of these global brands into their local markets (Harvey, 2005: 80; see also Stiglitz, 2002: 68). The global prominence, appeal, and impact of American corporate brands, products, and services has led some analysts to make reference to American economic and cultural imperialism, a process of Americanization and/or, in acknowledgement of the global impact of a range of specific commodities and organizational practices originating in the USA, 'coca-colonization' (Pendergrast, 2000), 'Disneyization' (Bryman, 2004), and 'McDonaldization' (Ritzer, 1998; Smart, 1999). Each of these terms conveys something more than simply the appeal or popularity of American products and services by implying that local cultures, customs, and practices, exposed to American consumer commodities, organizational practices, values, and lifestyles, to varying degrees have been vulnerable to, indeed have been subjected to, forms of colonization, homogenization, and/or standardization. Lending weight to such a view, Dawson, focusing specifically on the growth in global marketing operations, argues that in respect of three particular consumer constituencies, 'ordinary Europeans, ordinary Japanese … [and] Third World elites … commercial television, automobile transportation, fast food, and branded personal products have already gone far toward the global replication of the *American pattern of intensively commercialized and commodified lifestyles*' (2005: 127, emphasis added).

Notwithstanding all the qualifications that have been made by analysts armed with an array of concepts designed to qualify the impact processes of globalization have had on local customs and practices, it is evident that 'emulation has played an important role in global affairs. Much of the rest of the world has been entrained politically, economically, and culturally through Americanization ...[and] emulation of US consumerism, ways of life, cultural forms, and political and financial institutions has contributed to the process of endless capital accumulation globally' (Harvey, 2003: 41). Economic globalization, the relentless pursuit by corporations of markets for consumer products and services around the world, has led to the transformation of 'local' national industries, and given aspects of production, marketing, and consumption, in the particular locations in countries so affected, a 'cosmopolitan' character, providing new means for satisfying a range of existing local wants and tastes, as well as promoting new wants and tastes.

From early in the twentieth century American consumer commodities and services, in particular the iconic global brands which have emanated from corporate America to influence the lifestyles of people around the world, have played a very significant, if not hegemonic, role in the (trans) formation of local consumer tastes, wants, and desires. From Coca-Cola to McDonald's, from Nike to Gap and Apple, and from Hollywood and the film industry to Disney, MTV, and television series such as *CSI Miami* (the world's most popular show), *Lost*, *Desperate Housewives*, and *The Simpsons*, American consumer cultural forms have acquired international popularity and exercised an unrivalled influence on global consumerism. Such developments suggest that life in many places around the world, including 'in Europe and Japan has become more and more "American"' (Dawson, 2005: 127). In so far as lifestyles have become intensively commercialized and increasingly consumer orientated then such a conclusion may be warranted, however, qualification is necessary as American commodities, services, and lifestyle practices and values are themselves 'contextualized in local realities, and are thus transformed in the process' (Sassatelli, 2007: 179). Moreover, while American corporations and their iconic brands may predominate in the consumer marketplace there are other globally popular non-American brands deriving from Japan (Toyota, Nintendo), Korea (Samsung), Finland (Nokia), UK (Body Shop), Germany (BMW, Mercedes), Italy (Armani, Benetton) and the Netherlands (Heineken) (Stearns, 2001; Frost, 2002; Sassatelli, 2007). In short, if globalization in some respects and to some degree leads to forms of homogenization and/or standardization, the complex articulations that arise with local forms of life simultaneously promote new forms of difference. Increasing interconnectedness is now a feature of economic and cultural activity around the world, but while this is producing degrees of integration as global networks are formed and extended, rather than promoting convergence it is leading to new synergies and new forms of difference, to 'glocalization' or 'difference-within-sameness' (Robertson, 2001: 462; see also Gray, 1999; Wang, 2008).

The UN report 'Consumption for Human Development' drew attention to the respects in which globalization was creating degrees of integration in respect of a number of areas, including trade, investment, finance, and consumer markets. Local and national boundaries were perceived to be 'breaking down' and consumer markets were recognized to be increasingly open to 'a constant flow of new products' as competition increased and advertising became more and more aggressive. In particular, the report identifies the emergence of global consumer classes – 'elites' and 'middle classes' – following comparable consumer lifestyles, as well as the growth of 'global teens', a constituency of 'some 270 million 15–18-year-olds in 40 countries inhabiting a "global space", a single pop-culture world, soaking up the same videos and music and providing a huge market for designer running shoes, t-shirts and jeans' (United Nations Development Programme, 1998). In an analysis of global marketing and branding Klein also identified respects in which homogenizing effects were apparent in the form of the figure of the 'global teen', living in 'a global consumer loop: hot-linked from their cellular telephones to internet newsgroups; bonded together by Sony Playstations, MTV videos and NBA games ... middle class youth all over the world seem to live their lives as if in a parallel universe' (2001: 119). But the implication is not so much that teenagers around the world are becoming more American, although the growing preference of Chinese teens for Coca-Cola over green tea, Nike trainers instead of sandals, and KFC and McDonald's fast food instead of traditional rice dishes, does underline the appeal and market penetration of American brands and tastes, rather, as Klein observes, it is that global corporations intent on achieving global markets for their brands have sought to generate a placeless image of the global teen, a 'new demographic', one with which teens from different cultures can identify:

> Nationality, language, ethnicity, religion and politics are all reduced to their most colorful, exotic accessories, converging to assure us ... there is 'never an "us and them", but simply one giant "we"' ... a third notion of nationality – not American, not local, but one that would unite the two, through shopping. (2001: 120)

Globalization: for richer and poorer

While economic globalization has led to the erosion of local and national boundaries, to forms of integration in trade, investment, finance, and consumer markets, as well as to the emergence of a growing global consumer class, substantial numbers of the world's population have found themselves marginalized within, or excluded from, a burgeoning consumer culture. The globalization of consumer capitalist forms of life has led to increasing polarization between rich and poor (Sklair, 2002). For example, in the closing decades of the twentieth century consumption per capita increased in industrial countries by 2.3% annually and in East Asia by 6.1% annually, but there remained increasingly stark inequalities in consumption and around a quarter of the world's population, the 'desolately poor', were effectively being excluded from global consumerism and continue to be so. The United Nations reported that worldwide 'over a billion people are deprived of basic consumption', and further that of the 4.4 billion people in developing countries around 60% are without basic sanitation, 30% have no access to clean water, 25% lack adequate housing, and 20% have no access to modern health services (United Nations Development Programme, 1998).

Within the USA increases in inequality have meant that consumerism has rested 'more and more on the consumption habits of the top 10 per cent of the … population' (Harvey, 2003: 225; see also Davis and Monk, 2007: xi–xii), a pattern that has been replicated globally with the wealthiest fifth of the world's population accounting for the bulk of private consumption (76.6%) while the poorest fifth share less than 2% of the total (Shah, 2008b). Meanwhile, the number of people worldwide deprived of food, the most basic and essential of consumer goods, has remained unacceptably high. At the end of 2008 the Food and Agriculture Organization (FAO) of the United Nations reported that 963 million people were under-nourished, that is around one in six of the world's population, and that an additional 40 million people had been pushed into hunger in the course of the previous year due to higher food prices. Moreover, 907 million of the world's under-nourished people were living in developing countries, with seven – India, China, the Democratic Republic of Congo, Bangladesh, Indonesia, Pakistan and Ethiopia – accounting for 65% of the total (FAO, 2008).

While the global consumer class has been encouraged to live in expectation of ever-increasing consumption of a growing volume of goods and services, a very substantial number of the world's population have been living in poverty, lacking the resources necessary to achieve an adequate standard of consumption. As Davis and Monk comment, given 'more than 2 billion people subsist on two dollars or less a day', the growth of neoliberal dream-worlds – 'city-sized supermalls, artificial island suburbs and faux downtown "lifestyle centers"' – inflaming 'desires for infinite consumption … are clearly incompatible with the ecological and moral survival of humanity' (2007: xv). The acknowledged constraints of global ecological sustainability mean that the achievement of provision of adequate levels of consumption for those living in poor countries will require a degree of redistribution of global resources and that 'will entail reductions in consumption for better-off people all over the world' (Sklair, 2002: 311).

Notes

1. Gini coefficient is an indicator of inequality in respect of income or wealth distribution within a population. The coefficient ranges from zero, which indicates perfect equality, to one, which implies absolute inequality.

2. A further example of the problematic consequences of 'Coca-colonization' (Pendergrast, 2000) to which local communities are exposed is provided by Brazil. The first Coca-Cola bottling plant was opened there in 1942 and early in the twenty-first century Brazil had become the third largest market for the beverage. After its signature cola beverage the company's best selling drink is Fanta Orange, a drink containing, among its many ingredients, very limited quantities of orange juice concentrate, the percentage varying from country to country, with no juice content at all in some countries, including the USA, Mexico and India, 5% in the UK, and 10% in France, Italy, Argentina, and Brazil.

   Brazil is the world's largest producer of oranges, accounting for 27% of global production, and the 'largest exporter of orange juice', producing 53% of juice consumed worldwide. Coca-Cola is one of the main buyers of Brazil's orange crop with the fruit being used in the manufacture of the company's *Minute Maid* '100% pure juice' range. While Brazil leads the world in orange juice production 99% of its output is exported and within the country consumption of oranges and orange juice is 'very low and many Brazilians suffer from vitamin C deficiency'. Paradoxically, in volume terms Brazil is the largest consumer in the world of the Fanta Orange beverage (Dawson, 2005: 130; United States Department of Agriculture, 2005).

6
CONSEQUENCES OF CONSUMERISM

All manner of explanations have been advanced to account for people's seemingly inexhaustible propensity to consume, capacity to spend, spend, and spend again, to work longer hours to earn more, to use credit and run up debt, and willingness to withdraw equity from their homes in order to participate in 'consumer society', to fund the purchase of more and more consumer goods and additional services. If pleasure and enjoyment, both anticipated and experienced, are part of the story it is worth remembering that some of the goods selected for purchase are never used and a significant proportion end up being thrown away, including substantial quantities of edible foods, with one estimate from a UK report suggesting avoidable food waste over the course of a year amounted to 4.1 million tons (Ventour, 2008: 4: see also Stuart, 2009). The pleasurable experience that is anticipated to be a corollary of participation in consumerism, the status associated with being seen to own a particular commodity or being able to enjoy a specific service, and the satisfaction that may be derived from appearing to emulate others in one's circle of friends and acquaintances – 'Keeping up with the Joneses' or, increasingly, aspiring to appear like more distant iconic celebrity figures from the worlds of sport and entertainment, whose consumer lifestyles attract so much attention and publicity in the media – undoubtedly have contributed to people's seemingly inexhaustible propensity to engage in consumer activity, but such experiences, associations, and aspirations themselves have been formed through processes of transformation that have provided the 'life-blood of the consumer society' (Frank, 1998: 234).

Pursuit of Consumer Pleasure: Cool Individualism and Social Inclusion

An increasing propensity to consume and associated growth in late-modern forms of 'hedonistic' consumerism have been traced back by Thomas Frank (1998) to the articulation of specific economic and cultural developments that emerged in 1960s America, in particular signs of a growing correspondence between a rapidly developing and innovative business culture and what was regarded in the period in question, and in the early 1970s, as a 'counterculture' movement. The predictability, 'creative dullness', and conservative character of an over-organized culture in 1950s 'mass society' America produced a rich variety of creative reactions in the business world and in the field of popular culture. In particular Frank identifies a significant degree of common ground between critical reflections on and associated transformations in marketing practices and management thinking in the business world in the 1960s and radical developments simultaneously taking place in music, art, fashion, and popular culture (Frank, 1998). The suggestion is that an unanticipated affinity existed between the 'new values and anti-establishment sensibility' generated by the counterculture and 'the new values of consuming and managing', which an increasingly image-orientated business community was striving to embrace as it sought to 'accelerate the pace of consumption' (Frank, 1998: 26, 25). In sum:

> The counterculture served corporate revolutionaries as a projection of the new ideology of business, a living embodiment of attitudes that reflected their own ... Capitalism was entering the space age in the sixties, and ... old values of caution, deference, and hierarchy drowned creativity and denied flexibility ... when business leaders cast their gaze onto the youth culture bubbling around them, they saw both a reflection of their own struggle against the stifling bureaucracy of the past and an affirmation of a dynamic new consuming order that would replace the old. (Frank, 1998: 28)

Rather than consuming to fit in or impress the Joneses, Frank argues that the new order that emerged promoted systemically positive resistance to conformist consumerism by encouraging a 'rebellious', 'hip', or 'cool' individualism, an interest in continually fashioning the self that would be expressed in and through endless consumer activity. It effectively contributed to the development of a new species of consumerism, one that promoted increasing obsolescence in the guise of politically sanitized rebellion against the cultural conformity exemplified by established or prevailing forms of consumption, and represented for the business community 'a cultural perpetual motion machine ... which ... could be enlisted to drive the ever-accelerating wheels of consumption' (Frank, 1998: 31).

The world described by Frank is one of social and cultural upheaval, it is one in which individualism is promoted and the pace of consumption is accelerated, a world in which the solution to problems is deemed to be 'more consuming' (1998: 55). It is a world in which the social bonds of community have been weakened by the growing prominence of a culture of individualism, promotion of self-interest, and equation of increasing material acquisition with enhanced well-being. Reflecting on the increasing significance accorded to 'personal ambition and consumerism' in particular, Robert Bellah and his colleagues have suggested that a 'consumption-oriented lifestyle ... becomes a form of defence against a dangerous and meaningless world' (1996: 290–1). This idea, that participation in consumer activity brings meaning to people's lives, is endorsed by a number of other analysts who argue that increasingly it is in the shopping malls that we commune; it is in what have been described as our 'cathedrals of consumption' that we now seek to find 'community' and achieve a sense of identity and belonging (Kowinski, 1985; Crossick and Jaumin, 1999; Ritzer, 2005).

Consumption, Social Exclusion and Crime

An insatiable and intense consumerism has become increasingly prominent in contemporary social life and is argued to have displaced work and production as the fulcrum or linchpin of community existence and the principal source of belonging and identity (Bauman, 2007b). Elaborating on the increasing prominence of consumerism and perceived relative shift of emphasis away from the significance of work and productive activity in people's lives, Bauman comments that:

> Contemporary society engages its members primarily as consumers: only secondarily, and in part, does it engage them as producers. To meet the standards of normality, to be acknowledged as a fully fledged, right and proper member of society, one needs to respond promptly and efficiently to the temptations of the consumer market; one needs to contribute regularly to the 'demand that clears supply', while in times of economic downturn or stagnation being party to the 'consumer-led recovery'. All this the poor and indolent people lacking a decent

income, credit cards and the prospect of better days, are not fit
to do. (Bauman, 2007b: 125–6)

The fate awaiting those in consumer societies depicted as unable to respond
to the 'enticement to consume, and to consume more' is argued to be social
exclusion (Bauman, 2007b: 130). But such a dramatic sounding fate, ban-
ishment beyond the citadel of consumption, assumes that lack of (a decent)
income and appropriate access to credit will inevitably impede participation in consumer activity, will necessarily deprive those without legitimate
means from indulging in consumerism and in consequence lead to their
social exclusion. As the idiom 'where there's a will there's a way' suggests
and, more significantly, research in the field of criminology has effectively
demonstrated, if motivation is sufficiently strong, and more specifically if
the consumer dream merchants in marketing media have succeeded in
enervating consumer desire and promoting consumer fantasies, then it
is likely that self-interested, narcissistic individuals, whose sense of identity
is bound up with the symbolic and material value of consumer goods, will
avail themselves of other opportunity structures, even if they are illegiti-
mate, to secure access to the consumer goods and services they crave (Hall
et al., 2008). The lack of a decent job and the income it provides, and/or
the unavailability of credit, does not necessarily mean exclusion from pursuit of consumerism's seductive promise, for there are other means that
can be drawn upon, means that are to be found in what has been termed
the 'criminal economy' (Castells, 1998: 74).

The appeal of 'capitalism's culture of ornamental consumerism' (Hall
et al., 2008: 191) transcends differences between the employed and the
unemployed, those with wealth, a degree of disposable income, and/or
access to credit, and those without such means. The notion that such differences in employment status and financial resources necessarily lead to
a majority enjoying being a part of 'consumer society', achieving a sense
of social inclusion through consumerism, while a significant minority consider themselves to be marginalized as the victims of social exclusion is not
borne out by the research conducted by Hall et al., who report that 'None
of our respondents perceived themselves to be occupying a position of
"social exclusion"' (2008: 191). The individuals interviewed did experience relative material deprivation and hardship, a good many were reliant on welfare, and objectively they appeared to exemplify Bauman's idea
of 'social exclusion', but their responses clearly demonstrate that they did
not regard themselves as victims, as losers, or as 'flawed consumers'.

As much as anyone else living within a neo-liberal consumer capitalist
economic system, the individuals interviewed in the study demonstrated
that they had absorbed the values of a fiercely individualistic, narcissistic,
and materially acquisitive consumption-driven way of life and wholeheart-
edly expressed their belief 'that the good life should be understood in

terms of the acquisition and conspicuous display of commodities and serv-ices' (Hall et al., 2008: 48). A critical difference was that unable to access legitimate means, they turned to crime as 'a way of generating the cash necessary to indulge in their attachment to hedonism and conspicuous consumption' (2008: 48, 45). Hall et al.'s study demonstrates the cen-tral place consumerism occupies in contemporary social life, including within 'the lives of most young criminals … [which] revolve around the acquisition and display of consumer symbolism' (2008: 45). Few, if any of us, experience exclusion from the advertising induced and marketing enhanced cultural appeal of the seemingly endlessly proliferating range of enticingly presented consumer goods and services. Hall et al.'s insight-ful study suggests that individuals, preoccupied with their symbolic place on the consumer treadmill, will do virtually whatever it takes to convey the impression that they are moving on up, that they are 'able to consume and display' anything that is currently fashionable (2008: 196).

Consumer Pleasures and Delusions

Pleasure can be derived not only from participation in consumer activity, but also from anticipation of such activity, from the expectations that are aroused by the prospect of consumerism. Consumerism is widely recog-nized to promote experiences of emotional and aesthetic pleasure. Desires are provoked and fantasies are aroused by thoughts of participating in con-sumer activity, thoughts stimulated by a growing repertoire of persuasive techniques artfully deployed to entice or induce increasing levels of con-sumption. Advertising and marketing techniques contribute to pleasurable anticipation of consumer activity and the enjoyment consumer goods and services promise, and are expected, to deliver. Shopping and all the asso-ciated activities, including locating, ordering, and choosing specific goods and services for purchase, are generally represented, and indeed often experienced, as pleasurable, as enjoyable. In addition, and in contrast to the disciplined and more regulated character of the workplace and the 'bureau-cratized monotony of … productive lives', Frank remarks that participation in consumer activity can enable consumers to feel 'cool' and 'hip', and allows them to escape the routines and more sober values associated with the world of work, with all its attendant insecurities, by immersing themselves in the 'non-stop carnival' of hedonistic consumerism (1998: 232).

Furthermore, once purchased and owned, consumers generally derive some benefit or positive value from the functional utility aspect(s) of a good or service, although this experience may not be particularly durable, as the pleasure to be derived from a commodity's utility may be, and frequently is, transitory. Appreciation of the functional utility of a new product may not endure for long as consumers can quickly come to take a product for granted. In addition, subsequent techno-logical and design innovations frequently lead to a relative reduction in the perceived functional utility and value of a product and, in turn, stylistic innovations may erode its symbolic value, thereby contribut-ing further to the sense of a product's obsolescence and diminishing any prospect of pleasure to be derived from its use and/or possession (Frank, 1998).

As one keen observer of the plight of the consumer living amid a culture of abundance has observed, we are inclined to get used to the things we buy and pretty soon after we have acquired them and become accustomed to using them, they are taken for granted:

> My first desktop computer had 8 K of memory, loaded programs by cassette tape (it took five minutes to load a simple program) and was anything but user-friendly. I loved it and all the things it enabled me to do. Last year I dumped a computer with several thousand times that much speed and capacity because it was too clunky to meet my needs. What I do with my computer hasn't changed all that much over the years. But what I expect it to do for me has. When I first got cable TV, I was ecstatic about the reception and excited about all the choices it provided ... Now I moan when the cable goes out and I complain about the paucity of attractive programs. When it first became possible to get a wide variety of fruits and vegetables at all times of year, I thought I'd found heaven. Now I take this year-round bounty for granted ... I got used to – adapted to – each of these sources of pleasure, and they stopped being sources of pleasure. (Schwartz, 2005: 167–8)

Consumer behavior is both utilitarian and hedonistic, utility and pleasure are both closely associated with and represent goals of consumer activity. The utility of a good or service, the quality of practical use or serviceability, may be a source of pleasure and satisfaction. However, pleasure, an enjoyable sensation or emotion, may also be derived from goods and services where utility or usefulness is at best a secondary attribute, if not absent altogether, where it is some other quality anticipated and/or experienced in consump-tion that represents the primary, if not sole, source of appeal. Although con-sumer pleasure derives from both the utility of a good or service and its symbolic value, these are ultimately perishable 'commodities', their ability to deliver pleasure, to promote pleasurable experiences, diminishes over time. As another observer of contemporary consumer culture confirms:

> Human beings have a remarkable capacity to get used to things ... a capacity ... to get bored with stuff that used to thrill us: to overestimate how much pleasure any given purchase will

give and for how long. Thus the iPod eventually gets taken for granted, the visually thrilling high-end kitchen appliance simply becomes your stove, and the LiveStrong bracelet ends up in the back of a drawer. We all know that novelty fades ... What we're not good at judging is the "intensity and duration" of our feelings about events that haven't happened yet: the BMW, or the Nike Shima Shima 2 Air Max I's, or the Viking Range stove, or whatever, will not make us as happy as we believe it will, and certainly not for as long as we guess ... what adaptation research suggests is not that we don't know novelty fades, but that we're not good at figuring out how to factor this knowledge into our decision making. (Walker, 2008: 263)

As the pleasure we derive from our goods declines, as past experience leads us to expect it will given the continual emergence of newer, more contemporary looking, brighter, sleeker, more powerful or 'better' performing commodities, we eagerly pursue the new possibilities, new goods, and/or new services presented, stimulated by the enticingly marketed proliferating range of fresh options available to us, which promise to deliver pleasure and satisfaction, the appeal of which will, in turn, prove short-lived as further generations of appealingly marketed commodity choices emerge promising even more. There is always another choice on the horizon 'to spark that anticipation of pleasure', to re-ignite consumer desire and further stimulate consumer fantasies, a process which appears to be without end in an economic system seemingly inextricably wedded to the perpetual pursuit of economic growth (Walker, 2008: 264).

In a series of novel reflections on modern consumerism Colin Campbell (1989: 48) argues that to account for the seemingly insatiable appetite of modern individuals for consumer goods it is necessary to go beyond narratives that are overly preoccupied with the intrinsic utility of goods and services to recognize that consumerism is as much, if not more, about emotions and feelings as it is about function. An explanation of the seeming inexhaustibility of our consumer longings lies for Campbell in 'the imaginative pleasure-seeking to which the product image lends itself, "real" consumption being largely a resultant of this "mentalistic" hedonism' (1989: 89). The modern consumer is represented as inclined to engage in 'covert day-dreaming' and therefore as being vulnerable to succumbing to illusions about the promised pleasures new forms of consumption are promoted as being able to deliver. Goods and services appearing as new, as novel, appeal to the desire of consumers to experience something different from the things they currently use and do. Campbell argues that whether products ultimately deliver 'additional utility or a novel experience' is not really the point, what matters is that consumers believe in the possibility, that they imagine the goods on display, the goods promoted through marketing strategies and advertising techniques, will do so and they make their purchases on that basis. From this perspective what drives the continual growth in consumption is then not so much a desire to have more and more things as a longing to realize imagined pleasures, to experience the 'pleasurable dramas' which 'each "new" product is seen as offering a possibility of realizing' (Campbell, 1989: 90).

The reality experienced by consumers is however of a different order. The imagined pleasures that are a feature of consumer fantasies frequently prove illusory, at best fleeting, or temporary in character. The pleasures imagined, anticipated, and expected, amplified by marketing and advertising techniques, entice consumers to make purchases which appear to promise to convert the fantasy into reality, but what emerges, what is quickly realized, is disillusionment. It is not disillusionment with consumerism per se (although it is arguable that for some anti-consumerist movements that indeed has become the outcome), but rather with a particular purchase, a specific product, this one that I already have, rather than that one I am now fantasizing about buying, which (I think) I will feel differently about. The recognition that wanting this good or service was not such a wise idea, that purchasing it did not lead to a realization of the pleasures imagined, does not generally seem to dispel consumer desire, nor reduce the readiness of consumers to attempt to realize further imagined pleasures, to the contrary it serves, as Campbell notes, to sustain consumer momentum by maintaining the 'cycle of desire-acquisition-use-disillusionment-renewed desire' (1989: 90).

Anticipation of pleasure and enjoyment is a very important part of contemporary consumerism and significant marketing resources are devoted to generating representations that might nurture in potential consumers an association of imagined pleasures with particular commodities, services, and/or brands. But insofar as 'each purchase leads to literal disillusionment' the consumer's lot is a far from happy one (Campbell, 1989: 90). Satisfaction and contentment can not be achieved through constant consumerism, to the contrary, the continual nurturing of consumer interest in and desire for a seemingly endless range of new goods and services, which have to be produced within our economic system, the logic of which necessitates increasing capital accumulation through the generation of new markets, leads inevitably to feelings of frustration. 'Enough' does not appear in the lexicon of modern consumerism. The necessary corollary of a form of economic life wedded to the continual pursuit of growth in the production of goods and services, and with them capital accumulation and wealth calculated in monetary terms, is consumers 'permanently exposed to the experience of wanting, something which is only periodically and briefly interspersed with soon-to-be disillusioned consummations of desire' (Campbell, 1989: 95). 'More' is the watchword of modern economic life, more and more production and more and more consumption, for which the seeming 'inexhaustibility of wants which characterizes the behaviour of modern consumers' is truly a necessity, but it is not, as Campbell seems to imply at times, inevitable, not a corollary of being human (1989: 95). A 'desiring mode' may be a universal feature of the human condition, but it is not inevitable that its object of expression is ever-increasing levels of consumer materialism, for there are other potential sources of pleasure, possible alternative forms of hedonism (Soper and Thomas, 2006).

Consumerism is generally accorded a positive value in contemporary societies and is considered to play an important part in the constitution of identity. It has been pointed out a number of times that 'consumo, ergo sum', or *I shop therefore I am* (Saumarez Smith quoted in Hinsliff and Smith, 2007), represents an increasingly appropriate late-modern dictum, at least for a growing global consumer class (Levine, 2007: 209; Harvey, 2005: 170) Looking at consumer magazines, window-shopping, trawling through shopping malls, fantasizing about potential consumer purchases, as well as subsequent processes of selection, choice, and purchase of particular goods and services, are widely considered to be a source of pleasure and enjoyment in late modern consumer societies (Campbell, 1989). Participation in consumer activity is represented as a positive lifestyle choice, as synonymous with social inclusion, as constituting a means of achieving a personal sense of communal belonging and, in turn, displaying for others membership of, or inclusion within, the same. In addition, engagement in consumerism, going shopping, is sometimes described as 'retail therapy', one implication being that it may have some beneficial therapeutic effects on individuals by offering a temporary escape from the stresses and anxieties of modern existence, effectively constituting a feel-good factor in people's lives. The implication is that shopping may improve the consumer's mood or disposition, may provide comfort or consolation. Shopping has also been identified as an increasingly popular leisure pursuit or hobby (Euromonitor International, 2008).

More significantly, in some circumstances consumer activity has been presented as an important, if not patriotic, contribution to national economic and political well-being, as when, in the wake of the traumatic events of 9/11, President George W. Bush asked American citizens for 'continued participation and confidence in the American economy' (2001) and a few years later, in the course of a series of comments on the need to keep the economy growing, made in a press conference from the White House, he said to the American public 'I encourage all of you to go shopping more' (2006). With the implementation of neo-liberal economic policy initiatives from the mid-1970s the economic importance accorded to consumer activity by private individuals increased significantly. Consumer choices, consumer confidence, and the willingness of consumers to continue to shop, to make purchases, financed if, when, and where necessary through credit, have come to be recognized as critical for the well-being of the economic system.

While more shopping may have produced benefits of utility and pleasure for consumers, profits for businesses, and, through enhancement of economic activity, may have served to maintain, if not increase, employment levels and taxation revenues in national economies, there has been a simultaneous generation of social costs and a range of associated problems, in particular a growing realization that there are a number of respects in which consumerism is having a detrimental impact on some individuals, communities, and the environment as a whole, and that as a way of life it is ultimately not sustainable.

Consumerism's Costs and Disappointments

In a wide ranging analysis of the consequences of modernity Anthony Giddens (1990) draws attention to the double-edged character of modern life, to the dangers that continue to threaten our security and to the costs, frequently unanticipated, that are a corollary of the benefits of modern existence. The consequences of modern consumerism provide further confirmation of the double-edged character of modernity. Alongside the undoubted benefits and pleasures afforded by participation in consumerism, a variety of problematic consequences have been identified, including forms of dissatisfaction, frustration, and unhappiness arising from consumer activity, as well as a suggestion that increasing consumer materialism promotes moral malaise (DeAngelis, 2004; Schwartz, 2005). In addition, there is evidence of accumulating levels of debt borne by consumers in some parts of the world (Ritzer, 1995; Clugston, 2008; Credit Action, 2008); research indicating that the prospect of social exclusion of sections of the population from participation in consumer activity may promote forms of criminality (Bauman, 1998; Hall et al., 2008); and growing awareness of detrimental health consequences arising from the excessive character of certain consumer lifestyles, which has led to the identification of particular problematic shopping or buying behaviors as symptomatic of disorders, variously designated as 'emotional shopping'; 'compulsive shopping'; 'serial consumption'; and/or as signifying 'spending addiction' (Faber and O'Guinn, 1989; Koran et al., 2006).

Certain types of consumer behavior have been identified as manifestations of a disorder, 'compulsive shopping syndrome', or *oniomania*, a condition that is receiving serious consideration by researchers in psychology and psychiatry in particular. Whether shopping to excess genuinely constitutes a medical disorder of some kind remains controversial. Designating the behavior of some consumers who engage excessively in shopping, running up huge credit card liabilities, and in some cases engaging in fraudulent and other criminal activity to fund consumer expenditure, as symptomatic of an individual's pathological medical condition, distracts attention away from the social, cultural, and economic factors which routinely serve to promote the idea of the desirability of increasing consumption. There is a tendency to displace problems from the realm of social structure onto individuals, to translate social problems into individualized pathological psychological and biological conditions, to the detriment of an understanding of the cultural and economic factors that actually promote excessive consumer activity. Given our increasing exposure to persuasive advertising images, the identification of consumer activity as an increasingly important source of social inclusion, the promotion of shopping as an enjoyable leisure pursuit or hobby, the emphasis placed upon material possessions as the principal source of social status and worth, and the representation of consumer goods and services as increasingly significant in the constitution and expression of self-identity, it is not surprising that shopping has come to occupy such a prominent place in the lives of many people.

Research conducted in the USA at Stanford University in 2005 suggested that compulsive shopping disorder, or being unable to control spending, was affecting 'up to 8% of Americans, [that is] 23.6 million people', leading afflicted consumers to accrue unmanageable levels of debt and placing their personal relationships under enormous strain (cited in Zivalich, 2006: 6). In a series of critical observations on the matter Benjamin Barber (2007) suggests that from a marketing industry perspective the apparent addictiveness of consumer culture might be regarded as a sign of success, demonstrating that the industry's ambition has been realized. The compulsion to shop and spend is undoubtedly a problem for those individuals designated as suffering from, what is increasingly recognized as, a psychological and behavioral disorder, 'an impulse control disorder … [which] has features similar to other addictive disorders' (IIAR, 2008). Compulsive shopping disorder can affect people's capacity to work effectively, their personal relationships and family life, as well as their financial security, and the addictive potential of the condition is considered to be increased by a range of social, economic, and cultural factors. These include the preoccupation with material possessions and personal appearance in contemporary societies, the relatively easy availability of credit, and the increasingly easy accessibility of a wide range of goods through the emergence of a growing number of readily accessible shopping opportunities, for example 'online shopping and television programs devoted to buying goods 24 hours a day … [which means that goods] can be purchased and ordered by express delivery to arrive quickly without the buyer having to leave home or personally interact with anyone else' (IIAR, 2008). Compulsive shopping is also an issue in the UK with research placing the incidence of the disorder at around 10% of the population (Baker, 2000). Noting that a 'mental and spiritual disorder' associated with excessive shopping is recognized even in Russia, which has only relatively recently embraced consumer capitalism, Barber remarks that the phenomenon of 'shopping addiction appears to be as global as shopping itself' (2007: 242).

Happiness

At the hub of the capitalist market economy is the articulation of production–distribution–exchange–consumption, its dynamism deriving from the interconnected pursuit of ever-increasing rates of economic growth and capital accumulation, realized through the generation of ever-expanding consumer markets to absorb the growing volume of goods and services being produced. Significant improvements in productivity, the USA posted an eight-fold increase over the course of the twentieth century (Durning, 1992; Siegel, 2008), and continuing processes of product innovation and development made successful cultivation of consumer interest in and desire for emerging new commodities and services a necessity if increasing growth in rates of consumption was to be achieved. However, the continual emergence of new products and rising rates of consumption have not led to increasing levels of happiness for consumers. Beyond a relatively modest annual per capita income and associated level of purchasing power, human happiness levels are far more responsive to qualitative, non-material social factors, such as community involvements, friendships, and family than to further increases in income, wealth, and rising levels of consumption (Lane, 2000; Layard, 2005; Schwartz, 2005; Jackson, 2009). Increases in real incomes and consumer purchasing power do not necessarily produce corresponding increases in happiness. Feelings of well-being do not continually grow with rising levels of material consumption. In the second half of the twentieth century the purchasing power of the average American consumer increased substantially, by a factor approaching three, but while this made possible a significant increase in purchases of all manner of consumer goods and services, in the period 1957–2002 the number of people who said they were 'very happy' actually declined from 35% to 30% (Myers, 2007).

Research conducted by the economist Richard Layard confirms that, beyond a relatively modest level, increasing wealth does not

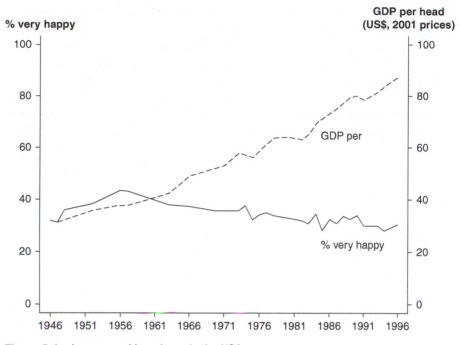

Figure 6.1　Income and happiness in the USA

Source: Layard (2003: 16) 'Happiness: has social science a clue?', Lionel Robbins Memorial Lectures 2002/3, 3–5 March, London School of Economics. Reprinted with permission from the author.

produce increases in reported levels of happiness – 'comparing countries confirms ... that, above $15,000 per head, higher average income is no guarantee of greater happiness' (2003: 20). Drawing on the US General Social Survey, Layard compared data on reported levels of happiness in 1975 and 1996 and noted that the distribution remained virtually unchanged over the period. Combining this data with comparable responses to an earlier US Gallup survey Layard noted that while GDP per head rose significantly from the mid-1940s to the mid-1990s in the USA the percentage of the population declaring themselves to be 'very happy' remained virtually constant as Figure 6.1. illustrates.

Drawing on comparable data from Japan and Europe, which lends further weight to the view that increases in income above a relatively modest level do not lead to increases in happiness, Layard concludes that:

> People in the West have got no happier in the last 50 years. They have become much richer ... they have longer holidays, they travel more, they live longer, and they are healthier. But they are no happier. (2003: 15)

Further confirmation of the lack of any significant correlation between growth in income, or per capita wealth, and increases in happiness is provided in Schwartz's analysis of the respects in which increasing consumer choice in a culture of abundance has not been conducive to improvements in psychological and emotional well-being:

> Once a society's level of per capita wealth crosses a threshold from poverty to adequate subsistence, further increases in national wealth have almost no effect on happiness ... In the last forty years the per capita income of Americans (adjusted for inflation) has more than doubled. The percentage of homes with dishwashers has increased from 9% to 50% ... with clothes dryers ... from 20% to 70% ... [and] with air-conditioning ... from 15% to 73%. Does this mean we have more happy people? Not at all. Even more striking, in Japan per capita wealth has increased by a factor of five in the last forty years, again with no measurable increase in the level of individual happiness. (2005: 106–7)

Once again it is non-economic factors, community involvements, friendships, family life, in short close social ties and social relationships that are identified as contributing most to well-being and happiness. The emphasis placed upon material wealth, consumption, and individualism, coupled with rising expectations, is argued to be associated with declining levels of happiness and increases in the prevalence of stress and clinical depression (Schwartz, 2005: 201–2).

Part of the explanation advanced by Schwartz to account for the discontents associated with consumerism rests with the fact that we consumers are inclined to become quickly used to the things we buy and 'start to take them for granted', perhaps even coming to regret not having made different choices (2005: 167). The process of taking things for granted is illustrated to some extent by the way in which new commodities, initially considered 'luxuries', come in a relatively short period of time to be regarded by consumers as 'necessities'. For example, in America in 1973 air-conditioning in cars was generally regarded as a 'luxury' with only 13% of the public considering it a 'necessity', but by 2002 this had increased to 41% (Schwartz, 2005: 169). In the 10-year period from 1996–2006 the percentage of the public reported to consider microwave ovens a necessity increased from 32 to 68%, with cell phones it rose from 0 to 49%, home computers 26 to 51% (in 1983 it was only 4%), dishwashers 13 to 35%, clothes dryers 62 to 83%, and high speed internet 0 to 29% (Walker, 2008: 217; see also Pew Research Center, 2006). The more income consumers have the more inclined they seem to be to regard 'goods and gadgets as necessities rather than luxuries' (Pew Research Center, 2006: 5).

The status of consumer products shifts from 'luxury' to 'necessity' as the novelty value declines, we get used to them, adapt to them, take them for granted, and as this occurs the pleasure derived wanes and 'comes to be replaced by comfort' (Schwartz, 2005: 172). Elaborating on this process of 'hedonic adaptation' Schwartz remarks that:

> The result of having pleasure turn into comfort is disappoint-ment, and the disappointment will be especially severe when the goods we are consuming are 'durable' goods, such as cars, houses, stereo systems, elegant clothes, jewellery, and comput-ers. When the brief period of real enthusiasm and pleasure wanes, people still have these things around – as a constant reminder that consumption isn't all it's cracked up to be, that expectations are not matched by reality. And as society's affluence grows, consumption shifts increasingly to expensive, durable goods, with the result that disappointment with consumption increases. (2005: 172)

From this perspective disappointment with things constitutes a neces-sary part of the consumer cycle, the common consumer response being to seek out new commodities represented as promising renewed experi-ences of pleasure 'whose potential has not been dissipated by repeated exposure' (Schwartz, 2005: 172). Alleviation of consumer disappointment through imagining potential experiences of satisfaction and pleasure to be derived from future purchases is conducive to the promotion of accel-erated consumption, to 'buying goods for the moment, discarding them quickly, and moving on to the next' (Frank, 1998: 122).

'Buy Now, Pay Later': Consumer Credit and Debt

To sustain growth in consumer expenditure, to ensure that consumers not only have the desire to keep on shopping, to continue buying, discard-ing, and buying again (and again), but significantly also have the means available to do so, it has become increasingly important that they are in a position, when and where necessary, to be able to go beyond drawing on present income, or that which has remained unspent from past earnings, accumulated in the form of savings, investments, and equity in property, and have the opportunity to gain access to credit, effectively that is to draw on prospective future forms of income (Ritzer, 1995; Calder, 1999). As one analyst has observed of the increasing dependence of consumer expenditure on credit:

> The economy is increasingly dependent on the expenditure of future income … That is, it is not enough for us to spend all of our cash in hand or in the bank. We must also spend an increas-ing portion of money we have not yet earned in order to keep

the economy humming at the level it expects and to which it has become accustomed.

Indeed, were large numbers of us to eliminate credit card debt, to begin living within our means, the effect on the economy would be disastrous. (Ritzer, 2005: 136)

A retrenchment of credit not only affects consumers whose spending is reined in. A reduction in consumer credit has very significant knock on effects for the economy as a whole, leading to 'slowing down and scaling back in goods production and service provision' and as Ritzer noted of the prospect, it would mean that 'we would likely face recession or depression' (2005: 136).

The global economy is driven by the pursuit of continuing growth in productive capacity, in output, and this in turn is necessarily articulated with promotion of consumer activity, with the achievement of continual increases in consumption, for which readily available consumer credit has been identified as an essential prerequisite. For the most part growth in production and consumption has been regarded as an unquestionable virtue, has constituted the principal goal towards which the economies of nation states and the operations of commercial corporations have been unquestioningly directed, a goal endorsed by politicians of all governing parties and shared by most citizen-consumers of democratic and non-democratic states alike, but one criticized by a growing number of analysts who have recognized the increasingly detrimental ecological impact of 'the pursuit of constant growth' (Gorz, 1983: 22; Bahro, 1984: 112; Princen, 2002; Gardner and Prugh, 2008; Jackson, 2009). The accumulation of scientific evidence on the impact of the relentless pursuit of economic growth and associated rising levels of consumption on the environment, most significantly on levels of greenhouse gas emission, biodiversity, and resource depletion, has led critics to conclude that a transition towards a sustainable form of economic life is now 'a financial and ecological necessity' (Jackson, 2009: 12; see also Conca, 2002).

The imperative of growth led to expanding economic production in pursuit of rising rates of profitability, development of new markets for goods and services, and increasing consumer indebtedness to finance increasing levels of consumption, especially in the USA and the UK. In the period of debt-led hyperconsumerism leading up to the global economic recession it was chief executive officers (CEOs) in commercial corporations and the financial sector who were the primary beneficiaries of the neo-liberal economic boom, as the following economic data illustrates.

Over the period 1965–2005 there were very significant increases in the ratio of CEO to average worker pay. At the beginning of the period CEOs in major US companies earned 24 times more than the average

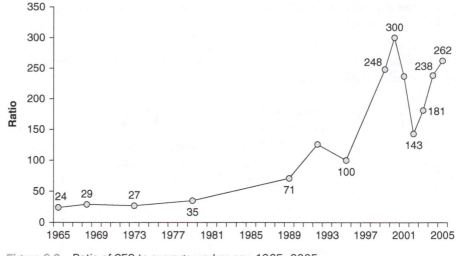

Figure 6.2   Ratio of CEO to average worker pay, 1965–2005

Source: Figure 32 from Mishel, Bernstein, and Allegretton (2007). *The State of Working America 2006/2007*. Reprinted with permission from the Economic Policy Institute, Washington.

worker but went on to reach 300 times the average worker's pay in 2000 before a fall in the stock market reduced the ratio to 143 times in 2002, subsequent growth taking it back up to 262 times the average worker's pay by the end of the period (see Figure 6.2). As Mishel (2006) notes, 'by 2005 the average CEO was paid $10,982,000 a year ... an average worker $41,861 ... a CEO earned more in one workday (there are 260 in a year) than an average worker earned in 52 weeks'. A comparison of remuneration at the top and bottom of American society in 2007 revealed an even wider margin with the average salary of CEOs in the top 500 US companies being US$15.2 million a year in contrast to a full-time minimum wage employee's annual salary of US$12,168 (DeCarlo, 2007).

US and UK consumer debt

In late 2008 consumer debt in the USA was estimated to have risen to US$2.588 trillion (US Federal Reserve, 2008a) while in the UK it had reached £235 billion (Credit Action, 2008). Home mortgage debt was recorded as US$10.6 trillion for the USA at the end of the second quarter of 2008 and £1.2 trillion for the UK by October 2008 (US Federal Reserve, 2008b; Credit Action, 2008). Significant increases in levels of personal debt in the USA coincided with growing income inequality and increases in the cost of living. Whereas in the period from World War II to the 1970s the gains accruing from increasing prosperity were more evenly shared, the predominant trend from the early 1980s through to the early 2000s was of worsening income inequality as the incomes of the wealthiest families in the country grew substantially, while middle- and lower-income families received at best only modest increases and in some years some families experienced a drop in income. As an analysis of state-by-state income trends revealed:

> On average, nationally, the incomes of the poorest fifth of fami- lies grew by $2,660 over the two-decade period, after adjusting for inflation. By contrast, the incomes of the richest fifth of fami- lies grew by almost that much ($2,148) each year over the course of the two decades, for a total increase of $45,100.
>
> The widening income gap is even more pronounced when one compares families in the top five percent of the income distribu- tion (rather than the top fifth) to the bottom 20 percent. In the 11 large states for which this comparison is possible, the incomes of the top five percent of families increased by 73 percent to 132 percent between the early 1980s and the early 2000s, by contrast, the incomes of the bottom fifth of families in these states increased by 11 percent to 24 percent over the same period.
>
> In the 11 large states analyzed, the increases in the average incomes of the top five percent of families ranged from $80,400 to more than $153,000. In five states — Massachusetts, Michigan, New Jersey, New York, and Pennsylvania — the increase exceeded $100,000. By contrast, the largest increase in average income for the bottom fifth of families in these states was only $4,000. In New York, for example, the average income of the top five percent of families grew by $105,000, while the average income of the bottom 20 percent increased by only $1,900. (Bernstein et al., 2006: 8–9)

Another report covering the same period drew attention to a consider- able degree of income volatility from year to year in the USA and noted that for 1980–1981 'when the US economy was in a recession and GDP growth was slowing, nearly one-in-five workers experienced a 50% drop in earnings, and nearly one-in-four experienced a 25% drop in earnings, adjusted for inflation' (Congressional Budget Office, 2007: 12). Later in 2002–2003, when the economy was growing only relatively slowly, around 20% of workers experienced a drop in income of more than 25% and around 15% had to cope with a decrease of more than 50% (Congressional Budget Office, 2007: 1). During this period of just over 20 years consumer debt in America rose from US$350 billion at the beginning of 1980, to US$1.54 trillion by January 2000, and to US$1.98 trillion by the beginning of 2003 (US Federal Reserve, 2008a).

In the year ending October 2008 total UK personal debt had risen by 4.7% to £1455 billion, a higher figure than UK GDP which stood at £1410 billion (Credit Action, 2008). Average UK household debt, excluding mortgages, was estimated to be £9633, but when calculated on the basis of the number of households who had some form of unsecured loan the figure rose to an average of £21,952 (Credit Action, 2008). Data on UK credit card transactions published at the beginning of 2006 revealed debt outstanding at £56.35 billion, a figure which represented two-thirds of total EU credit card debt (Credit Action, 2006). In the USA at the end of 2006 'revolving credit' (credit card debt) stood at US$875 billion and non-revolving credit (e.g. car loans and 'big ticket items') was estimated to be US$1.5 trillion – by September 2008 these had increased respectively to US$971 billion and US$1.6 trillion (US Federal Reserve, 2008a). Over the period 1984–2003 easier access to credit markets and the willingness of households and individuals to assume greater levels of consumer debt meant that, while there was a sharp increase in income inequality and 'a large widening of wealth inequality', the increase in consumption inequality was relatively small in scale (Iacoviello, 2005: 22–3).

In late-modern, neo-liberal, capitalist economies consumer expenditure constitutes the largest element of total GDP, with estimates in 2003 ranging from 70% in the USA, 68% in the UK, 58% in Germany, and 57% in Japan. In such societies consumer expenditure has been, and indeed remains, the engine for economic growth and employment (Skousen, 2007). However, following the sub-prime mortgage crisis in the USA in 2007, which triggered a major global financial crisis in the course of 2008, there were dramatic reductions in credit availability. Prevailing US levels of consumer debt, which had risen from 113.7% of disposable income at the end of 2003 to reach 133.7% by late 2007, and associated patterns of consumer expenditure were no longer sustainable (Iacoviello, 2005; Weller, 2008). Consumer expenditure became subject to a range of inhibiting factors. Real incomes had not been rising significantly, if at all, for a number of years for the majority of those in work, house prices were in decline, and deteriorating property equity levels had curbed additional mortgage borrowing to fund expenditure above current income. In addition, unemployment was growing, stock market values had plummeted, household savings were in many cases negligible, credit was not so readily available, some living costs had risen, and by October 2008 consumer confidence had reached an all-time low level. Given this 'perfect storm' a decrease in consumer expenditure was to be expected, but some observers speculated that it would be more than a temporary interruption, arguing that the four-decade long growth in consumer spending had reached its end and that hyperconsumerism and conspicuous consumption would be replaced by a 'new frugality', the economic implications of such a transformation, if indeed it takes place, will be far-reaching (Palmer, 2008; The Conference Board, 2008; Weller, 2008).

Psychological distress and anxiety provoked by worries about comparative social standing, the endlessness of the circuits of consumption in which participation is necessary if 'the desire to have the best of everything – to maximize' is to be sustained and, no less important, displayed for others, and the rapidly upward spiraling of credit indebtedness, are some of the more problematic outcomes of the growth of consumerism and the accelerating proliferation of choices to which consumers have been increasingly exposed, and to which there have been a range of anti-consumerist and anti-shopping responses (Schwartz, 2005: 221; see also Klein, 2001; Schor, 2004; Levine, 2007). Such consequences, along with a range of other costs associated with the growth of consumerism, including such undesirable by-products as rising levels of waste and pollution, and increases in noise and congestion levels, call into question the common assumption that increasing consumerism promotes greater happiness and pleasure (Layard, 2003, 2005; Soper, 2007b). However, beyond such negative consequences, which are a corollary of the benefits and pleasures to be derived from consumerism, it is increasingly alarming signs of wide-ranging environmental costs arising from our consumption-driven way of life, the unsustainability of which has been recognized more and more as it has become increasingly global in scope and intensity, which are giving most cause for concern (Princen et al., 2002; Soper and Thomas, 2006; Jackson, 2009; Smart, 2009).

7

AN UNSUSTAINABLE
ALL-CONSUMING WORLD

Economic growth has meant raised levels of productivity and has made possible the consumer lifestyles enjoyed by a global consumer class of around 2 billion people. Over the course of the twentieth century global economic output grew 18-fold and in the period 1950–2005 the total value of all goods and services produced around the world, based on purchasing power parity, increased from US$7 trillion to US$61 trillion (Gardner and Prugh, 2008: 8; see also Mygatt, 2006). Consumer expenditure on goods and services by private households increased four-fold in the period 1960–2000 rising from US$4.8 trillion to US$20 trillion (Gardner et al., 2004: 5). However, the consumer way of life, which has become second nature to those who participate in it, has also led to a number of serious consequences, including a significant squandering of resources, in many instances relatively scarce if not irreplaceable natural resources, the production of increasing quantities of waste, various forms of pollution, and, perhaps most significantly of all, increasing evidence of global warming, the consequences of which are proving detrimental to the well-being of individuals, communities, and the environment that constitutes our life-support system.

From the mid-twentieth century there has been an accelerating process of global diffusion of the Western consumption-driven lifestyle promoting the values of material acquisition and consumer choice, a process which has been stimulated by increasing competition between commercial corporations in pursuit of new markets for an endlessly proliferating range of consumer products and services, global population flows (for example, tourism and travel, as well as migration in pursuit of work and refuge), enhanced global media communication of seductive images promoting enticing consumer commodities, and not least by the emergence and growth of a global consumer class with access to the financial resources necessary to participate in Western forms of consumerism. However, the resource and energy intensive, materially acquisitive, consumer lifestyle that has become synonymous with the routine practices and mundane assumptions of everyday life for the majority of people in North America, Western Europe, Australasia, and Japan, and is growing in appeal in a number of other countries, especially Brazil, Russia, India, and China, where private consumption is increasing rapidly, cannot be sustained on a worldwide basis.

There are material limits to the growth of global consumption, limits to the prospect of being able to participate in a Western materially acquisitive consumption-driven lifestyle. Early in the twenty-first century it was estimated that 'humanity uses the equivalent of 1.3 planets to provide the resources we use and absorb our waste. This means it now takes the Earth one year and four months to regenerate what we use in a year' (Global Footprint Network, 2008). It is simply not possible for everyone on the planet to consume at the rate that Americans and Europeans have come to take for granted. At a time when global population stood at 6.6 billion it was calculated that the Earth's resources were sufficient to sustain only 2 billion people at the standard of living being enjoyed in Europe. Extrapolating through to the mid-2030s, on the assumption that current population and consumption trends continue, it is suggested that 'we will need the equivalent of two Earths to support us' (Global Footprint Network, 2008: see also Figure 7.1).

There is now a substantial body of scientific evidence on the ecological consequences of Western consumerism, including the increasing quantities

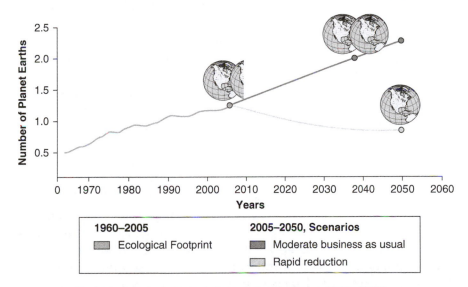

Figure 7.1   Ecological footprint calculations and projections, 1960–2050

Source: Global Footprint Network 2006, http://www.footprintnetwork.org/en/index.php/GFN/page/world_footprint (accessed 11 February 2009). Reprinted with permission.

of waste being produced and the various forms of pollution affecting air, soil, and water quality, as well as other forms of environmental degradation (Princen et al., 2002; *New Scientist*, 2008; Jackson, 2009). As Jonathan Porritt, Chairman of the UK Sustainable Development Commission has cautioned:

> Consumerism puts consumption at the very heart of the modern economy and everything is done to persuade us to go and consume more ... Almost unnoticed, consumerism has become our principal pastime, our zeitgeist, our ideology, all rolled into one. It's a very seductive idea, but it's also a lethal idea .... Scale up all of these individual acts of consumption multiplied by several billion people and stand back and watch the disaster unfold. (2007)

Taking stock of consumerism's impact on our environment, in particular increases in carbon dioxide and other greenhouse gas emission levels and their effect on climate, it is clear that current consumption-led economic growth is not sustainable 'because levels of consumption are already undermining life support systems on which we depend' (Smith, 2007b).

Consumer Waste

A growing volume of waste is one of the direct consequences of Western-style consumerism and it has led to a landfill or 'trash' crisis as sites in the USA and the UK, and in a number of other consumer societies around the world, including the Republic of Ireland, Belgium, Luxembourg, the Netherlands, and Japan, approach capacity (Svoboda, 1995; Tammemagi, 1999; Clapp, 2002; Moreton, 2006; DEFRA, 2007). 'Consumption' and 'consume' derive from the Latin term *consumere* meaning to use up, eat, or waste and there are at least five respects in which waste can be considered a corollary of modern consumerism. First, in addition to its aesthetic or symbolic significance consumption constitutes a process of extraction of use-value, from which waste in some shape or form is an inevitable and unavoidable by-product; it represents a normal outcome of the process of consumption and in this sense is sometimes referred to as 'post-consumer waste'. Second, waste can arise from the fact that a commodity may fail to become an object of consumer choice and remaining unsold or having become impossible to sell is disposed of. The precise fate of unsold goods is not always easy to determine. However, studies of food production and consumption have revealed substantial quantities of edible food are wasted at every stage in the process from farm to plate. For example, supermarkets routinely throwaway into lockable skips substantial quantities of perfectly edible food products that are at, or just past, their sell-by-dates and restaurants and sandwich chains operate in a comparable manner (Ventour, 2008; Stuart, 2009). There are also unsubstantiated reports of export markets for some unsold American goods in Latin America, North Africa, and the Middle East, some goods are given to charity, and a proportion end up in landfill, but the scale of unsold merchandise, a manifestation of overproduction, is difficult to calculate and is not given the consideration it warrants.

A third form of waste is exemplified by the tendency for consumers to neglect to use a proportion of the commodities they have chosen for purchase, including food, clothing, electronic goods, books, and a variety of other products. A fourth and related form of waste arises from the fact that consumers are encouraged, if not continually exhorted, to consider replacing or 'retiring' existing functional commodities with later, improved, more contemporary, and fashionable models (Slade, 2006). It is here that product design, marketing, advertising, and media promotion of appealing and/or luxurious consumer lifestyles may exert an influence over consumer desires and aspirations. Rising consumer expectations have meant that a potentially realistic prospect of keeping-up-with the neighbor next door has been displaced by the fantasy of enjoying the seductive attractions promoted in images of the luxurious consumer lifestyles of the rich and famous, but the excesses associated with celebrity consumer lifestyles are destined to remain continually unattainable for most people whose best efforts to 'live the dream' generally allow them to do little more than maintain their place on a more mundane consumer treadmill (Schor, 1998: 2004).

Finally, there is a growing awareness that the widening of consumer choice, the bringing of a 'cosmopolitan character to production and consumption', the cultivation of new tastes and consumer expectations not constrained by the vagaries of the seasons and 'requiring for their satisfaction the products of distant lands and climes' (Marx and Engels, 1968: 83, 84), along with the development of a global division of labor, have led inexorably to new forms of waste. These have taken the form of finite or scarce local resources being reduced, used up, and/or destroyed in the course of production for global consumer markets. Take the example of the production of salad food items and flowers out of season for Northern European consumer markets. The increasing scale of the production of such popular consumer goods on the African continent is intensifying the shortage of water in local communities, increasing the hardship of those who find that their supplies of water have been appropriated by large commercial enterprises catering for global markets, and is leading to permanent environmental damage (Pearce, 2006). In turn, the long-distance transportation of such produce adds to global carbon dioxide emission levels and constitutes an additional detrimental impact on the environment (Nugent, 2006).

Critical analyses of waste

Writing in the late 1960s Jean Baudrillard (1998[1970]) noted a growing concern about waste and the global squandering of natural resources. In his discussion of consumer society he describes the 'fragility, built-in obsolescence and … transience' of many of the goods produced by the production system, the contribution of advertising in promoting the 'fashion-value' of commodities, which serves to increase the prospect of the 'ever earlier replacement' of goods, and the 'environmental nuisance' arising from the dynamic of economic growth and associated 'structures of consumption'. Consumer society may have delivered more and more goods, but it has also led to waste and 'degradation of our shared living space … noise, air, and water pollution [and] environmental destruction'. In this context waste is described as a 'spectacular squandering' and argued to have a functional role, providing 'economic stimulus for mass consumption' (Baudrillard, 1998: 39, 46). Reflecting critically on the systemic place of wastage within the production system Baudrillard remarks that:

> What is produced today is not produced for its use value or its possible durability, but rather with an *eye to its death* … Now we know that the order of production only survives by paying the price of this extermination, this perpetual calculated 'suicide' of the mass of objects, and that this operation is based on technological 'sabotage' or organized obsolescence under cover of fashion. (1998: 46)

While Baudrillard's analysis of the functionality of wastage, exemplified by everything from built-in obsolescence, the effect of advertising on the fashion-value, durability and replacement of commodities, and the sacrifice of social wealth through 'military budgets and other state and bureaucratic prestige expenditure' (1998: 46) continues to have analytic relevance for making sense of aspects of contemporary consumer society, subsequent increases in the scale of waste production, and wasteful overproduction associated with consumption, have increased concerns about related environmental consequences that have become far more significant than the brief dismissal of them as a 'nuisance' allows. What has changed is that while waste continues to be 'integrated into the economic system', as Baudrillard (1998: 197) noted, the gravity of the environmental consequences arising from the global diffusion of a wasteful and excessive consumerist way of life now makes action an urgent matter.[1]

In a series of critical reflections on the extent to which life in a late modern or 'liquid' modern society revolves around consuming, Zygmunt Bauman remarks that the 'society of consumers is unthinkable without a thriving waste-disposal industry' (2007b: 21). Desired goods are rarely, if ever, cherished for long once they are owned as the forms of obsolescence to which they are all vulnerable ultimately guarantee that they will end up as waste and, almost inevitably, be replaced by new commodities. The intensification of economic competition has meant that increasing emphasis has been placed on the need to raise turnover, to speed up the rate at which goods are sold, which in turn requires more rapid retirement and disposal of the things consumers already own and use. As Bauman observes, insofar as a 'consumerist economy thrives on the turnover of commodities' it necessarily comes to 'rely on excess and waste' (2007b: 36–8).

As is the case with Baudrillard's analysis of consumer waste, the focus for Bauman is on the various ways in which waste is engineered in a 'consumption-oriented economy' (2007b: 46). The continual production of consumer waste through the engineering of product obsolescence, retirement, and/or disposal is an essential part of the consumer cycle. While the waiting may be taken out of wanting, as the 1970s Access credit card slogan promised, the wasting cannot be. Waste is a direct corollary of the objective at the center of consumer society, to continually increase the supply of commodities by constantly 'inventing, developing, and redesigning consumer goods' and cultivate 'demand for the products so developed', by devising, as Galbraith noted, appropriate marketing strategies, '"selling points" and "advertising pegs" or ... [accelerating] "planned obsolescence"' (1963: 224–5). The aim being to achieve a regeneration or renewal of consumer needs, wants, and desires by turning today's 'useful and indispensable objects, with but few exceptions ... [into] tomorrow's waste' (Bauman, 2004a: 96).

Food, electronic goods and clothing

Western consumerism has led to increasing levels of waste and problems of resource depletion, waste disposal, and environmental pollution. The promotion of consumer choice and the goal of maximizing private consumption have led consumers to routinely over-consume, to purchase goods whose use-value in some instances is never realized. For example, research shows that consumers fail to use a significant proportion of the food they buy. A project conducted at the University of Illinois revealed that 12% of domestic grocery products purchased are never used and are wasted (Wansink et al., 2000). In 2004, research conducted by Timothy Jones, an anthropologist at the University of Arizona, Bureau of Applied Research, produced a comparable figure, namely that on average, household's waste 14% of their food purchases. An average family of four was found to dispose of unused meat, fruit, vegetables, and grain products to the value of US$590 per year and nationwide that added up to food waste in the order of US$43 billion. Even more worrying the research revealed that 'forty to fifty per cent of all food ready for harvest never gets eaten' (foodnavigator.com).

In Britain in 2005, it was reported that in the food industry 'large-scale manufacturing and rigid supply chains are creating very significant quantities of waste' to the tune of between £8 billion and £16 billion a year (Vidal, 2005). In 2006, it was estimated that 6 million tons of household food was being discarded in the UK and that the average household was throwing away food to the value of £424 each year (WRAP, 2006). Food wasted by consumers in the UK in 2009 was estimated to be in the region of 5.4 million tons each year, representing around 25% of the quantity bought (Stuart, 2009). A comparable study in Sweden revealed that around 20% of the food produced is wasted, the largest single source of which was 'plate-waste' of 11–13% of the quantity of food served. The economic value of wasted food is substantial and in the case of the Swedish study it was estimated to be equivalent to the food produced from 1.5% of the arable land under cultivation (Engstrom and Carlsson-Kanyama, 2004). The most wasteful nation in food terms is Japan, which imports 60% of its food. As the world's leading food importer Japan is 'top of the Food Miles shame list compiled by UK-based environment group Safe Alliance' and is estimated to throw away '¥11 trillion (US$101.6 billion) worth of food' each year (Fitzpatrick, 2005).

The research findings which have emerged from the USA, UK, Sweden, and Japan suggest a considerable wastage of food products, but wasteful consumption extends beyond food to clothing and a variety of other consumer commodities, including electronic goods such as computers and mobile phones, which are being jettisoned at an increasing rate as new more powerful models are designed, produced, and marketed. In the UK in 2005 an insurance survey estimated the value of items of clothing that women had purchased but never worn at £7.3 billion and in 2008 it was reported that while over the previous five-year period clothing prices had fallen by 25%, the quantity of clothing purchased had risen by almost 40%, and that textiles had become 'the fastest-growing waste product in the UK … [with around] 74 per cent of the two million tonnes of clothes' purchased each year ending in landfill sites (Churchill Insurance, 2006; Fletcher, 2008). Research conducted in Australia in 2004 indicated that on average each household wasted AUS$1226 on items purchased but not used and while food represented the most significant item, other wasteful forms of consumption included clothes, shoes, gym memberships, books, and CDs (Hamilton et al., 2005).

Consumer commodities such as games consoles and mobile phones have built in obsolescence to stimulate sales of later generations of products (Parnell, 2002). Computers too are being replaced at an increasing

Figure 7.2 Electronic waste

Source: http://media.canada.com/gallery/Greenpeace%20Guide/1.jpg (accessed 8 June 2009)
Reprinted with permission from Greenpeace UK.

rate. It has been estimated that in 2004 in the USA 'about 315 million working PCs were retired ... 10 percent would be refurbished and reused but most would go straight to the trash heap ... [representing] an enormous increase over the 63 million working PCs dumped into American landfills in 2003' (Slade, 2006: 1). As the rate of obsolescence accelerated most organizations were calculating that new models would be outdated within three years (Flynn, 2006). In 2005, 100 million cell phones were 'retired' by US consumers leading Slade to remark that '50,000 tons of still usable equipment joined another 200,000 tons of cell phones already awaiting dismantling and disposal' (2006: 1). While some recycling is possible with PCs Slade suggests that the design of cell phones, in particular their compactness, makes recycling a less viable economic proposition and that in consequence they tend to be discarded and represent 'a toxic time bomb waiting to enter America's landfills and water table' (2006: 2) (see Figure 7.2).

Products that are working perfectly well are discarded for a variety of reasons, for example, because in technical or stylistic terms they have come to be regarded as 'obsolescent', that is they still work but are not comparable to the technical specification of later models, or they have become unfashionable because of the emergence of what are represented as more contemporary designs. A corollary of obsolescence in all its various forms – 'technological, psychological or planned' (Slade, 2006: 3–6) – is an accelerating accumulation of waste, a good deal of which may contain toxic elements, and this is now recognized to be threatening, if not overwhelming, our capacity, and that of the environment we inhabit, to deal with it.

Consuming Landscapes

In an analytic 'tour' of what are described as 'new means of consumption' – phenomena such as franchises, chain stores, shopping malls, catalogues, superstores, and electronic shopping centers – George Ritzer makes reference to the contribution of American corporations to the rapid growth in consumption, to the respects in which 'American-based corporations are intent on, and aggressive about, exporting American consumer goods and the American way of consuming them' (2005: 38), and how people all around the world have taken to 'the American way of consuming' (2005: 39). Many of the means of consumption identified as 'new' are relatively longstanding and do not signify a 'revolutionary change' (Ritzer, 2005: ix). For example, franchising, which became increasingly popular from the late 1950s, can be traced back to America in the 1850s and Singer's establishment of a network to sell its sewing machines to the public. Chain stores were being established from 1859 when the Great Atlantic & Pacific Tea Company (A&P) was set up. Shopping centers were developing from the 1880s and by the late 1890s over a thousand mail-order concerns were competing for the business of over 6 million customers (Leach, 1993: 57, 44, 26).

While there is a great deal more continuity than the notion of a 'revolution in consumption' suggests, it is true that there has been an increasing 'proliferation of settings that allow, encourage, and even compel us to consume' (Ritzer, 2005: 2) and to describe the growth of such settings, in particular the increase in locations where two or more franchises, superstores, chain stores, or malls are situated, the notion is introduced of 'landscapes of consumption' (Ritzer, 2005: xi). The term is intended to reflect the growth in scale of consumer activity and the increasing density of consumption settings in particular 'geographic areas'. To that end consideration is given to a number of such examples, including 'the Strip' in Las Vegas, 'the area around the main cathedral in Milan, Italy', and a new 'landscape' in Columbus, Ohio (Ritzer, 2005: 155; for data on Britain's biggest shopping centers see Richards and Burgess, 2009). In turn, potential problems associated with consumption, for example, the extent to which Americans are 'obsessed' with it, spend too much on it, and may in consequence get into debt, are briefly noted and there is recognition of the need for structural initiatives to deal with the agencies 'that play such a large role in hyper-consumption and overspending' (Ritzer 2005: 31–2, 191–2). However, there is no consideration of the systemic economic growth imperative that drives the continual promotion and expansion of consumer activity, a lack of any sustained critical engagement with the contribution of business marketing, advertising, and branding to the promotion of excessive consumption, and no recognition of the ways in which 'landscapes of consumption' have consumed – quite literally have devoured, wasted, exhausted, and destroyed – irredeemable *ecological* landscapes, not just where the shopping malls and centers are physically situated, but also where the commodities they display and sell have been produced, increasingly with globalization, in remote low labor cost, low tax, and lightly regulated locations, and further, where the growing volumes of waste from the consumer cycle are ultimately deposited, far removed (and safely concealed) from the artfully contrived retail emporia that are designed to enchant consumers and induce them to make purchases.

With the globalization of economic life, significant environmental costs arising from the production of consumer goods are not borne by the societies in which the goods are consumed, but 'locally' in the producer countries to which manufacturing has been outsourced and to which post-consumer waste is exported for recycling and disposal. For example, between 2002 and 2005 China's carbon dioxide emissions increased by 45% with half of the increase being attributable to production of consumer goods for export, 60% of which were destined for Western countries (Guan et al., 2009; see also Clapp, 2002; Conca, 2002; Princen, 2002; Wang and Watson, 2009). The limitation of analytic focus to matters of consumption alone and neglect of the close articulation with production leads to a diminished understanding of consumerism and an omission of any consideration of significant environmental consequences and concerns arising from increases in consumption flowing from developments in economic production. As one of America's leading critics of the social and environmental consequences of consumerism has remarked, 'if you want to understand consumption, you have to analyze it in the context of production. I think the linkage between production and consumption is really important' (Schor cited in Holt, 2005: 9). Social analysis of consumption has not been well-served by a 'cultural turn' which has led to 'increasingly marginal postmodern theories of fantasy consumption, an under-theorized notion of identity consumption, emphasis on "simulacra" and spectacle, ... the positing of the consumer as a sovereign agent' and a simultaneous neglect of influential, if not determining, 'structural constraints' and 'economic processes' (Schor, 2002: 3).

Images of Consumer Waste

The problematic environmental consequences that have become more and more apparent with the growth in consumerism and increasing pervasiveness of a materialistic consumer mentality have been the focus of a series of powerful artistic representations created by Chris Jordan (2007) a Seattle-based photographic artist. Jordan's work (2003–2005, 2006–2009) provides a series of compelling images of the scale of the consumer waste that is a corollary of the cycles of 'creative destruction' that generate new consumer goods, new designs, and technological refinements and upgrades that encourage replacement and renewal of commodities that frequently remain in good working order. In contrast to the 'enchanted, sometimes even sacred, religious character' attributed to the landscapes occupied by 'new means of consumption' (Ritzer, 2005: 7), Jordan directs a critical aesthetic gaze on to the problematic consequences flowing from the consumer process, notably the growing number of consumer goods that get prematurely 'retired', the waste that accumulates, the extraordinary variety of things that get excreted at the end of the consumer cycle. These aspects have tended to be marginalized or neglected altogether, especially when the future anticipated is one that 'will bring with it unimagined palaces of consumption filled to capacity with a cornucopia of goods and services' (Ritzer, 2005: 207), a conception of the future that appears oblivious to the destructive impact consumerism has had, and is continuing to have, on natural resources and the environment (Hertwich, 2005; Cohen, 2007).

The aim behind Jordan's *Running the Numbers* series is to expose viewer-consumers to the problems arising from consumerism through photographic images that powerfully represent 'the tiny incremental harm that every single one of us is doing as an individual' as we consume, images that are intended to get viewer-consumers to think about how 'the cumulative effect of hundreds of millions of individual consumer decisions is causing the worldwide destruction of our environment' (Jordan, 2007). The images presented of the rate of consumption of various commodities in America include the following:

> 11,000 jet trails, the number of commercial flights taken every 8 hours
>
> 28,000 42-gallon barrels, the amount of oil consumed every 2 minutes
>
> 60,000 plastic bags, the number used every 5 seconds
>
> 106, 000 aluminum cans, the number used every 30 seconds
>
> 320,000 light bulbs, the number of kilowatt hours of electricity wasted every minute

426,000 cell phones, the number 'retired' each day

1 million plastic cups, the number used on internal airline flights every 6 hours

1.14 million brown-paper supermarket bags, the number used every hour

2 million plastic beverage bottles, the number used every 5 minutes

8 million toothpicks, representing the number of trees harvested every month to make the paper for mail order consumer catalogues

15 million sheets of paper, the quantity used every 5 minutes. (Jordan, 2006–2009)

A subsequent series, *Running the Numbers II*, provides images of *global* mass consumer related phenomena, including the average number of tuna fished from the world's oceans every 15 minutes (20,500) and the estimated weight of plastic pollution dumped in the world's oceans every hour (2.4 million pounds). The latter work, entitled 'Gyre', presents an image that depicts the threat posed to 'the world's marine ecosystem' by phenomena such as the 'Great Pacific Garbage Patch' (Jordan, 2009). There is an 'island' of plastic waste floating in an area of the northeastern Pacific, variously estimated to be twice the size of Texas or France and to contain an estimated six million tons of material. There is a 'Western garbage patch' stretching from Japan to Hawaii and an 'Eastern garbage patch' which flows from Hawaii to California, collectively they are known as the 'Great Pacific Garbage Patch' or the world's biggest 'landfill', one containing a variety of plastic debris to a depth of up to 10 meters, and including bottles and caps, toothbrushes, Styrofoam cups, detergent containers, pieces of polystyrene packaging, plastic bags, and smaller unidentifiable plastic 'chips' deposited in the oceans and carried by currents to the North Pacific central gyre (Allsop et al., 2006). More than 200 billion pounds of plastic is produced worldwide each year and of that 'about 10 percent ends up in the ocean ... Seventy percent of that eventually sinks, damaging life on the ocean floor ... The rest floats; much of it ends up in gyres and the massive garbage patches that form there, with some plastic eventually washing up on a distant shore' (http://science. howstuffworks.com/great-pacific-garbage-patch.htm, accessed 2 May 2009, see also Figure 7.3).

The Consumer Juggernaut

The ecological implications of contemporary patterns of global consumption have not always been accorded the critical analytic consideration their significance warrants. For example, it has been suggested

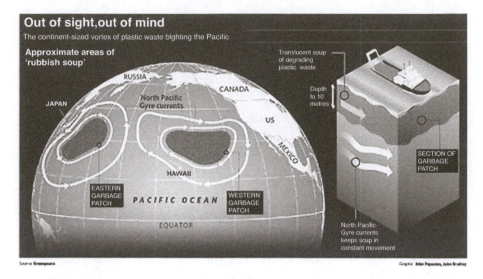

Figure 7.3   The Great Pacific Garbage Patch

Source: http://www/treehugger.com/files/2008/02/great_garbage_pacific_garbage_patch.php (accessed 5 June 2009). Reprinted with permission from Greenpeace UK.

that sociologists have tended to be preoccupied with 'the status and meaning of consumption in modern society' (Princen et al., 2002: 11) and 'have made almost no reference to the environmental impact of rapidly expanding levels of consumption' (Shove and Warde, 1998: 3). And where there has been a sociological acknowledgment of the environmental impact of consumption reference has tended to be, at best, cursory (Gabriel and Lang, 2006: 22–4). Undoubtedly more critical consideration needs to be given to the environmental consequences of consumption and to what have been aptly designated as the 'hedonistically repressive' effects of consumerism, that is effects that blunt our 'sensibility to sensual delight itself', such matters as light pollution and noise, and the variety of other assaults on our senses that have become commonplace in the metropolitan and suburban consumer environments that increasingly dominate the habitats of the majority of the world's population (Soper, 2007a: 221).

As evidence has accumulated on the growing scale, scope, and range of detrimental consequences arising from consumer activity, unfavorable associations have begun to be (re)attributed to consumption (Gabriel and Lang, 2006: 24). Analysts have made critical references to the hollow experience of living on a hedonic consumer '*treadmill*' (Offer, 2006) and have termed the ethos of consumer capitalism 'infantile' (Barber, 2007). Elevation of 'the value of novelty above that of lastingness' and an associated acceleration of the cycle of desire, possession, gratification, rejection, and disposal have been identified as manifestations of a problematic 'consumer *syndrome*' (Bauman, 2004b, 2007: 85–6). In addition, modern consumption has been described as 'juggernaut' like in character, as out of control (International Institute for Sustainable Development [IISD], 1999; Maniates, 2002; Renouard, 2007), and consumerism has been identified as having an increasingly damaging impact on the environment and on those individuals and communities subjected to the global 'gale of destruction', which has been a corollary of the pursuit of growth in production and consumption under the ethos of neo-liberalism (Chomsky, 1999; Princen et al., 2002; Starke, 2004; Schor, 2005). It is in this context that calls to 'consume differently' have been articulated and that organizations such as Friends of the Earth International have added their voice to those urging people to 'consume less, live more' (Gorz, 1983; Maniates, 2002; Soper and Thomas, 2006; Soper, 2007a, 2007b).

The notion of the 'juggernaut' provides a compelling image of modern consumerism as a powerful, fast moving and seemingly unstoppable form of life (Giddens, 1990). The apparent lack of control that exists in respect of our 'runaway' consumer society, the design faults and operator failures that contribute to the unintended and unwanted consequences of consumption that are a by-product of the complexity of the global 'free-market' economic system, and the impact that new generations of commodities, new forms of consumption, and associated new consumer lifestyles and related courses of action, have on both the *social* world, continually altering 'its nature, spinning it off in novel directions', and, no-less significantly, on the *natural* world, make the term particularly appropriate to describe the overwhelmingly expansive and transformative character of contemporary consumerism (Giddens, 1990: 153).

Since the beginning of the twentieth century the growth of consumption has been truly relentless. The number of products and services produced and consumed has grown inexorably and promises to continue to do so as more of the world's population aspires to the lifestyles that have come to predominate in 'overdeveloped' and 'over-consuming' countries (Renner, 2004). Until the recession of 2008 the growth in per capita consumption was showing no sign of abating, to the contrary, a few years earlier it was reported to be 'expanding eight to twelve times faster than population growth' (Princen et al., 2002: 4) and in the USA alone between 1993 and 2004 'real personal consumption expenditures per capita' rose by 33% (Schor, 2005). Notwithstanding the accumulation of scientific evidence on the seriously damaging, quite possibly irreversible, environmental impact of the growth orientated and consumption-driven capitalist organization of the global economy, the common response of political administrations around the world to the global economic downturn and threat of a 1930s style depression was to attempt to regenerate consumer confidence, to restore consumer demand, in effect to return to the *status quo ante*, to promote the very consumerist form of economic life that scientific research had shown was putting the world's ecology in peril (Clapp, 2002; Conca, 2002; Tucker, 2002). Moreover, rather than the combination of an economic crisis and an ecological crisis spelling the end of neo-liberalism and a more significant interventionist role for the state, it has been suggested that 'neo-liberalism lite' appears to be a more likely outcome as political administrations attempt to restore the global economy to its early August 2007 pre-credit crunch form (Elliott, 2009).

While the consumerist form of economic life has come to seem 'natural', one to which more and more people aspire and to which it seems policymakers consider there can be no alternative, in the face of the 'perfect storm' of two interconnected globally extensive crises, our highly materialistic and individualistic consumer culture and the growth oriented model of economic life with which it is inextricably connected, have been called into question by critical social and environmental analysts (Gardner and Prugh, 2008; Flavin and Engelman, 2009; Jackson, 2009).

Unsustainable Consumption

From the late nineteenth century analysts have expressed criticism of a consumption-driven lifestyle, which over time has become second nature for a growing number of people. In America towards the close of the nineteenth century in a study of the growth of consumption Thorstein Veblen noted how 'the lines of demarcation between social classes' were growing 'vague and transient' as people were increasingly aspiring to the consumer lifestyle 'in vogue in the next higher stratum' (1994: 84). Furthermore, once a standard of consumption or lifestyle, which had been an aspiration, had been acquired and lived, it was suggested by Veblen that its attractions would wane, its status would be inclined to diminish, its value to decline. With familiarity and use the 'luxury' would quickly acquire the status of 'necessity'. What might start out as a conspicuous form of consumption and might constitute an example of conspicuous waste, 'frequently ... [becomes] in the apprehension of the consumer a necessary of life' (1994: 99).

Veblen implicitly recognized the problem of endless accumulation which is symptomatic of modern consumerism, remarking that the standard of consumption to which consumers might aspire, 'the amount and grade of goods consumed, ... is flexible and ... *indefinitely extensible*', that yesterday's novelty or luxury commodity very quickly becomes today's necessity as it is 'incorporated into the scale of decent consumption, and so ... *become[s] an integral part of one's scheme of life ... as hard to give up [as those commodities] that maybe necessary to life and health'* (1994: 102–3, emphases added). In addition, Veblen anticipated that increased industrial efficiency, driven by the 'capitalistic system' in pursuit of 'profits on investment', would require continuing increases in consumption and that to this end the 'production of customers by sales-publicity' would become increasingly important to encourage people to strive to acquire more and more goods (2005[1904]: 7–8, 2006[1923]: 306 n12). His views on the respects in which advertising and salesmanship utilize envy and emulation to increase motivation to consume, continue to inform critical analyses of business marketing practices (Dawson, 2005).

Insofar as he presents a critical analysis of the growth of wasteful consumption in the 'capitalistic ... modern industrial system' Veblen's (2005: 7) work provides a classical sociological perspective on environmental problems which subsequently have increased in gravity as the economic practices and consumer lifestyles he identified have grown in scale and scope. Veblen was particularly concerned with the ways in which developments in 'the industrial arts' led to 'complex and extensive technology' which increased output and risked creating a problem of overproduction, of production overtaking the market (2006: 111). It was in this context that the business of 'sales-publicity' grew, its brief being to turn 'credulous persons into profitable customers', primarily through their 'fear of losing prestige' (2006: 310).

In addition to being critical of the conspicuous waste associated with modern forms of consumption Veblen drew attention to the wasteful and inefficient ways in which business appropriated natural resources. Veblen describes how natural resources are converted to 'absentee ownership' and private gain and that this 'has been worked into the texture of American life and culture' (2006: 168). A range of natural resources, which have been subjected to 'progressive seizure' or converted from 'community goods to private gain', are listed, including agriculture and real estate, gold and precious metals, timber, coal, petroleum and natural gas (2006: 168, 171). Critically reflecting on 'the American plan of exhausting the country's resources by seizure and conversion' Veblen states that the country's supply of timber, affected by 'land-grabbing' and soil cultivation, and its oil resources, subjected to hasty development 'without afterthought', have been 'disembowelled' (2006: 185, 191, 198). From this standpoint waste and inefficiency are deemed to be routine features of the process of business enterprise seizure, conversion, and consumption of natural resources. In Veblen's view, as Ross Mitchell observes:

> business interests are foreordained to exploit and squander resources. Sane, rational, efficient use of the environment and its resources is cast aside as externalities in cornucopian revelry. Any socioeconomic and political system built on the belief

of 'getting something for nothing' has no other choice but to
satisfy its vested interests, leaving the rest of humanity to pay
the costs of reduced availability of resources and environmental
degradation. (2001: 402; see also Mitchell, 2007)

In the early years of the twentieth century the German sociologist Max
Weber, a figure who frequently lamented the modern reticence to reflect
upon the values guiding conduct, echoed Veblen's concerns, cautioning
that '[w]e must not forget that the boiling heat of modern capitalistic
culture is connected with heedless consumption of natural resources, for
which there are no substitutes' (1970[1906]: 366). In the century that has
passed since Weber (1976: 181) expressed criticism of the 'inexorable
power' exercised by material goods over people's lives, consumerism
has increased in extent and intensity, as have the problematic consequences which have followed in its wake. The industrial capitalist form
of life both Veblen and Weber expressed concern about was described
by Arthur Penty, an English guild socialist, as 'a blind alley from which
we must retrace our steps or perish' (1922: 53). Penty drew attention to
the impact technological innovations were having on productivity, work,
and employment, the respects in which increases in production and consumption were leading to pollution, waste, and environmental degradation, and was led to conclude that 'it is simply impossible for civilization
to continue on the road it is traveling' (1922: 123). While his judgment
that modern industrial civilization had run its course was premature the
implication that it is ecologically unsustainable has been endorsed by
later social and environmental analysts.

A number of late twentieth-century analysts argued that consumerism
was unsustainable, that the appropriation and transformation of natural
resources in increasing circuits of production and consumption was having a damaging impact on the environment and creating a 'wasteland'
(Roszak, 1972), that the 'organization of the entire economy toward the
"better" life has become the major enemy of the *good* life' (Illich, 1985:
102, emphasis in original), and would in due course precipitate a collapse
of the biosphere and with it our whole way of life (Bahro, 1984: 144). In his
discussion of the global ecological crisis Rudolph Bahro argued that continuing to pursue growth in production and consumption would prove
to be a 'complete disaster', that the consumer lifestyle of 'Washington,
London and Paris' cannot be transferred to the rest of the world, and
that existing 'excessive use of natural resources will take far too long to
correct … [and is] at the expense of generations to come' (1984: 112,
110, 144). Taking stock of the consequences of economic growth and the
increasing production of consumer goods, Bahro, in an expression of
concern bordering on bewilderment which has lost none of its relevance
in the subsequent quarter century, remarked that:

> The world's material resources ... are fast being depleted. Our civilization, with its established technology and structure of needs, cannot be maintained. I don't understand how one can refuse to face this. (1984: 115)

In the intervening 'neo-liberal' years production and consumption have increased significantly by virtue of innovations in technology; consumer needs, wants, desires, and wishes have accumulated; resources have been further depleted; and awareness of the impact of modern industrial lifestyles on the planet has grown, but we have continued to head down the same path and only now are we (too) slowly beginning to face up to the enormity of the consequences we have already set in train.

Consumption Beyond Bio-capacity

The global production and consumption of goods and services now extends far beyond those needed to sustain a secure and happy life (IISD, 1999). In so far as growth remains the virtually unquestioned goal of economic activity, then consumption remains paramount, essential, sacrosanct, a necessary corollary of which is that products are, indeed have to be, regularly and routinely displaced – discarded, disposed of, and/or 'retired' (Princen et al., 2002: 4–5). As one critical sociological observer of contemporary consumer culture has commented:

> Every cultural product is calculated for maximal impact (that is, for breaking up, pushing out and disposing of the cultural products of yesterday) and instant obsolescence (that is, shortening the distance between the novelty and the rubbish bin ... quickly vacating the stage so that nothing should stand in the way of the cultural products of tomorrow). (Bauman, 2004a: 117)

While a growing number of contemporary observers and analysts consider the growth of global consumption to be unsustainable, a substantial volume of resources have continued to be directed to marketing and advertising to promote increasing levels of consumption (Princen et al., 2002; French, 2004).[1] Even at the mid-point of 2008, a period of growing concern about the prospects for the global economy as an international banking and credit crisis increased in intensity, global advertising expenditure for 2007 was estimated to have been US$485.5 billion and the reported expectation was for further growth in subsequent years (ZenithOptimedia, 2008a). With the neo-liberal turn in economic policy from the 1970s the production–consumption–obsolescence–disposal–replacement cycle accelerated as the mobility of global capital and associated downward pressure on labor costs led to lower commodity prices and an increasing tendency to regard a growing range of commodities as 'disposable' (Schor, 2005). The subsequent accelerating globalization of mass production and mass consumption has given rise to a mounting problem of 'mass waste' which is having detrimental environmental and social consequences (Clapp, 2002). It is not enough to assume that future technologies capable of delivering more-efficient and cleaner forms of production and the prospect of a 'new type of service economy' will resolve such matters, for the danger remains that 'the consumer juggernaut will overwhelm even the most sophisticated methods and technologies that can be devised to make consumption lean and super-efficient' (Renner, 2004: 111).

In 2006 the World Wildlife Fund reported that global human consumption had been in excess of the earth's bio-capacity since the 1980s and that by 2003 global consumption 'overshoot' was running at 25%. As the report states:

> The Earth's regenerative capacity can no longer keep up with demand – people are turning resources into waste faster than nature can turn waste back into resources. Humanity is no longer living off nature's interest, but drawing down its capital. This growing pressure on ecosystems is causing habitat destruction, or degradation, and permanent loss of productivity, threatening both biodiversity and human well-being. (2006: 4)

In a series of critical reflections on the emergence of neo-liberal policy responses to an earlier crisis of capitalism, which developed in the 1970s, Andre Gorz noted how growth in production and consumption had come to depend upon 'individual solutions to collective problems' (1985: 16). The neo-liberal pursuit of economic growth through an expansion of market relations has involved a policy combination of deregulation and privatization, and the increasing deployment of 'technologies of information creation and capacities to accumulate, store, transfer, analyze, and use massive databases to guide decisions in the global marketplace' (Harvey, 2005: 3). The dominant principle promoted and implemented has been that wherever and whenever possible 'all problems and needs ... must be answered by *individual* consumption of marketable goods and services' (Gorz, 1985: 16, emphasis in original). Neo-liberalism, as David Harvey has remarked, 'seeks to bring all human action into the domain of the market' and the associated promotion of market forces or 'freer trade [has] allowed a consumer culture to flourish' (2005: 3).

Rising levels of production and commensurate increases in the purchase of goods and services have been considered to be not only economically beneficial, but also conducive to the achievement of increases in personal satisfaction and happiness. While the global spread of the neo-liberal free-market led to 'free trade zones ... [and] ... consumption in the wealthiest countries ... increasing six-fold in less than twenty-five years' it also promoted increasing environmental degradation and destruction (Beck,

2000: 74). Accumulating evidence of the detrimental environmental consequences precipitated by neo-liberal policies and the 'consumerist vision',
which has constituted a necessary corollary, led David Harvey to caution:

> If we are entering the danger zone of so transforming the glo-
> bal environment, particularly its climate, as to make the earth
> unfit for human habitation, the further embrace of the neo-
> liberal ethic and of neo-liberalizing practices will surely prove
> nothing short of deadly. (2005: 173)

Supportive criticism of 'unrestrained consumption' and 'unconstrained
growth', and in particular the damaging environmental consequences of
consumerism, has come from an unlikely industry source. Sir Martin Sorrell,
Chief Executive Officer of WPP the world's second biggest advertising
group, was reported in 2008 to have declared in a number of speeches that
the industry's instinct to continually encourage people to consume more
and more, to engage in 'super-consumption' or 'conspicuous consumption',
is not productive, and should be discouraged. In a series of related critical
comments on product obsolescence, created by continual manufacture of
new models in the electronics industry in particular, Sorrell expressed concern about the burden being placed on the environment and the respects
in which obsolescence fostered 'a mindset of super-consumption, where
expensive items made at vast cost to the earth's resources quickly become
unfashionable and are not expected to last'. While this practice may prove
profitable in the short run Sorrell is reported to have commented that 'it is
not sustainable and it is not responsible' (cited in Benady, 2008).

The damaging impact of modern industrial consumption-driven ways
of life on the environment has attracted a series of warnings from critical
social analysts and even, of late, from consumer industry insiders, but the
overriding response to repeated forewarnings about a growing ecological
crisis has been to resort to 'business as usual', in short, to continue pursuing economic growth, increasing production of goods and services, and
creatively cultivating increases in demand by promoting consumerism.

Note

1. The increase in the financial resources devoted to advertising and marketing is confirmed by data from the USA, where annual spending on advertising directed to the
   cultivation of consumers for products and services the industry promotes, is reported
   to have increased steadily from US$6.5 billion in 1950, to US$56 billion in 1980,
   and to around US$170 billion in 2000 (Hemsley, 2007), rising to US$179 billion by
   2007 (ZenithOptimedia, 2008a). It was reported that in the UK 'advertising spend ...
   topped £19bn for the first time in 2006' (Advertising Association, 2007). Towards the
   close of the twentieth century it was estimated that each day in the USA people were
   being exposed to around 3000 advertisements promoting brand names, logos, and
   consumer activity (Bordwell, 2002: 239). Stealth advertising, experiential marketing
   and mobile campaigns, as well as search engine marketing have added to the range of
   techniques available to producers to cultivate increasing consumption.

8

CONSUMING FUTURES I: BUSINESS AS USUAL

Writing at the end of the twentieth century Ulrich Beck observed that one consequence of 'the neo-liberal free-market utopia' was the transformation of paid work, 'the spread of temporary and insecure employment', and consequently the increasing precariousness of people's lives (2000: 1). In his discussion Beck directs attention to the employment implications of knowledge's growing role as the primary source of wealth generation, in particular the respects in which the deployment of information technology promotes the capacity to raise productivity without commensurate increases in paid employment, and he explores a number of the alternative scenarios proposed in response to the end of the 'normal work society', but finds the majority to be of limited value insofar as they ultimately exemplify a lack of political imagination, demonstrated by an inability to come up with anything beyond a reform of the work society (2000: 63).

Visions of the Future from Work to Consumption

The alternative vision of the future proposed by Beck outlines a different way of life to that conventionally associated with an industrial, work-centered modernity secured within the territorial boundaries of the 'national state', one in which social, cultural, and economic conditions are considered to be subject to transformation by the modernization of modernity itself. What is described is effectively a counter-model, a 'second modernity', one marked by increasing uncertainty and risk and requiring 'strong states capable of transnational market regulation' to counter the detrimental consequences of 'neoliberal deconstruction' (2000: 20–3, 175). In his vision of the future Beck explains:

> The counter-model to the work society is based not upon leisure but upon political freedom; it is a multi-activity society in which house-work, family work, club work and voluntary work are prized along-side paid work and returned to the centre of public and academic attention. For in the end, these other forms remained trapped inside a value imperialism of work which must be shaken off. Those who wish to escape the spell of the work society must enter political society (in a new historical meaning of the term) – a soci-ety that gives material form to the idea of civil rights and transna-tional civil society, and thereby democratizes and gives new life to democracy. (2000: 125)

The criticism of future scenarios for remaining confined 'within the magic circle of the work society' is warranted and, in turn, the attention devoted to 'civil labour' and other possible alternatives to paid work in subsequent discussion is appropriate and necessary (Beck, 2000: 63; see also Gorz, 1982, 1985). However, it is surprising that more consider-ation is not given to consumption in the analysis provided, because it has been consumerism that has helped the work society cast its spell by providing it with its *raison d'être*, its necessity, if not its enduring appeal, as productivity has grown and been met, not with the reductions in work-ing hours, which could have been a possibility, but with the production of increasing quantities of goods and services and continually rising rates of consumption of the same (Durning, 1992; Schor, 1998; Siegel, 2008). The global growth and appeal of consumerism, as Beck (2000: 74) very briefly acknowledges, has 'spun practically out of control' in the wealthi-est countries and has had significantly detrimental consequences for the environment, contributing to rising levels of greenhouse gas emission precipitating climate change, leading one critical analyst to caution that 'the single biggest thing you can do to save carbon emissions' is to con-sume less (Jackson, 2008b: 43). Consumption, as much as work and pro-duction, warrants a prominent place in any consideration of visions for the future.[1]

A decade later neo-liberal policies, which had continually extolled the virtues of market forces, promoted their deregulation, and unreservedly celebrated wealth-creators and risk-taking bankers and financiers and their conspicuous consumer celebrity cousins, were being called into question following the 'economic Chernobyl' that radiated out from the US mort-gage market to produce a global economic recession bearing comparison, in some respects, with the 1929 'Great Crash' (Galbraith, 1992; Beck, 2000: 47). What began in the US financial and banking sectors triggered a global 'credit crunch', which, in turn, created a recession throughout the global economy affecting manufacturing and service sectors alike as consumer confidence and consumer demand plummeted, leading some prominent industry insiders, including the chief executive officer of WWP, the world's number two advertising group responsible for 'trillions of dollars of consumer spending worldwide', to speculate about 'the end of consumerism' (cited in Benady, 2008).

In this period, with the exception of some high-end luxury goods and consumer commodities and services designed specifically for the rich and famous, most indicators pointed to a significant decline in consumer expenditure with the automobile industry being particularly badly affected. For example, in the USA car manufacturers reported continuing falls in sales for the year up to March 2009 with America's 'big three', General Motors, Ford, and Chrysler each registering substantial reductions of 53%, 48%, and 44%, respectively, while US subsidiaries of Toyota, Honda, and Nissan also posted significant falls of 37.3%, 35.4% and 37%, respectively (Halliday, 2009). Then in June 2009 General Motors entered bankruptcy procedure and the US Government prepared to take a 70% stake. As Michael Moore commented, 'the company which invented "planned obsolescence" – the decision to build cars that would fall apart after a few years so that the customer would then have to buy a new one – has now made itself obsolete' (2009). In Western Europe as a whole, car sales were down by 25.4%, with significant falls being recorded in the UK of 30.9%, Italy 33%, Spain 41.6%, Denmark 50.8%, and Ireland 66.3%, but with lower falls recorded in France and Germany of 7.9% and 11.2%, respectively (Just-auto, 2009). As Michael Renner commented:

> Beset first by rollercoaster oil prices, then by a global financial crisis, the world's automobile industry is clearly in deep crisis. Automakers are closing plants, shedding jobs, reducing working hours for their employees, and trying to reduce their inventories through heavy discounts. At the same time, there is growing pressure on the industry to produce more-efficient and less polluting cars in the face of the gathering climate crisis. (2009)

The immediate short-term response of most governments around the world with car industries was to introduce schemes to encourage consumers to scrap their current vehicles and purchase new or nearly new vehicles, which it was anticipated would be more fuel efficient and likely to emit lower quantities of pollutants, including carbon dioxide. In Europe the introduction of financial incentives by governments lifted spring 2009 car sales but also raised industry concerns about the likely collapse of demand once the schemes had ended. More significantly the environmental benefits of the 'scrappage schemes' were argued to be, at best, debatable as reductions in carbon dioxide emission levels in vehicles manufactured after 1995 have been at best modest and governments have tended not to factor in full car lifecycle carbon costs into their replacement-scheme calculations. Scrapping a vehicle requires energy and has a carbon dioxide emission cost, as does the production of the new or nearly new vehicle that will replace it, courtesy of taxpayer funded financial incentive schemes, which could have been deployed to develop alternative 'CO$_2$ saving' forms of energy generation – 'geothermal energy … [and] mini hydroelectric schemes' – as well as other forms of energy efficiency, public transport initiatives, and additional measures such as 'cycle lanes … coach lanes … [and] better enforcement of speed limits', offering potentially far higher 'carbon payback' benefits (Monbiot, 2009).

In the USA the car industry is central to the entire economy, a major source of direct and indirect employment, with around 15% of the labor force involved in manufacturing, sales and marketing, driving in some professional capacity, repairing and servicing, insuring, licensing, administering, and policing, as well as building and maintaining roads and/or highways (Giddens, 2009). It was anticipated that the US government would follow the example of European administrations and introduce a comparable scrappage scheme, which they duly did in July 2009 with the implementation of the 'US Car Allowance Rebate System'. An initial US$1 billion program was announced offering consumers trading in vehicles up to 25-years-old and doing fewer than 18 miles per gallon a discount of between US$3500 and US$4500 from car and truck dealers for purchase, or lease, of a new 'greener' model, up to a value of US$45,000, capable of at least 22 miles per gallon (BBC, 2009a). While a modest improvement in fuel efficiency and security was one stated objective of the US government 'cash for clunkers' intervention, stimulating the economy through the promotion of increasing vehicle consumption and production was of even greater significance, as was the case with the equivalent European schemes.

Business as Usual

In 2009, governments around the world faced two interconnected crises, one economic, the other environmental. The financial crisis which had erupted in 2007 in the USA triggered a global economic recession. The environmental crisis had been gestating for some time and the accumulating ecological impact of growth orientated modern industrial economies and the associated consumer lifestyles they so vigorously promoted had been identified as a serious and growing problem from the 1970s, if not earlier (Roszak, 1972; Gorz, 1983[1975]; Illich, 1985[1973]; Hirsch, 1995[1977]). Although there has been an increasing accumulation of scientific evidence on and growing international concern over climate change and other forms of environmental degradation arising from a resource and energy intensive consumption-driven way of life, which has become increasingly global in scope and intensity, it is economic problems that have tended to be accorded greater political priority.

Whether as a consequence of a lack of political will, imagination, or understanding, for the most part consuming futures have continued to be presented as simple linear extrapolations from the present. Governments have continued to extol the virtues of economic growth and have proceeded to introduce various measures designed to revive it through a regeneration of consumer demand. What emerges in such instances is a false sense of comfort that by means of economic policy readjustments and appropriate scientific innovations and technological developments, which are presented as promising to deliver 'green' or 'renewable' solutions to environmental problems, a highly materialistic and increasingly global consuming way of life can be sustained indefinitely. The clear message conveyed is effectively 'business as usual', that economic growth, continually rising production, and ever-increasing levels of consumption of goods and services continue to be both desirable and possible.

There are other responses which present a rather different view of consuming futures, which outline the necessity for a radical transformation of lifestyles, especially in the 'consumer societies' that have grown accustomed to a seemingly endless, upwardly spiraling supply of consumer goods and services provided increasingly by those 'producer societies' to which a significant quantity of manufacturing has been outsourced and associated greenhouse gas emission levels exported (Princen et al., 2002; Starke, 2008; Giddens, 2009; Jackson, 2009; Watts, 2009). In consumer societies commodities are continually being marketed, purchased, and consumed in some shape or form, only subsequently to be displaced, 'retired' or disposed of, dumped in over-flowing landfill sites, or (too rarely) recycled, as they are rendered obsolete by the introduction of innovative new generations of products (Dawson, 2005; Slade, 2006). People consuming more and more things, and being ready to continue to do so over and over again, is a necessary corollary of the perpetual pursuit of economic growth, but as a growing number of analysts now argue this growth orientated way of life is not sustainable in a world of finite resources (Princen et al., 2002; Schor, 2005; Daly, 2008; Jackson, 2008a, 2008b, 2009).

Conceptions of consuming futures range all the way from versions of 'business as usual', through various forms or shades of green consumerism, to more radical and critically informed positions that place emphasis on the importance of 'sustainability' and present arguments for consuming differently and/or consuming less, especially in those parts of the world occupied by the global consumer class, while simultaneously recognizing the need for an overdue redistribution of resources to raise the standards of living of those long suffering from scarcity and poverty, those who have not benefited significantly, if at all, from the 'consumer revolution'. At one end of the spectrum it seems from policy pronouncements that 'any alternative to growth remains unthinkable' (Jackson, 2008b: 42), but at the opposite end the accumulating weight of scientific evidence convincingly demonstrates the need for a radically different model of economic life, one not wedded to perpetual growth and increasing consumption, one that factors into the equation that consumerism, the hyperconsumer way of life indulged in by the global consumer class, is quite simply unsustainable (Simms et al., 2006; Porritt, 2007; Global Footprint Network, 2008; Jackson, 2009; see also Figure 8.1).

A 'precautionary approach' to the issue of the ways in which increasingly interdependent economies and associated modern ways of living impact negatively on the environment was outlined at the United Nations Conference on Environment and Development in Rio de Janeiro in 1992. The conference outlined a series of principles designed to create new forms of cooperation between states, which would serve to 'respect the interests of all and protect the integrity of the global environmental and developmental system' (United Nations Environment Programme [UNEP], 1992). The 'Rio Declaration', as it has become known, emphasized that nation states should adopt a 'precautionary approach' to protect the environment, 'reduce and eliminate unsustainable patterns of production and consumption', and not allow 'lack of full scientific certainty ... [to] be used as a reason for postponing cost-effective measures to prevent environmental degradation' (UNEP, 1992: Principles 8, 15). However, rather than a precautionary approach the intervening period has been very much one of 'business as usual', a period marked by the relentless pursuit of more economic growth, and commensurate increases in production and consumption, leading not to a reduction, but to a significant *increase* in global emissions of carbon dioxide:

> The tragedy of these two wasted decades is that during this period the world has moved from a situation in which roughly a billion people in industrial countries were driving the problem – the United States, for example, has 4.6 percent of the world's population but accounts for 20 percent of fossil-fuel CO_2 emissions – to today's reality in which the far larger populations of developing countries are on the verge of driving an even bigger problem ...

> Between 1990 and 2008 U.S. emissions of carbon dioxide from fossil-fuel combustion grew by 27 percent – but emissions in China rose 150 percent, from 2.3 billion to 5.9 billion tons. (Flavin and Engelman, 2009: 7)

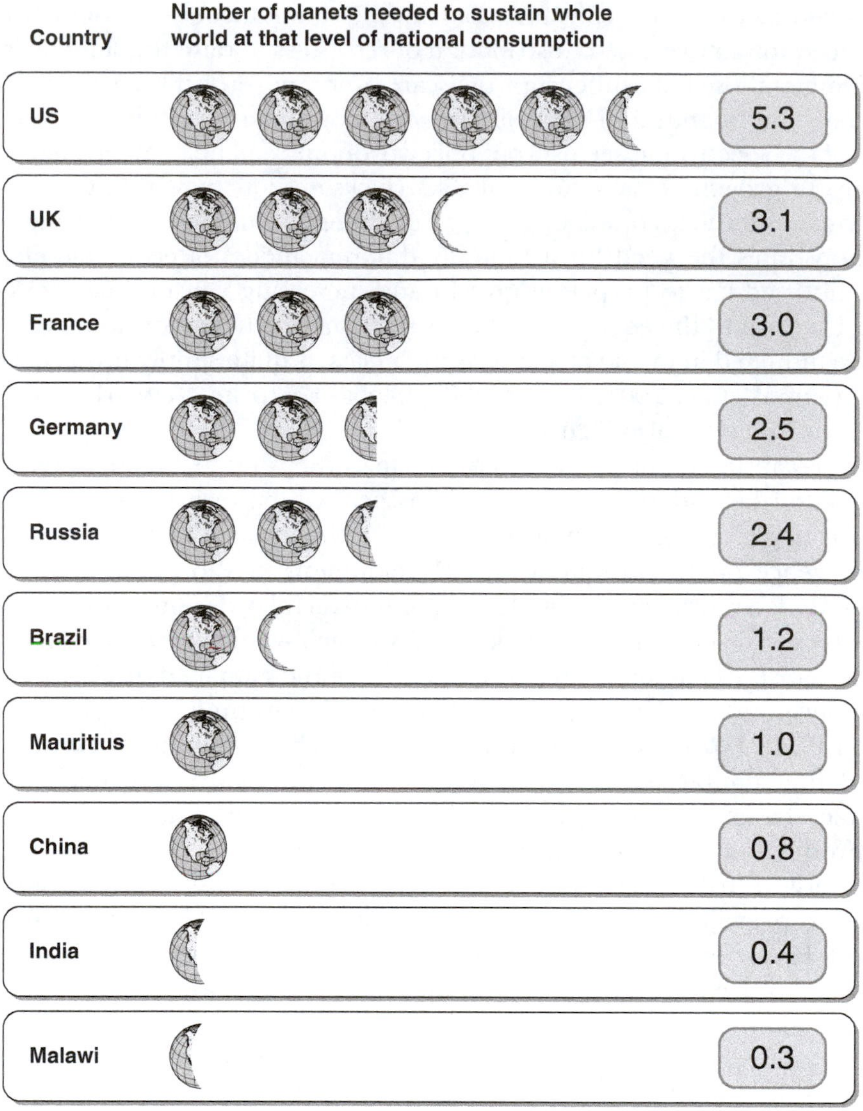

Country	Number of planets needed to sustain whole world at that level of national consumption	
US		5.3
UK		3.1
France		3.0
Germany		2.5
Russia		2.4
Brazil		1.2
Mauritius		1.0
China		0.8
India		0.4
Malawi		0.3

Figure 8.1   Global Unsustainability of current national consumption levels

Source: Simms et al. (2006: 15). The UK Interdependence report: How the world sustains the nation's lifestyles and the price it pays, London, New Economics Foundation p15. Reprinted with permission.

While the general principle of reducing and ultimately eliminating unsustainable patterns of production and consumption has been endorsed, the policy response has been disappointing and for the most part lacking in urgency, with relatively few effective measures being introduced that might make a substantial contribution to reducing emissions, or promoting sustainability, and too frequent recourse being made to the prospect of future 'technological ingenuity' saving us from having to change our ways to avoid 'climate disaster' (Jackson, 2008b). It is not so much that nothing of any great significance has yet been done, rather that the practical measures introduced by governments rarely seem to reflect the urgency of the situation, the gravity of the growing ecological crisis, with the result that to date 'no nation ... gets even close to what might be regarded as an effective performance in terms of reduction of greenhouse gas emissions' (Giddens, 2009: 74). The abiding impression too often conveyed by the political establishment is that the problems represented by climate change can be resolved through future, generally unspecified, untried and untested, technological innovations and that increasing economic growth and materially acquisitive consumer lifestyles can continue unabated.

(Bl)airlines

In a revealing interview conducted on Sky News in January 2007 Tony Blair, at the time UK Prime Minister, declared that he had no intention of restricting his use of long-haul flights in order to reduce his carbon footprint. The idea of encouraging people to take fewer flights and holiday closer to home was described as 'impractical', something that would be avoided by any politician interested in remaining in office. Describing the imposition of targets on travelers as 'unrealistic' Blair added:

> You know, I'm still waiting for the first politician who's actually running for office who's going to come out and say it – and they're not ... It's like telling people you shouldn't drive anywhere ... I think that what we need to do is to look at how you make air travel more energy efficient, how you develop the new fuels that will allow us to burn less energy and emit less. How – for example – in the new frames for the aircraft, they are far more energy efficient. (Quoted in Watt, 2007)

Air travel constitutes a significant aspect of global consumption. It facilitates global population flows through the provision of a consumer service in the form of flights to commercial-work and holiday-tourist destinations and both of these forms of air travel were on the increase from 1990 through to the onset of the economic recession in 2007/8. In 2004, the International Air Transport Association (IATA) reported that a record 1.8 billion passengers were carried and it was anticipated that between 2005 and 2008 global growth would be in the region of 6% per annum, a figure that was revised downward in December 2008 as economic recession affected the global economy. While recorded passenger growth for 2007 at 6.4% was as anticipated, in 2008 growth in passenger

numbers declined to 2% and for 2009 the expectation was of a fall in
passenger numbers (BBC News Online, 2004; IATA, 2008). In the period
1990–2004 the number of people using airports in the UK had risen by
120% and the impact of air travel on the environment increased significantly. There was a 79% increase in consumption of energy through air
travel and carbon dioxide emissions almost doubled (Monbiot, 2006).

Notwithstanding awareness of the environmental impact of air travel
and agreements made to meet reduced carbon dioxide emission targets
outlined in the Climate Change Act 2008, early in 2009 the UK Labour
Government, led by Prime Minister Gordon Brown, gave approval for
a third runway and a sixth terminal to be built at Heathrow Airport in
London. The announcement represented the start of a long planning
process. The proposed new runway was anticipated to raise the number of flights using Heathrow from in the region of 480,000 a year in
2008 to 702,000 by 2030. In anticipation of opposition Geoff Hoon, the
Transport Minister, informed members of parliament that he remained
confident that 'environmental targets' could be met and that the government would place '*an initial cap* on additional flights from the new
runway of 125,000 each year, would ensure new slots were "green slots"
used only by the "cleanest planes" and would set a new target on aircraft
emissions – that they would be lower in 2050 than in 2005' (BBC News,
2009b, emphasis added).

The optimistic responses, exemplified by Blair's remarks and those
of Geoff Hoon, on the prospect of potential future technological innovations making possible significantly more efficient and environmentally friendly air travel, effectively serve to promote the possibility of a
'business as usual' consuming future. The continuation of our current
consumer way of life is assumed to be a realistic proposition, one made
possible by anticipated future innovations achieved through progressive
developments in science and technology. Business as usual has pretty
much remained the default setting for democratic politicians' responses
to accumulating scientific evidence of the impact of a materially acquisitive, resource and energy intensive, consumption-driven way of life on
the planet. As Tony Blair is reported to have commented, 'The answer
to climate change ... is the development of science and technology' which
will enable global emission target reductions to be met 'without pain:
westerners can keep flying, driving and consuming while those in developing countries can realistically aspire to the same things' (Leake, 2009).
Promoting the prospect of achieving a resolution of problems identified
in the present through future scientific research and associated technological innovations constitutes a highly speculative and risk-laden
response, but one which accords perfectly with the limited career cycle of
the democratic politician who can safely assume that he/she will not be in

office to be called to account when the future duly arrives. Who by 2050 will remember Geoff Hoon, or recall that, 41 years earlier, in his capacity as Transport Minister in a New Labour administration, he had pledged that aircraft emissions by mid-century would be significantly lower than they were in 2005 and expressed confidence that environmental targets would be met?

Kyoto Protocol

Another example of a 'business as usual' response on the part of the political establishment to concerns expressed about the environmental impact of our consumption orientated way of life is provided by the administration of George W. Bush, the 43rd President of the USA. Bush presented a relatively uncompromising view of consuming futures and his administration's response was for the most part one of outright denial of any urgent environmental problems arising from modern lifestyles (Giddens, 2009). On assuming office in 2001 Bush disbanded the President's Council on Sustainable Development (PCSD), launched by former President Bill Clinton in 1993, and his administration implemented a domestic agenda that systematically sought to 'dismantle many of the country's cornerstone pieces of environmental legislation' (Cohen et al., 2005: 59).

Throughout his two terms in office George W. Bush's administration steadfastly refused to countenance any measures that might interfere with the routine running of the American economy and the consumer lifestyles of its citizens and continually expressed criticism of the Kyoto Protocol, an international agreement composed in 1997 which advocated that developed countries endorse legally binding targets to reduce greenhouse gas emissions in a first commitment period (2008–2012), to around 5% below 1990 levels. The predominant tendency throughout the Bush years was to regard economic growth as sacrosanct, to consider it to be necessary to raise standards of living, to promote increases in 'material affluence', measured in terms of continuing quantitative growth in the production and consumption of goods and services. The possibility that continual pursuit of growth in production and consumption, so central to the existing organization of social and economic life, might be environmentally problematic and globally unsustainable, did not receive serious consideration (Jackson, 2009: 76).

When, in a speech delivered in 2002, President Bush did briefly acknowledge the possibility that global warming might represent a potential future threat, he merely advocated 'voluntary efforts' and 'market forces', rather than the mandatory measures outlined in the Kyoto Protocol, which he considered were unacceptable as they would lead to a 'loss of $400 billion in industry and 4.9 million US jobs' (UN Wire, 2002). In February 2005 the Kyoto Protocol finally came into effect with 141 nations, accounting for in the region of 61% of greenhouse gas emissions, ratifying the treaty and pledging to cut emissions by an average of 5% by 2012. But while all European and the majority of other developed industrial nations ratified the Protocol, Australia and the USA abstained from doing so for 'economic reasons', in addition fast-growing developing countries such as China and India remained outside the framework. In any event, the targets finally agreed after rounds of negotiations and associated compromises have proven to be too low to make a sufficient impact on global warming. As Giddens comments:

> Because the Kyoto agreements were not adopted until 2005 most countries were slow in making any progress at all towards reaching even the modest targets that had been set. In practice so far, little has been achieved ... Emissions in Spain have gone up by over 30 per cent since 1990. In the US, emissions grew by 13 per cent during that period overwhelming whatever progress the EU countries might make. (2009: 189)

The uncompromising 'business as usual' approach promoted by President Bush seemed to have come to a close with the inauguration of the 44th President, Barack Obama, who assumed office pledging to tackle the problem of climate change through the introduction of taxation incentives and financial subsidies to stimulate the development of climate-friendly technologies, energy sources, and fuels, alongside measures to increase energy efficiency. Initial policy measures proposed to promote greener production and consumption stopped short of levying a charge on businesses and households for the carbon-intensive energy used to manufacture commodities and provide commercial services on all the things consumed routinely everyday. However, on his first overseas trip as President, with the world's media hanging on his every word, Obama made no reference to the ecological crisis, but emphatically placed renewed emphasis on ' the need for immediate, concerted action to restore economic growth' (CBC News, 2009).

Notwithstanding the evident priority accorded to the restoration of economic growth, US policy on the dangers of global warming changed significantly under the Obama administration. At a symposium on climate change held in London in May 2009 the US Energy Secretary Steven Chu promised decisive action on energy security and efficiency fronts, the aim being to decrease US dependency on imported oil, promote 'green energy', and reduce the world's carbon footprint. Action included passing legislation committing the USA to reduce greenhouse gas emissions to 80% of 1990 levels by the year 2050 and a series of other measures, including introduction of tougher energy standards for appliances and new fuel standards for vehicles, as well as investment to improve the energy efficiency of commercial buildings and houses and to develop new renewable energy technologies (Chu, 2009). A combination of high oil prices and economic recession had already led to a 2.8% reduction in energy-led carbon dioxide emission levels in the USA in 2008, but 5.8 billion tons of carbon dioxide had continued to be released into the atmosphere in the course of the year. Moreover, although energy demand had declined in 2008 by 2.2% it was a decline of 6% in oil-related emissions that accounted 'for the bulk of overall reduction in energy-related carbon-dioxide emissions' (Energy Information Administration, 2009).

In 2006, China had overtaken the USA as the country responsible for the largest share of global carbon dioxide emissions, an unenviable position the latter had occupied for a century. The top five emitters – China (24%); USA (21%); EU (15 countries) (12%); India (8%); and the Russian Federation (6%) – were responsible for 71% of global carbon dioxide emissions. However, if population size is factored in the rankings change considerably to reveal significantly higher emissions of carbon dioxide per person in the USA, reflecting the country's much higher level of economic development and the effect of its energy-intensive, materially acquisitive, consumption-driven lifestyle – USA (19.4 metric tons); Russian Federation (11.8); EU (8.6); China (5.1); and India (1.8) (Netherlands Environmental Assessment Agency, 2007). The critical test for US greenhouse gas emission reduction policy initiatives will come, post-recession, when global economic activity picks up, production rises, demand for fossil-fuels increases, and the prospect of consumption-driven economic growth returns.

Transforming factories, offices, households, and lifestyles and the energy systems on which they have come to depend, to make them less dependent on environmentally damaging technologies and stabilize greenhouse gas emissions at an acceptable level, will prove costly. Estimates of cost have ranged from '4–5% of world GDP, with average estimates of around 2–3% of world GDP … [that is] around one year of trend growth' down to the 1% of global GDP initially proposed in the Stern Review, a figure which was subsequently revised upward to 2% of global GDP when the need for a lower stabilization level was recognized (Hawksworth, 2006: 9; Stern, 2007: xii; see also Annex to Climate Group Report [2009] for additional cost estimates). Making businesses and citizen-consumers pay more for goods and services, particularly in circumstances where they are already facing economic difficulties, as was the case in the face of the global economic recession that gathered momentum through 2008, is likely to prove highly unpopular with electorates. As Blair's comments about air travel and Bush's remarks on the potential impact of the Kyoto Protocol on the US economy imply, the relatively short-term democratic electoral cycle means that elected politicians are generally unlikely to countenance the introduction of any measures which, while necessary if not essential in the medium- and/or long-term, risk proving to be unpopular and potentially politically damaging in the short 'electoral' term.

The prospect of an exhortation to consume differently, to downshift, or 'consume less, live more' finding a place on the manifesto of a mainstream political party, or within government policy in a hyperconsumer society, where it would be both appropriate and highly beneficial, currently seems remote in the extreme, as the range of policy responses to the global economic crisis, universally directed towards a regeneration of credit and a restoration of consumer confidence, demand, and expenditure served to demonstrate. As one critic has perceptively noted, you can be confident that 'one piece of advice you will not see on a government list is "buy less stuff"', because within the governing paradigm economic growth must be maintained, 'protected at all costs' (Jackson, 2008b: 43, 42). An appropriate example of political unwillingness and/or an inability to imagine anything else beyond business as usual is provided by Blair's successor as UK Prime Minister, Gordon Brown, in an address in the USA to the joint session of Congress. While making reference to change being essential, and of the need not simply 'to manage our times but to transform them', the response to global economic recession ultimately offered holds out no meaningful prospect of a transformation of our times as it returns to the familiar trinity of economic growth, rising production, and increasing consumption:

> An economic hurricane has swept the world, creating a crisis of credit and of confidence. History has brought us now to a point where change is essential. We are summoned not just to manage our times but to transform them. Our task is to rebuild prosperity and security in a wholly different economic world, where competition is no longer local but global and banks are no longer just national but international ... while today people are anxious and feel insecure, over the next two decades literally *billions of people in other continents will move from being simply producers of their goods to being consumers of our goods and in this way our world economy will double in size. Twice as many opportunities for business, twice as much prosperity, and the biggest expansion of middle class incomes and jobs the world has ever seen.* (Brown, 2009, emphasis added)

G20 2009

The major policy measures introduced to date to promote global economic recovery reveal a common view, namely that recovery hinges on the successful stimulation of economic growth and parallel reinvigoration of consumerism:

> Recovery ... is taken to mean business as usual. Kick start the
> circular flow of the economy and watch it grow. The outcome
> (assuming it works) will be thoroughly predictable. Business inno-
> vation (creative destruction) and consumer demand (positional
> spending) will drive consumption forwards. And with employment
> depending on it, there's no means of anyone getting off the tread-
> mill. (Jackson, 2009:72)

The G20 summit held in London in April 2009 in response to the global
economic crisis provides an appropriate illustration of the priority accorded
to economic growth. On the eve of the summit climatologists and environmental scientists expressed concern that action on climate change, for example
re-establishing international agreement on carbon dioxide emission-
reduction timetables, targets, and amounts, was taking second place to
dealing with the global economic crisis. A report submitted to the G20 summit by environmental advisers cautioned that 'climate change poses a far
more serious threat to the global economy in the long term than do temporary economic downturns' and, expressing concern that fiscal stimulus
packages intended to revive the global economy were not directing a sufficient level of resources into low-carbon 'green' measures, argued that there
needed to be a 'greening' of fiscal stimuli (Bauer et al., 2009: 6, 17).

The final statement, outlining the measures agreed upon by the leaders of the 20 nations present at the summit, nations whose economies
account for around 85% of global output, revealed that greater emphasis
was being placed upon the global economic crisis and the perceived need
to regenerate and sustain economic growth and consumer demand, than
the ecological crisis and climate change. The final G20 statement con-
tains repeated references to 'growth', including commitments to 'restore
confidence, growth, and jobs' (clause 4: bullet point 1); 'deliver the scale
of sustained fiscal effort necessary to restore growth' (clause 6); 'accelerate the return to trend growth' (clause 10) and 'restore global demand'
(clause 11); 'support sustainable global growth' (clause 13) and 'growth
in emerging markets and developing countries' (clause 17); and ensure
that 'resources can be used effectively and flexibly to support growth'
(clause 18). Concluding clauses lend further weight to the significance of
economic growth by noting that 'World trade growth has underpinned
rising prosperity for half a century', that in the face of a global decline
in demand 'Reinvigorating world trade and investment is essential for
restoring global growth (clause 22), and that the G20 are 'determined
not only to restore growth but to lay the foundation for a fair and sustainable world economy' (clause 25) and will 'support employment by
stimulating growth' (clause 26).

In a number of places token reference is made to the importance of
economic growth being 'sustainable', but surprisingly there are relatively

few references to ecological, environmental, or climatic matters. Moreover, where there is an explicit address of sustainable globalization early in the statement the factors identified, on which rising prosperity is considered to be based, do not include the environment – 'We believe that the only sure foundation for sustainable globalisation and rising prosperity for all is *an open world economy based on market principles, effective regulation, and strong global institutions*' (clause 3, emphasis added). There is a subsequent very brief reference to building 'an inclusive, green, and sustainable recovery' (clause 4) and the fiscal stimulus is described, amongst other things, as accelerating 'the transition to a green economy' (clause 6), but no clarification is provided and no specific policy proposals are outlined. It is only towards the very end of the statement that reference is made to using the fiscal stimulus to invest in programs (unspecified) that it is hoped will promote 'a resilient, sustainable and green recovery', programs that are described as making possible 'the transition towards clean, innovative, resource efficient, low carbon technologies and infrastructure' (clause 27). Then, almost as an afterthought, 'the threat of irreversible climate change' is acknowledged and a commitment 'to reach agreement at the UN Climate Change conference in Copenhagen in December 2009 (clause 28) is reaffirmed (G20, 2009).

The G20 identified the global economic crisis as urgent and considered immediate action was required to restore economic growth, whereas the environmental crisis and the problem of climate change were considered deferrable to the end of the year. As Tim Jackson notes:

> When the economy falters, the clarion call from every side is to get the economy 'back on the growth path'. And this call is not just to increase the GDP. It is, for the most part, to stimulate consumption growth: to restore consumer confidence and stimulate high street spending. (2009: 68)

In short, while there is a compelling shared assumption that growth needs must be restored post-haste, comparable consideration is not given to the growing body of scientific work that details the detrimental environmental consequences of a growth dependent form of social and economic life, or the alternatives outlined that may offer a potential resolution to both the global economic crisis and the growing ecological crisis (Princen et al., 2002; Gardner and Prugh, 2008; Daly, 2008b; Jackson, 2009).

It is not surprising to find democratic politicians wary of displeasing their electorates by introducing measures that would have a negative impact on existing materialistically acquisitive consumer lifestyles, for example the imposition of various restrictions, or additional costs, on forms of consumption that are recognized to be environmentally damaging. As Giddens observes, 'such a difficulty is to some extent intrinsic to democratic politics, given the push and pull between political leaders, interest groups and the public – coupled to the need to win elections' (2009: 89). Some analysts regard the prevalence of vested interests in democracies as a critical impediment to the introduction of the long-term social and economic policy measures necessary to effectively address ecological problems, measures that it has been suggested authoritarian forms of government may find easier to introduce and enforce. Reflecting on the 'unfettered ecological consumption patterns' that have been a feature to date of democracies deploying neo-liberal policies in pursuit of economic growth, one critic argues that authoritarian forms of government may find it easier to enforce the 'draconian' measures now required to move towards sustainability (Nair, 2008: 4). However, as Giddens points out, while liberal democracies may indeed encounter difficulties in mobilizing public opinion to respond positively to the introduction of measures necessary to deal with climate change, it is liberal democracies which have encouraged 'the open development of science' and allowed environmental movements, pressure groups and NGOs to emerge. In contrast, authoritarian states have exercised a high degree of surveillance and regulation over civil society organizations and to date have had 'poor or disastrous environmental records' (Giddens, 2009: 73).

It is perhaps predictable that the interconnected goals of increasing economic growth, raising rates of production, and promoting ever-rising levels of consumption of goods and services seem to have remained sacrosanct within the policies of governments of all political persuasions. However, free of the judgment of the ballot-box scientific analysts are in a position to be able to take a more detached and considered view of our materially acquisitive, consumption-fixated way of life, to reflect critically on its consequences and engender debate about where it is leading us and what consuming futures are probable, possible, and/or preferable. It is to a brief consideration of alternative consuming futures, those that extend beyond business as usual, that discussion below is primarily directed, although analysts too may succumb to a business as usual view of consuming futures, as the following example serves to demonstrate.

A Future Cornucopia of Goods and Services

In the conclusion to a wide-ranging analysis of some of the ways in which consumption has been transformed in the course of the twentieth century, George Ritzer notes how consumerism has continued to expand and suggests that the 'future will bring with it unimagined palaces of consumption filled to capacity with a cornucopia of goods and service' (2005: 207). What is anticipated is more stuff, effectively a version of business as usual, a future involving a 'further escalation of ... consumerism ... [and/or] continued growth of consumption' (2005: 208). In attempting to explain the anticipated continuing future expansion of consumption, analytic consideration is not directed to the logic of the prevailing economic system, necessarily wedded as it is to perpetual growth and increasing capital accumulation, achieved primarily through continual increases in the production of goods and services designed for private consumption. Rather the focus of the analysis is deliberately confined to 'consumption in general, and the means (and landscapes) of consumption in particular' (Ritzer, 2005: 188).

Although there is a very brief acknowledgment of the influence of modern advertising and the corporate requirement for ever-increasing profitability and there are a few passing references to some of the problems that are a direct consequence of the hyperconsumption that has become a feature of a way of life that began in America but has subsequently become global in scope, for example growing levels of debt, a decline in savings, and increases in working hours to service debt-led consumption, ultimately such matters are at best marginal to the discussion. The contentious matter of the relationship between increasing consumption, possession of more and more material goods, and levels of human happiness is similarly marginalized. While a reference is made to public opinion polls casting doubt on the latter matter, there is no discussion of the substantial body of research which very effectively challenges the conventional wisdom promoted through business marketing and advertising, that ever-increasing consumption and possession of more and more material goods leads to rising levels of happiness for consumers (Faber and O'Guinn, 1989; Layard, 2003, 2005; Gardner and Assadourian, 2004; Schwartz, 2004).

Where there is recognition of potential problems that might be associated with increases in consumption and the global diffusion of American consumer lifestyles, responses are confined to an acceptance of the fact that 'the exportation of American means of consumption to the rest of the world involves a process of Americanization' and that there are a 'series of potential drawbacks not the least of which is the fact that people … have become voracious consumers' (2005: 45). However, the potentially critical import of this acknowledgment is heavily qualified, indeed largely neutralized, by the accompanying assertion that the 'explosion' of American-led consumerism has brought 'benefits such as lower prices and a cornucopia of consumer goods unheard of in human history' (2005: 45).

There is a fleeting admission that a precondition for consumption assuming 'center stage in American society' is that 'more and more basic production is taking place in other nations … especially in developing nations' (Ritzer, 2005: 26), but the implications lurking in the statement are not explored. How lower prices for consumer goods have been achieved, chiefly through the exporting of manufacturing to lower-wage cost economies and export processing zones, where workers receive derisory rates of pay, where children are prevailed upon to engage in various forms of labor (an estimated 158 million worldwide), and where there is little if any health and safety protection, is not addressed. The question of who the primary beneficiaries of the production of a 'cornucopia of consumer goods' have been is not posed and in consequence inequalities in respect of the social distribution and consumption of such commodities, which have remained largely unavailable to a significant majority of the world's population, are not considered. The growth in global consumption has come at a considerable cost, especially for those numerous 'invisible' others who have largely been excluded from the benefits of increased consumption, those whose terms of employment and working conditions, following the globalization of economic production, are frequently far removed from the 'enchanting' landscapes, 'cathedrals of consumption', malls and other retail sites, both real and virtual, through which the commodities they produce are purchased and consumed (Klein, 2001; Bauman, 2004a; Labour Behind the Label, n.d.; UNICEF, n.d.).

Also omitted from the discussion of the 'new means of consumption' is any consideration of the increases in inequality in income, wealth, and consumer activity which have been a corollary of the neo-liberal, free-market driven growth in consumption. Within the USA, and for that matter around the world as a whole, inequality increased significantly from the early 1970s through to the present, with the exception in the former of a very brief period in the early 1990s (Demos, 2006; Shah, 2008b; Johnson and Shipp, n.d.). As Tim Jackson notes:

> A fifth of the world's population earns just 2% of global income. Inequality is higher in the OECD nations than it was 20 years ago. And while the rich got richer, middle-class incomes in Western countries were stagnant in real terms long before the recession. Far from raising the living standard for those who most needed it, growth let much of the world's population down. Wealth trickled up to the lucky few. (2009: 6)

Over the period 1979–2005 'the top five percent of American families saw their real incomes increase 81 percent ... [while] the lowest-income fifth saw their real incomes decline' (Demos, 2006:1). The growth in inequality in America during this period contributed significantly to 'status competition in consumption' (Schor cited in Holt, 2005: 12, 17). A much more unequal society emerged, one in which media promotion of celebrity lifestyles and emulation of the rich and famous prompted pursuit of status through purchase and display of valued branded consumer goods and services, a pattern that has been replicated in the UK, another country in which inequality increased significantly over the period in question, and has been followed, albeit to a lesser degree, in other parts of the world.

However, the most significant problem with the analysis is the absence of any consideration of the growing body of work that documents the range of highly damaging consequences modern consumer lifestyles have for the environment (Durning, 1992; Princen et al., 2002; Gardner et al., 2004; Jordan, 2007). While a notion of 'landscapes of consumption' (Ritzer, 2005) is introduced, the term merely serves to decorate discussion of some aspects of the geographical reconfiguration of 'new' means of consumption. The more significant impact of means of consumption on physical surroundings is not addressed and there is no recognition of the conveniently distanced, detrimental environmental consequences arising from the 'outsourcing' of the production of the consumer goods on display throughout the commercialized 'landscapes of consumption'.

In the discussion of the growth of spectacular retail environments there is relatively little critical analysis of consumerism and the consequences that have followed from the proliferation of 'means of consumption'. In consequence, the opportunity to help dispel illusions by producing an appropriately critical analysis of a way of life already overly enchanted with consumerism is missed, as is the prospect of outlining a vision of a different consuming future by engaging with the pressing matter of sustainability and the plight of those excluded from the global consumer class. Notwithstanding an admission that Americans spend too much on consumption, a recognition of the uncertainty of social and economic life, and a brief acknowledgment of the possibility that 'developments ... might disrupt or even derail the seemingly inevitable development and expansion of ... consumption', in the final instance the future anticipated is one of continuing growth in which the means of consumption will become 'even more central than they are today' (Ritzer, 2005: 209).

Consumers are deemed unlikely to change their behavior because they are considered to be having 'fun', finding the displays provided within the emporia of consumption spectacular, if not 'entertaining'. Even the prospect of a 'deep recession or depression' is considered to represent little more than a temporary interruption to socioeconomic life, the expectation being that consumers will continue to 'demand more' and that the means of consumption 'will be back, bigger and better, with the next upturn in the economy' (Ritzer, 2005: 193). In consequence, the future envisioned is effectively more of the same: 'today's means of consumption will ... be supplanted by even newer means that are infinitely more enchanted, spectacular, and effective as selling machines' (Ritzer,

2005: 207). However, the unintentionally disturbing vision outlined, of hyperconsumerism without end, is simply unsustainable as research within the discourse of 'ecological political economy' has demonstrated so effectively (Princen et al., 2002; Simms et al., 2006; Gardner and Prugh, 2008; Jackson, 2009).

Note
1. In a later discussion of potential forms of opposition to the global power of neo-liberal capitalism, Beck suggests that in the global age the 'counter-power' to capital resides in civil society and is 'based on the figure of the political consumer' (2005: 7). It is the capacity of the consumer to refuse 'to make a purchase, at any time and in any place' that constitutes the potential threat to the power of capital. By deliberately choosing to refrain from buying certain products the consumer is deemed to be 'casting a vote against the politics of corporations' (2005: 7). However, for the 'counter-power of the political consumer' to be effective there has to be 'good networking and carefully planned mobilization', as well as effective organization, and in their absence the threat to the power of capital posed by consumers employing the 'weapon of non-purchase' is recognized to be no more than unrealized potential, 'a blunt weapon' (Beck, 2005: 7). Beck alludes to the relentless systemic growth of consumption, remarking that there are 'no limits, in terms of either manufacture or use' (2005: 7), but offers no consideration of the accumulating body of scientific evidence on ecological limits in respect of which organized alternatives to global consumerist capitalism are increasingly being mobilized (see Chapter 9).

9

CONSUMING FUTURES II: 'GREEN' AND SUSTAINABLE ALTERNATIVES

Concerns about consumerism and attempts to promote alternatives have a long history, almost 'as old as capitalism itself' (Etzioni, 2003: 7). Forms of consumer activism and campaigns arising from problems associated with capitalist market-exchange-based forms of consumption can be traced back to at least the mid-nineteenth century and the reaction of working-class communities in England to 'excessive prices and poor quality goods, food in particular', which led to the establishment of a modern cooperative movement offering consumers the possibility of forming mutually benefi-cial consumer cooperatives providing good quality products and services at the lowest cost, as an alternative to conventional profit-seeking consumer businesses. Consumer cooperatives are now to be found around the world (Flanders, 2006: 80–3; Gabriel and Lang, 2006: 156–8; International Cooperative Alliance n.d.). The growth of commercial corporations in the course of the twentieth century and the potential impact of their increasing economic power on the interests of consumers precipitated other expres-sions of consumer activism, including 'value-for-money' and product design and safety campaigns. But it was only in the course of the 1970s that a number of alternatives to mainstream consumerism emerged campaign-ing on a variety of 'green' concerns about the ways in which the production of consumer goods and services impacted on the environment, resources, the welfare of animals, and the health and well-being of both workers and consumers (Gabriel and Lang, 2006: 166–8).

There are now a range of critical responses and anti-consumerist alternatives to modern consumption-driven forms of economic organization and associated lifestyles, including the voluntary simplicity movement, downshifters, the freecycle network, freeganism, eco-villages, and the 'transition movement', as well as organizations such as Adbusters, which aims to subvert corporate consumerism through anti-ads and culture jamming activism, as well as by promoting an annual 'Buy Nothing Day' and a 'No TV week' (Adbusters, n.d., accessed 8 June 2009; Klein, 2001; Doherty and Etzioni, 2003). A common concern shared by critics of modern consumption-driven lifestyles and those exploring alternatives is that modern consumerism is unsustainable and that to redress ecological decline and climate change wealthier societies in particular need to take the lead in 'radically increasing energy efficiency' and shifting 'toward lower resource consumption', by placing less emphasis on materialistic values and lifestyles and more on the benefits to be derived from a 'higher quality of life' (Ryan and Durning, 1997: 67–70; Jackson, 2008a; Giddens, 2009: 106–8, 136–7).

In a manner that bears comparison with current concerns, Andre Gorz and Rudolph Bahro drew attention in the late 1970s and early 1980s to two closely articulated global crises, one economic in origin, the other ecological. Bahro was particularly preoccupied with accumulating signs of a developing ecological crisis and expressed the view that a radical transformation of the macro-economy was necessary, that the emphasis had to move away from 'the capitalist type of growth' because the planet's material resources were rapidly being depleted and the prevailing way of life 'with its established technology and structure of needs cannot be maintained' (1984: 112, 115). What Bahro advocated was a dramatic shift in social and economic emphasis, away from the pursuit of increasing economic growth and production of more and more consumer goods, and towards the generation of 'a new consumption pattern geared to the *qualitative* development of the individual' (1984: 102, emphasis in original). In a broadly comparable manner Gorz drew attention to the ecological consequences of capitalism's constant pursuit of growth and in the course of developing criticisms of 'the goods produced, the pattern of consumption which capitalism promotes, and the inequality which drives it' (1983: 27), argued that it is possible, and indeed necessary in the more developed societies, to consume less and live better. However, Gorz simultaneously cautioned that the capitalist economic system possessed considerable flexibility and, in particular, the creative capacity to 'assimilate ecological necessities as technical constraints, and adapt the conditions of exploitation to them' (1983: 3). As Gorz anticipated might be the case, a number of subsequent responses to the accumulation of scientific findings on the environmental impact of increasing economic production and expanding consumer life-styles have assumed the form of adaptations to ecological constraints and cultivation of forms of 'green consumerism', promoting the prospect of further scope for economic growth and capital accumulation through the generation of new businesses, products, and services, represented as sig-nifying the development of a 'more caring, considerate capitalism' (Gorz, 1983: 4–7; Gabriel and Lang, 2006: 167, 171).

Green Consumerism

Responses to accumulating evidence of the environmental consequences of modern ways of living have ranged from critical ecological political economy analyses, which consider environmental problems to derive from the logic of growth intrinsic to the economic system and call for sys-tem-wide changes in response to evidence of a growing ecological crisis (Gorz, 1983; Bahro, 1984; Jackson, 2009), related radical challenges to the notion of market supremacy, which advocate alternatives to consumerism and reductions in consumption, to various shades of 'green consumer-ism', promoting the idea that adoption of recommended 'environmentally friendly' products and/or practices will be conducive to the maintenance of economic growth and the promotion of forms of consumption that are not detrimental to the environment and indeed may even prove to be ben-eficial (Gabriel and Lang, 2006), and forms of 'natural capitalism', which hold out the future prospect of 'reintegrating ecological with economic goals' (Lovins et al., 1999: 158; Nordhaus and Shellenberger, 2007).

With green consumerism the implication seems to be that consum-ers made knowledgeable about environmental problems will be able to demand of manufacturers of products and providers of services that their commodities and services are environmentally safe or neutral. There are a growing number of books and websites emerging that claim to be designed precisely for that purpose, to assist consumers make the right 'green' choices.[1] The growing number of products represented as 'environmen-tally friendly' appearing on the market may suggest that producers and consumers are responding appropriately to environmental concerns, but it is questionable whether 'buying green' constitutes a sufficiently effective response to the scale and gravity of environmental concerns. Ultimately the ecological crisis will not be resolved by individual, private 'green' shop-ping decisions, by individuals 'buying so-called earth-friendly products', because as virtuous as the intentions behind eco-consumer activities might be the cumulative global environmental impact of consumerism 'remains enormous and hazardous' and what is required to deal effectively with the fundamental economic factors and industrial processes contributing to climate change is 'more transformative political action', not green consumer 'chic' or 'eco narcissism' (Williams, 2007; see also Monbiot, 2007; Giddens, 2009; Goleman, 2009).

The Body Shop

Established in 1976 the Body Shop represents an early UK example of a business that promotes itself as oriented towards green consumerism, presenting an image of itself as a caring company concerned to protect the environment and the rights of indigenous people, as well as opposing animal testing in the cosmetics industry, offering minimal packaging, and selling products made from natural ingredients. By 2009 the Body Shop (n.d.) had become a truly 'global retailer of toiletries and cosmetics' with in the region of 2500 outlets in over 55 markets around the world.

However, its green credentials have been challenged by critics who have questioned the naturalness of products by suggesting that in a number of lines (unspecified) there has been use of non-renewable petrochemicals, synthetic coloring, fragrances and preservatives, and that in many instances only very small quantities of botanical-based ingredients are used. Furthermore, as a commercial corporation the Body Shop, like other corporations, has of necessity to continually aim to improve its performance, to satisfy its shareholders, by increasing profitability through reductions in manufacturing costs and increases in sales of its products, achieved by innovations in and outsourcing of production, capturing a larger share of the market, and by growing the market for its goods, which are unnecessary items, effectively luxury goods. The accusation is that precisely like other consumer goods corporations the Body Shop contributes to ever-increasing levels of consumption by promoting the idea that personal well-being can be enhanced through consumption and that this necessary subscription to the logic of economic growth is ultimately detrimental to the environment (London Greenpeace, 1998).

In 2009, the company identified the development of cosmetic product ranges designed for men as a potential area for further growth and produced a marketing strategy to raise men's awareness of their appearance and promote products they might use.[2] The consumer market segmentation identified was 'urban cosmopolitan' men aged between 20–35 years and earning £25,000–55,000 per year and the central objectives of the marketing strategy identified were as follows:

> Review and refresh product portfolio to ensure at least 30% of the target demographic indicated likelihood to buy ... Promote awareness of the Body Shop core brand and specific men's

grooming product offerings through targeted channels such
that at least 35% of the target demographic is aware of the products and the unique values of the Body Shop ... Build loyalty to
brand products so that at least 10% of the target demographic
becomes repeat buyers ... by the end of 2009. (Chernenko
et al., 2009: 17–18)

The Body Shop and all other commercial corporations aspiring to green
consumer credentials still have to comply with the prevailing economic
logic, which means continually working to increase profitability by expanding markets for products, that is increasing consumption by 'creating ...
induced wants' through appropriate marketing strategies and relevant
advertising campaigns (Sklair, 2002: 166). The processes of product innovation, development, and marketing associated with the generation of green
consumerism and cultivation of other ostensibly 'eco-sensitive' consumer
lifestyle choices exemplify some aspects of the fundamental impulse of 'creative destruction' that Joseph Schumpeter identified as a necessary feature of capitalist economic life, providing it with its dynamism, its motion,
by 'incessantly' transforming the economic structure 'from within' (1975:
82–5). Increasing awareness that a range of existing productive technologies and practices and product lines are damaging the environment and
need to be replaced has provided additional new, potentially profitable,
business opportunities in respect of the development of methods of production, new goods and services, and even new consumers. In that sense
green consumerism contributes to the regeneration of consumer capitalism
by offering new opportunities for commercial exploitation, renewed scope
for profit making and capital accumulation, realized through the design
and manufacture of new green(er) products and the establishment of associated new markets through the promotion of green consumer demand
(Gabriel and Lang, 2006; Heartfield, 2008).

The 'green' consumer niche market and the rise of 'green' advertising

The idea of consuming in a manner that is environmentally friendly and
compatible with appropriate conservation of resources for future generations gathered momentum through the 1980s and encouraged consumers
to think about products and services in terms of their ecological impact. As
Gabriel and Lang remark:

consumers were offered a message that it was politically right
to set out to influence production directly: buy this rather than

that product and you can help good producers to out-compete bad producers. 'Good' and 'bad' were defined in environmental but also moralistic terms. If you consume badly, the implications will be felt by more than you the consumer. Other generations, the environment, the climate, might be affected. (2006: 166)

Green consumerism undoubtedly has stimulated a variety of corporate responses to the environmental impact agenda, including the introduction of genuinely new, more environmentally sensitive, production practices and products with recyclable components; self-initiated or voluntary environmental audits to identify potential problems and strategies for targeted correction, which may, or may not, in due course lead to improvements; but also, more calculatingly, employment of a 'greenwash' strategy to publicly promote an environmentally friendly corporate image. The latter strategy has been employed by, among other commercial interests, 'Big Oil', and is illustrated by British Petroleum's attempt to re-brand itself as 'Beyond Petroleum', Conoco's promo depicting dolphins jumping, flamingoes leaping, and whales breaching to the sound of Beethoven's Ninth Symphony while a narrator proclaims, 'In the Gulf of Mexico where the first tankers will operate …', and Shell attempting to cultivate green credentials by showing a 'groovy solar scientist and a gorgeous cultural anthropologist' advising 'indigenous peoples on how to coexist with oil development' (Marquit, 2007).[3]

Advertising campaigns have become increasingly important to corporations seeking to establish their green credentials. Expenditure in the UK on advertising containing 'green' signifying copy, words such as emissions, carbon dioxide, carbon, recycle, or environmental, increased in value from £448,000 in 2003 to £17 million in the period between September 2006 and August 2007, that is in the region of a 40-fold increase, with the biggest contributors being companies not generally thought of as 'green', notably Veolia Environmental Services ('the United Kingdom's leading waste management provider'), Exxon Mobil, the UK Government, BSkyB, and Marks & Spencer (Futerra Sustainability Communications, 2008: 7). Taking stock of the increase in corporate green image promotion one critical observer has expressed concern about the consumer confusion and cynicism created by 'greenwash':

you want to buy green, you expect companies to be green and as a result they just cannot quite resist the temptation to tell you that they are, often, unfortunately, without good reason or justification for doing so… Greenwash is essentially undermining consumer confidence in advertising and as a result only 10 per cent of consumers trust green information from business or government. (Gillespie, 2008: 4–5)

There are good grounds for being cautious about 'green consumerism' as a category, because while it might seem to introduce an environmentally friendly dimension into marketplace transactions and indirectly encourage consideration of sustainability in some shape or form, for example by promoting the consumption, wherever possible, of locally made and/or recycled goods, as well as foods that are in season locally, too rarely is the critical subject raised of how much is being consumed, that it might be healthier to consume less, and that in wealthy consumer societies it is now arguably environmentally necessary to do so. In some respects green consumerism has come to resemble a form of conspicuous consumption, with iconic green commodities such as solar panels and mini-wind turbines, along with celebrity-endorsed hybrid vehicles, displaying 'how conscientious (and how rich)' their owners are (Monbiot, 2007). As eco-product sales have grown awareness of the potential market for goods promoted as green has increased significantly, designers have become more eco-conscious, and being seen to be green has been argued to have become a signifier of social status for 'eco-narcissists' and 'eco-fashionistas', for whom 'green is the new black' (Williams, 2007; Winge, 2008).

The focus on individuals and the emphasis placed on the greening of their particular consumer preferences represents at best an encouraging gesture rather than a particularly significant contribution to the environmental challenges arising from economic growth and the global diffusion of materially acquisitive, consumption-driven lifestyles. Shifts in consumer preferences may have helped 'to drive interest in green products of all kinds', but whatever the products, whether reference is made to hybrid cars, compact fluorescent lightbulbs (CFLs), or organic foods, notwithstanding relatively impressive rates of growth, such 'sales constitute just a small share of the consumption of each product line – US sales of CFLs in 2007 accounted for only 5 percent of lightbulb sales, and organic agriculture is practiced on less than 1 percent of global agricultural land' (Gardner and Prugh, 2008: 16). Green consumerism may even be counter-productive, 'depoliticizing' as George Monbiot (2007) describes it, constituting 'another form of atomization – a substitute for collective action'. It may serve to promote complacency and lead to people who consider they have gone green simply carrying on 'buying and flying as much as ever before', prompting the understandable fear that while 'the whole world religiously buys green products ... its carbon emissions continue to soar' (Monbiot, 2007).

To move in a significant way towards truly sustainable lifestyles patterns of consumption have to change significantly. The warnings issued by environmental scientists are that the worst-case scenario trajectories outlined by the IPCC (Intergovernmental Panel on Climate Change) are already being realized, or exceeded, and that for 'many key parameters, the climate system is already moving beyond the patterns of natural variability within which our society and economy have developed and thrived' (International Scientific Congress, 2009). The response of global energy companies, such as BP, Shell, and Iberdrola Renovables to economic recession in 2009 did not induce optimism about the prospect of appropriate measures being taken to promote sustainable lifestyles as they reduced investment in alternative, renewable, 'green' sources of energy, a development that led one member of the UK's Renewable Advisory Board to state that 'the renewables sector was heading for crisis and ... [that] climate change targets would not be met' (Macalister, 2009: 26; see also Pagnamenta, 2009).

Consuming Differently

There is a substantial and growing body of work calling into question the sustainability of the growth model of economic life, the objective of which is to produce ever-increasing quantities of goods and services destined to be marketed to and purchased by a growing global consumer class with seemingly limitless appetites for all manner of products and services (Princen et al., 2002; Daly, 2008b; Jackson, 2009). As Andre Gorz noted in the mid-1970s, in the course of a series of comments on the impact of logging in the Amazon rainforest on the planet's regenerative capacity, the degeneration of air quality in big cities, growing problems of water supply and water quality, and other manifestations of environmental degradation associated with growth in production and consumption, 'the bond between "more" and "better" is broken ... the underside of the growth of production can be seen in the even greater growth of the damage it causes' (1983[1975]: 64).

People may be consuming more but they are not necessarily living any better, indeed they may be 'living worse'. Gorz certainly believed that was the case and warned that 'our present mode of life is without future', that *our* world is ending; [and] that if we go on as before, the oceans and the rivers will be sterile, the soil infertile, the air unbreathable in the cities' (1983: 12, emphasis in original). For the most part we have proceeded to 'go on as before' and subsequently the concerns raised in Gorz's critical 'ecological realist' narrative have been amplified by scientists warning of the continuing damaging impact of our consumer way of life on the environment, in particular, rising levels of greenhouse gas emissions promoting climate change and leading to increasing acidification of the oceans and growing food insecurity as 'the ecosystem services upon which long-term food and fiber production depend – healthy watersheds, pollination, and soil fertility' – are undermined (Scherr and Sthapit, 2009: 30–1; see also DiGregorio, 2009; Flavin and Engelman, 2009; Lovejoy, 2009).

As well as being ecologically unsustainable the 'benefits' that have accrued from the growth model of economic life have been unfairly distributed and unequally consumed. While global economic output increased 'more than 18-fold between 1900 and 2000 … extreme deprivation … [has remained] the norm for a huge share of humanity' (Gardner and Prugh, 2008: 8). The United Nations reported in 2006 that 'wealth accumulation at the top of the global income distribution has been more impressive than poverty reduction at the bottom' and that, independently of any asset wealth, the 500 richest people in the world 'have an income of more than \$100 billion … [and that] exceeds the combined incomes of the poorest 416 million' (United Nations Development Programme, 2006: 269). Undoubtedly economic growth has delivered higher levels of GDP and promoted increasing levels of consumption, but a high-consuming lifestyle is still only enjoyed by a minority and, in any event, should not be assumed to be an appropriate, or indeed accurate, measure of societal or individual welfare (Gardner et al., 2004). Taking into account the respects in which consumption may be 'detrimental to personal health, to others, or to the environment' it is clear that higher levels of consumption do not necessarily correspond to an overall higher quality of life (Talberth, 2008: 19; see also Jackson, 2009).

Those currently enjoying high consuming lifestyles are dependent for their low-cost products and services, necessary supplies of essential natural resources, and the recycling and disposal of waste required to sustain the consumer juggernaut, upon multitudes of excluded others working in the global economy (Maniates, 2002; Renouard, 2007). The growing global appeal of high consuming lifestyles is a consequence of a range of factors, including the relentless pursuit by commercial corporations of additional markets for their products and services, the widespread use of advertising, marketing, and branding to promote consumer awareness and generate demand, the endorsement activities of iconic globally identifiable celebrity figures from the worlds of entertainment and sport serving to attract interest and induce emulation, as well as the more mundane influence of travel and tourism by members of the consumer class from hyperconsumer societies bearing their cultural cargo, displaying their styles of dress, tastes in food, and standard of living in globally dispersed 'consumer enclaves', those exotic locations especially developed to attract and cater for them, which in turn serve to modify the consumption patterns and aspirations of local communities (Davis and Monk, 2007).

If in 1961 the population of the world, which then stood at just over 3 billion, had wanted to emulate the consumer lifestyle of the average UK citizen 'the Earth could just have supported the demand on its ecosystem'

(Simms et al., 2006: 3). However, by 2006 the global population had more than doubled, reaching 6.2 billion (rising to 6.7 billion by 2008), and consumption levels in the UK had risen very significantly, which meant that the materialistic, energy intensive consumption-driven way of life familiar to the average UK citizen, and those people living in other comparable hyperconsuming societies, could not be shared by the citizens of the world:

> Today, if everyone consumed as much as the average UK citizen, we would need more than three planets like Earth to support them. *To live within our overall environmental means, and give people around the world a chance to meet their needs, means the UK will have to reduce the burden its lifestyles create.* (Simms et al., 2006: 3, emphasis added)

Ecological limits mean not only that the whole world cannot live as Europeans and North Americans have become accustomed to, cannot 'adopt "our" rapacious ways of production and consumption', but that the global consumer class itself has no choice but to change its ways (Gorz, 1983: 66). As Juliet Schor has noted:

> One thing we do know is that consumerism is disastrous for the environment. The last half-century of growth has been the most ecologically destructive in human history, and the United States, with its big malls, fast food, and lots of private (versus public) consumption has developed the most ecologically damaging pattern of consumption in the world. (1995: 28)

To move towards sustainability the global consumer class has to reduce its consumption of the Earth's resources and its greenhouse gas emission levels, while allowing less wealthy and poorer countries to continue to develop and grow in order to improve their standards of living. Giddens argues that there will need to be 'two separate trajectories of "development"' involving significant contraction of emissions in wealthier countries, while poorer states are permitted, by international agreement, to increase emission levels for a time so that they can reach an agreed standard of wealth, following which progressive emission convergence will be necessary (2009: 64–5, 201).

Technological panaceas

There has been speculation about other possible ways of redressing the damaging impact our consumer way of life is currently having, and is projected to continue to have, on the environment, notably future technological innovations delivering solutions, for example, in the form of greater energy efficiency and lower greenhouse gas emission levels, and significant reductions being achieved in global population. Insofar as global population is anticipated to increase to 9.1 billion by 2050 the prospect of any meaningful medium term reductions on that front can probably be discounted (Optimum Population Trust; Porritt, 2009). But more to the point, research indicates that the most significant increases in population are taking place in poor countries, which have longstanding low carbon dioxide emission rates, and that they will continue to contribute little to climate change, in contrast to wealthy 'over-consuming' countries which are most responsible for greenhouse gas emission levels (Satterthwaite, 2009; Simms et al., 2009). The idea of technological innovations providing solutions, for example in the form of significant energy efficiency gains and commercially viable carbon capture and sequestration, is understandably attractive as it raises the possibility that 'limits to growth' may not be necessary and that significant lifestyle changes may not be required (The Climate Group Report, 2009). Analysts advocating a 'breakthrough' technological solution argue that market-led investment and innovation is the way to proceed and that 'an explicitly pro-growth agenda' and promotion of 'new high-tech businesses' will lead to the development of a 'new clean-energy economy' (Nordhaus and Shellenberger, 2007: 12).

While technological innovation should be encouraged it cannot provide a 'quick fix' and does not constitute an alternative to significant (and necessary) changes in lifestyle (Giddens, 2009). The idea that the solution to the environmental problems associated with climate change lies with innovations in technology is problematic, because scientific evidence to date indicates that 'gains in technological efficiency are simply being swamped by the sheer scale of rising aspirations and an increasing population' (Jackson, 2008a: 47). Moreover, given technological innovations at some point in the future do deliver economically viable environmentally friendly and efficient energy sources, there still remains the significant matter of the continuing consumption and depletion of other limited natural resources, such as platinum (vital component in catalytic converters and fuel cells), indium ('consumed in unprecedented quantities for making LCDs for flat screen TVs'), tantalum (used in compact electronic devices such as cell phones), as well as uranium and more common elements like copper, tin, nickel, and phosphorous (used in fertilizers). *New Scientist*'s audit of earth's natural resources, drawing on US geological survey reports and UN global population data, estimated the impact of changing lifestyles and living standards on mineral supply on the basis that consumption by every human on the planet was at half the rate of the average American in 2007:

> The calculations are crude – they don't take into account any increase in demand due to new technologies, and also assume

that current production equals consumption. Yet even based on these assumptions, they point to some alarming conclusions. Without more recycling, antimony, which is used to make flame retardant materials, will run out in 15 years, silver in 10 ... zinc could be used up by 2037, both indium and hafnium – which is increasingly important in computer chips – could be gone by 2017, and terbium – used to make the green phosphors in fluorescent light bulbs – could run out before 2012. (Cohen, 2007)

While acknowledging that, like per capita consumption of iron in the US around 1980, consumption of metals and minerals may not continue to grow in the future, the audit cites research which challenges the universality of the plateau notion by revealing that consumption of copper 'shows no sign of levelling off, and based on 2006 figures for per capita consumption ... by 2100 global demand for copper will outstrip the amount extractable from the ground' (Cohen, 2007).

The message is clear. Technological innovation is important, but behavior needs to change dramatically too. That will mean not only minimizing waste of resources, finding substitutes for materials, reclaiming and recycling, but also that established lifestyles dependent upon the interconnected objectives of ever-rising economic growth, continually increasing production of goods and services, and perpetually escalating levels of consumption have to be radically revised and reconfigured. Technology may ameliorate some of the effects of a consumer-driven way of life, may bring some temporary efficiency gains, but these are frequently neutralized by population growth and changes in behavior as consumers feel at liberty to consume more. For example, following energy efficiency improvements in fridges, it has been noted that consumers are encouraged 'to expect larger ones and it becomes normal to own two. Then along come the promotions for ice-makers and beer-chillers'. Cars provide a further example. Gains in fuel efficiency led to people using their cars more, driving further, and becoming more car dependent with the result that in the 'UK CO_2 emissions from road transport in 2004 were 9 per cent higher than 1990' (Sustainable Consumption Roundtable, 2006: 4).[4]

Technological innovations alone will not be sufficient to redress environmental problems. What is required in addition is a wide-ranging economic and cultural transformation of a way of life, now global in scope, which is '"locked in" to consumption growth by forces outside the control of individuals', a task which has been described as 'colossal' but not impossible (Jackson, 2008a: 57; see also Flavin and Engelman, 2009: 10). However, to achieve the order of transformation required, placing emphasis upon individual consumers and their expressions of choice, as tends to be the case in many versions of green consumerism, will not be sufficient. While citizen-consumers undoubtedly have a part to play, the global scale of the problems involved makes international as well as national initiatives, involving governments and business corporations, essential.

Choice editing

In the Sustainable Consumption Roundtable (SCR) report *I Will If You Will* government, business and people are each identified as having an important part to play in creating 'the opportunities and responsibilities to accelerate change' but it is government that is accorded the primary role, being recognized to be 'best placed to coordinate a collective approach to change' (2006: 1, 6). The measures outlined as examples of what is required to move towards achieving a sustainable form of consumption range from the exceedingly modest, those needing very little intervention in or change of lifestyle, for example introducing wind turbines and energy savings through cutting television standby power usage, to more significant attempts to change behavior by encouraging people to return to seasonal diets, reduce electricity consumption by turning off appliances and lighting whenever they are not strictly necessary, and walking or cycling for short journeys rather than resorting to use of a car, through to what are described as 'innovations and measures that allow people to change behavior or aspirations in more fundamental ways, such as around air transport' (SCR, 2006: 1–2). Recognition that responsibility cannot simply be left with consumers exercising choice means that the range of goods within which choices are made must first be 'edited', restricted, or limited to products that are not environmentally damaging and are truly sustainable. The report states that 'choice editing makes sense' and that consumers benefit from not having to 'grapple with ... complexities themselves' (SCR, 2006: 16).

To move towards a sustainable economy mainstream consumer product markets need to be transformed, or as the report states, 'more socially beneficial' or more sustainable products need to be made prominent in the marketplace, situated in the mainstream of economic life, and this cannot be left up to consumers. While in certain circumstances 'green consumers' may act as catalysts, adoption of more sustainable products within mainstream product markets is argued to depend upon 'choice editing' by government, retail businesses, and manufacturers, especially those producing influential brands. By setting standards and performance criteria and introducing appropriate regulations, government can 'act as choice editor on behalf of citizens who often struggle to understand what issues of concern mean for their shopping routines' (SCR, 2006: 22). Likewise, retailers can determine that the products they sell to consumers are sustainable and 'big-brand manufacturers can shift their product portfolio towards sustainability', thereby 'editing out' unsustainable choices consumers might otherwise be led to make (SCR, 2006: 22).

In respect of 'choice editing' the chief responsibility lies with government and business. Consumer behavior needs to change, but government, and retailers and manufacturers in particular, must take the initiative in creating the conditions in which sustainable products become part of the mainstream. Concerns articulated by retailers and manufacturers about the problems represented by the vagaries of consumer choice are, as the report implies, little more than unconvincing excuses for inaction:

> Too often we hear 'we cannot do this because consumers do not ask for it'. But the consumer did not ask for the iPod. Inspired marketers recognize the signs, or insights, translate these into anticipated future behavior and then launch products, branded, to meet these anticipated needs. Or, technological advances are made and then sold in a way that creates a 'want'. We appeal to business to do more of this, but in more sustainable ways.

> Often, the climate for change can be accelerated by civil society and campaigners. But we have also shown that successful products are rarely sold on either a 'do-good' platform or on a negative platform. Advertising and promotion can play a vital role ... by ensuring that the consumer sees the product as equal to, or better than, the competition. (SCR, 2006: 23)

While responsibility for change in the direction of sustainability involves government, business, and consumers, ultimately it is government that is in the best position to determine what is required to protect 'the social good' and able to introduce the policies required to generate 'an infrastructure of sustainability' (Jackson, 2008a: 58; see also Giddens, 2009: 91–4).

Consumerism and the Political Economy of Sustainability

Consumerism, a dominant feature initially of American social and economic life before becoming global in scope and appeal, has precipitated forms of over-consumption harmful to individuals, communities, and the environment. Individuals have become over-attached to material possessions and in consequence psychologically stultified, vulnerable to incurring debt as they succumb to the temptations of a 'buy now, pay later' cultural economy and, in turn, the appeal of 'rampant egoistic acquisition' has diminished community solidarity and encouraged 'artificial competition to accumulate' (Cohen et al., 2005: 60). This has led to elevation of the interest of the private 'consuming' individual in pursuit of the trappings of material affluence – a seemingly endless range of consumer goods to be desired, purchased, possessed, displayed and, not before too long, replaced – over and above the welfare of the public 'citizen' and provision of the goods and services required to foster the well-being of the community as a whole. An unbridled and uncritical consumerism, a corollary of the neo-liberal globalization of economic life, has led to consumers indulging in assembly of 'a large arsenal of inexpensive products, many ... produced under exploitative conditions', frequently in far removed locations scattered around the world, the full cost of which includes natural resource depletion, environmental degradation, and rising levels of greenhouse gas emission (Cohen et al., 2005: 60; see also Klein, 2001; Sklair, 2002; Jackson, 2009; Labour Behind the Label, n.d.).

If the prospect of achieving a sustainable future is to be enhanced then the wealthier or 'developed' countries need to break away from the assumption that economic growth is synonymous with progress, improvement, and a better life, for '[a]bove a certain level of affluence, growth no longer correlates highly with wider criteria of welfare' (Giddens, 2009: 8; see also Jackson, 2008a: 50). Rather than producing significant increases in subjective well-being, more growth, more production, and more consumption have delivered limited returns and a variety of unwanted personal and environmental costs, including rising global carbon dioxide emission levels. It is this realization which has led analysts to conclude that lifestyles in wealthy consumer societies need to become 'more modest' and less materialistic, and that, in turn, a significant measure of redistribution needs to be introduced to 'resolve social ills stemming from an inequitable distribution of wealth' (Cohen et al., 2005: 60; Giddens, 2009: 64–5).

Sustainability

There are a number of interrelated matters that sustainability scenarios need to consider, including standard(s) of living or level(s) of consumption, global inequalities and associated disparities in lifestyle, as well as the difficult issue of emissions directly attributable to economic activity within one country, but where a significant proportion of the products manufactured are exported and consumed in other countries. The latter constitutes a highly contentious matter because 'levels of emissions produced by the developed countries would be higher than they currently are without ... "transfer of emissions" eastward' (Giddens, 2009: 90). Research estimates that half of the 45% increase in emissions of carbon dioxide in China in the period 2002–2005 was due to export production,

60% of which was consumer goods, including HD televisions and laptops, shipped to Western countries (Guan et al., 2009) and that the UK's emissions would have risen 'by 20% relative to 1990 if imports and international transport were factored into the total' (Watts, 2009: 17).

What in practice would a 'more modest', less materialistic and sustainable level of consumption look like in the wealthier, highly developed countries and how might it be achieved? For what period of time might developing countries be exempted from reducing carbon dioxide emission levels while they pursue rates of economic growth which will allow a degree (how much?) of lifestyle and wealth convergence with more highly developed countries? Recognition of the intrinsic limitations of GDP as a measure of progress, improvement, or welfare represents a necessary starting point from which to begin to explore alternative pleasurable ways of living capable of contributing to the achievement of sustainable and more equitable levels of consumption in both developed and developing countries. GDP is a measure of the market value of all that is produced in a national economy over the period of a year, irrespective of matters of quality, durability, or effect on individual producers, consumers, communities, and the wider environment. Environmentally damaging and harmful goods and services are included alongside those economic products and activities that have more benign or progressive social and environmental effects. Whether they are 'goods' or 'bads' they 'appear to be wealth-generating in GDP measures' and this has led to calls for alternative and broader indices to be deployed to measure social welfare, sustainability, and progress (Giddens, 2009: 65, 66–7; see also Gardner and Assadourian, 2004; Renner, 2004; Gardner and Prugh, 2008; Jackson, 2008a: 2009; Talberth, 2008).

Understandably countries, communities, and individuals with lower material standards of living, with lower levels of consumption, aspire to improve their lot, strive to live better. Frequently that has led to emulation of a consumer way of life that takes its bearings from America, from American global brands, communications media, and associated cultural contents that promote the values of consumerism, the goal of endless material acquisition, a way of living in which 'more' is always assumed to mean 'better'.

Housing provides an appropriate example of the way in which 'consuming more' has become such a prominent feature of the American way of life. In the period from 1950 through to 2002 the average size of new homes in the USA more than doubled, increasing from 1100 to 2340 square feet, while average household size declined from 3.67 to 2.62 members, which meant that 'living area per family member ... increased by a factor of 3' (Wilson and Boehland, 2005: 278). The level of resources, materials, and land consumed in construction increased significantly over this period. Energy use also increased significantly as a consequence of the construction process itself and the subsequent energy-intensive ways people have lived in their homes. Notwithstanding the potential environmental benefits accruing from technological innovations, in the form of more energy efficient materials and higher insulation standards in particular, the significant increase in the size of new homes and increased number of 'higher performance' appliances provided in the 'McMansions', 'Hummer houses', or 'starter castles', as critics have described them, meant that energy use and greenhouse gas emission levels actually increased over the period. The growth in the closing decades of the twentieth century in the size of homes and number of domestic appliances provided as standard, along with the increase in number and size of vehicles purchased, and rapid growth in other forms of consumerism, led to carbon dioxide emission levels in the USA rising to more than double those of most other industrial countries. This led analysts critical of the environmental impact of consumerism to argue that, unappealing as it might at first sight appear, significant lifestyle changes are required and that it will be necessary to 'learn to live without – oversized cars and houses, status-based consumption, easy and cheap world travel, meat with every meal, [and] disposable everything' (Flavin and Engelman, 2009: 10), in short, that 'reduced levels of consumption ... are necessary to avoid massive climate change' (Kasser, 2009: 125).

Consume Less and Live Better

Taking stock from the mid-1970s of processes of economic transformation associated with the deployment of neo-liberal economic policies and 'post-industrial' information technologies, the French critical analyst Andre Gorz drew attention to the ecologically destructive impact of economic growth and rising consumption, the way the world of work was changing, and the scope represented by increases in productivity for formulating a policy of time which would allow people to 'work less, live more' (1983[1975]: 41, 1982: 134: see also Gorz, 1985). Although matters of consumption were not the immediate focus of Gorz's various deliberations on economic life the views he presents on the environmental consequences of increasing material affluence, associated deteriorations in the quality of life, and the scope for moving away from a consumption-driven 'work and spend' model of socioeconomic life to live differently by reducing necessary working time, extending the possibility for 'autonomous, self-determined, optional activity' (1985: 58), and nurturing non-market goals and values, broadly correspond with a number of subsequent critical reactions and responses to consumerism.

For example, those engaged in changing their consumer lifestyles by downshifting and practicing forms of 'voluntary simplicity' to free-up time and increase their autonomy, groups participating in the freecycle network and freeganism who enjoy the use-value of goods but avoid market exchange wherever and whenever possible, and people living in sustainable settlements, in eco-village communities like Findhorn (http://www.ecovillagefindhorn.org/, accessed 18 April 2009), display comparable concern about the consequences of perpetual economic growth, the impact of the capitalist market based production system and its consumerist culture on the environment, and endorse in practice Gorz's belief that to live better it is necessary 'to consume less, to work less, [and] to live differently' (Gorz, 1983: 68–9; Schor, 1998; Doherty and Etzioni, 2003; Jackson, 2009).[5]

Forms of voluntary simplicity, or living simply, emerged in the late 1970s and 1980s as a reaction to the excesses of consumerism and rising consumer debt, and shared longstanding concerns about a way of life predicated on 'ever higher levels of consumption of goods and services' associated with the development of modern industrial capitalist forms of production (Etzioni, 2003: 6). Participants in what is sometimes described as the voluntary simplicity movement frequently express dissatisfaction with conspicuous consumption and 'the quality of life afforded by ... consumer society' and voice concern about increasing environmental degradation (Grigsby, 2004: 1). What this ultimately means in terms of how people actually live varies considerably, leading one analyst to distinguish between three forms of voluntary simplicity. 'Moderate' styles of simple living, where the scale of downshifting may still allow a relatively wealthy and stylish existence to be lived and status to be maintained – 'you can display the objects of poverty in a way that makes it clear you are just rolling in dough' (cited in Etzioni, 2003: 8). 'Strong simplifiers' who elect to live on a much reduced income and forego the status that accompanies the consumer lifestyle they have chosen to leave behind. And 'holistic simplifiers' for whom simplicity constitutes an anti-consumerist life philosophy involving radical changes in the scale and pattern of consumption, especially in more highly developed consumer societies (Etzioni, 2003: 8–13).

Concern about the impact of consumer lifestyles on the environment is shared by the freecycle network which was established in Tucson Arizona in 2003 and is now a worldwide organization with 4755 groups with just under seven million members. The aim of the nonprofit network is to promote reuse of goods by making it possible for people who have things they no longer want to pass them on for free to others in their community who can make good use of them, thereby keeping perfectly adequate, functioning goods out of landfills (http://www.freecycle.org/, accessed 29 May 2009). Freegans are also concerned about the environmental consequences of the consumption-driven economic system and promote a number of strategies 'for sustainable living beyond capitalism'. Their aim is to have only limited participation in the market economy, to practice minimal resource consumption, and to promote a form of community life based on 'generosity, social concern, freedom, coopera-tion, and sharing in opposition to a society based on materialism, moral apathy, competition, conformity, and greed' (http://freegan.info/?page_ id=8, accessed 29 May 2009). The highest profile freegan strategy is sorting through the things thrown into bins and skips by supermarkets, restaurants, retailers, households, offices, and other establishments to recover goods that are frequently 'safe, useable, clean, and in perfect or near-perfect condition', what was designated in the early 1990s as 'dumpster diving' or 'urban foraging' (Hoffman, 1992).

In developing his criticisms of our growth-dependent, production and consumption fixated throwaway lifestyle, Gorz argued that there is more to life than market-dependent forms of consuming, that there are other, more profound pleasures to be enjoyed:

> activities unrelated to any economic goal which are an end in themselves: communication, giving, creating and aesthetic enjoyment, the production and reproduction of life, tender-ness, the realization of physical, sensuous and intellectual capacities, the creation of non-commodity use-values (shared goods or services) that could not be produced as commodities because of their unprofitability. (1982: 80–1)

In support of the popular appeal of alternative pleasures to market-dependent forms of consuming Gorz refers to a Norwegian Government Food and Health Agency poll conducted in the mid-1970s, which revealed that 76% of the respondents considered 'the standard of living of their country was "too high"' and expressed a preference for a calmer, simpler life (1982: 121n2). In a survey conducted in the late 1980s, 75% of working Americans said they would like to see less emphasis placed upon material success to allow people to live more simply (Etzioni, 2003). By the late 1990s it was estimated that around 19% of the population were respond-ing to the stresses and strains of hyperconsumption and an overwork cul-ture by choosing to downshift and live more simply (Schor, 1998). A study in Australia in 2003 revealed 83% of respondents believed their society was 'too materialistic' and 23% of adults aged 30–59 said they had vol-untarily reduced incomes and consumption levels – 'downshifted' – over the previous 10 years (Hamilton and Mail, 2003: 8). A comparable study in the UK in the same year indicated that 25% of those aged 30–59 had 'downshifted over the last ten years' (Hamilton, 2003: 12).

The relentless pursuit of growth in rates of production and levels of consumption has led to a range of unanticipated costs and unwanted consequences. These include, increased hours of work and levels of debt incurred by consumers pursuing the 'consumer dream' (Schor, 1992). The very minimal, at best, impact of ever-growing quantities of goods and services on the sense of well-being, satisfaction, and happiness of consumers, once a relatively low threshold of material possessions has been passed (Layard, 2005; Schwartz, 2005; Jackson, 2009). 'Private' consumer interests in material goods acquisition being accorded priority over 'public' resource provision serving community interests (Dawson, 2005). And the ecological impact of rising energy use and resource depletion, increasing pollution and the accumulation of waste, and most significantly of all the urgent threat posed by accelerating climate change (Conca, 2002; Flavin and Engelman, 2009; Giddens, 2009). A move away from a perpetual growth orientated form of social and economic life, in which progress or improvement is calculated in terms of quantitative increases in GDP, towards a sustainable, steady-state, 'qualitative development' model, utilizing a variety of alternative indicators such as the 'Index of Sustainable Economic Welfare, the Genuine Progress Indicator, the Ecological Footprint, and the Happy Planet Index', a model which can be accommodated within 'the regenerative and assimilative capacities of the ecosystem', is now not only environmentally necessary, but also socially and economically desirable (Daly, 2008a: 47, 2008b: 2–3).

Achievement of a sustainable steady-state form of social and economic life will require far-reaching macro-economic changes, a radical reorganization of production and the world of work, and a dramatic transformation of consumer lifestyles, in wealthier societies in particular (Gorz, 1985, 1999: Daly, 1996; Beck, 2000: Renner, 2004; Jackson, 2008a, 2009). There are two essential requirements for a steady-state form of economic life. One is for 'aggregate matter and energy throughput' in the production and consumption of commodities to remain constant. But while there may be no growth, 'steady' does not have to mean 'static'. Increases in scientific knowledge and technological innovation may promote positive developments, such as qualitative improvements in resource use, and 'stocks of artifacts ... may grow temporarily as a result of technical progress that increases the durability and reparability (longevity) of artifacts' (Daly, 1996: 31–2). The second essential requirement is that the constant matter and energy throughput must be 'ecologically sustainable for a long future for a [global] population living at a standard or per capita resource use that is sufficient for a good life' (Daly, 1996: 32).

The possibility of achieving a globally beneficial and sustainable form of life is bound up with international recognition of the biophysical, ethical and social limits to growth and agreement over associated, necessarily substantial, changes in economic production and consumption.

Our existing form of economic life, 'predicated on continual expansion of debt-driven materialistic consumption is unsustainable ecologically, problematic socially, and unstable economically', and has to change (Jackson, 2009: 103). As well as identifying a range of measures to promote a sustainable macro-economy (e.g. investment in more efficient use of resources, renewable energy, clean technologies, more effective and appealing public transport, and environmentally positive and appropriate business initiatives), Jackson lists a number of other policy initiatives which are necessary to move towards sustainability. These include the need to free people from the social logic of materialistic consumption by implementing reductions in working hours to improve the work–life balance and enhance people's quality of life; tackle 'systemic inequality'; overturn the equation of prosperity with increasing economic output and consumption and introduce socially and ecologically more appropriate indices of well-being; build more resilient and empowered local communities; and perhaps most significantly of all, reverse 'the culture of consumerism' (2009: 105–6).

Specific measures proposed to counter consumerism's hold include more effective regulation of commercial media, a ban on advertising to children, improvements in trading standards and consumer protection, and action on fair trade and the durability and sustainability of products. For example, in place of endless waves of technologically engineered, aesthetically fashioned, and socially cultivated forms of product obsolescence, which have provided the consumer cycle with its dynamic momentum, manufacturers need to work towards the fabrication of ever-more durable consumer goods, with longevity and reparability, in short sustainability, as the primary objective, rather than premature 'retirement' of existing product lines induced by the marketing of continually emerging generations of new commodities (Slade, 2006). The emphasis needs to shift away from 'fast fashion' in respect of consumer goods and 'a culture of rapid purchasing and disposal' which is a necessary corollary (Allwood et al., 2006: 39), towards goods being built to last and reparable, their lifespan extended, towards consumer commodities becoming genuinely '"durable" rather than … ephemeral' (Giddens, 2009: 71).

To date, international action to combat the worst effects of our consumption-driven lifestyles on the environment has been modest in scale and impact. In respect of energy policies and efficiency initiatives in response to the threat of climate change, the best performing countries around the world have made only 'relatively limited' progress (Giddens, 2009: 88; see also Flavin and Engelman, 2009). Much remains to be done if we are to begin to establish a sustainable global economy and promote sustainable consumer lifestyles, as the following two examples of the damaging impact of our way of life on the planet's ecosystem serve to underline (Gardner and Prugh, 2008).

Fish is a popular food and global consumer demand is increasing, but it has been estimated that in the region of 75% of global fish stocks are now 'fully exploited' or 'over-fished' and that not only is there a risk that the most popular species will be extinct within a few decades, but that if current practices continue all fish stocks will become commercially exhausted. In short, current global fishing industry practices and increasing global consumer demand for fish products are simply unsustainable (Clover, 2006; see also http://endoftheline.com/, accessed 6 June 2009). Consumption of fish needs to be tempered, reduced in scale, by knowledge of the seriousness of stock depletion reports which indicate that the number of large fish in the world's oceans has been reduced by 70–90%, 'just gone, because we ate them' (DiGregorio, 2009). Fishing is now a very big business, the industry is technologically very sophisticated, and the largest fishing vessels have enormous capacities, employ ultrasound to detect fish stocks and use trawl nets with the capacity to hold three 747s. To prevent further deterioration in fish stocks governments, industry, and consumers need to respond in a manner that may be experienced as against immediate self-interest. Large marine reserves need to be established, scientific fishing quotas adopted, fishing fleets cut, and only sustainable seafood should be purchased and consumed (DiGregorio, 2009). As Charles Clover cautions:

> we are entering a world of scarcity and the likelihood is that by depleting the fish in the oceans we are taking away food that people in developing nations need to survive, wiping out species that we will need to eat generations into the future, and accelerating global warming by affecting the oceans' ability to absorb carbon dioxide. (Interview response, DiGregorio, 2009)

The second and related example involves the impact of the rising global demand for beef cattle on the Amazon rainforest and the world's climate. The Brazilian government has invested heavily to promote the country's dominance of the global market for agricultural commodities in anticipation that by 2018 the country will be supplying around two-thirds of beef traded on international markets. Following a three year investigation, a report in 2009 of the global trade in cattle products revealed how growing demand for meat, hides for leather shoes and trainers, fat rendered and used to make soap, face creams and toothpaste, and gelatin used in yoghurt and sweets was contributing to illegal deforestation of the Amazon Rainforest to provide pasture land for cattle ranches. The cattle sector was identified by Greenpeace (2009) as the key driver responsible for 80% of all deforestation in the Brazilian Amazon and for 14% of annual deforestation worldwide. Self-interest motivated the Brazilian government to extend a US$41 billion credit line to finance expansion of agricultural and livestock production and form alliances with a few major Brazilian corporations in the sector, allowing the latter, in turn, to seize an opportunity to increase their share of the global market. Self-interest led the major Brazilian processing corporations to allow 'hundreds of ranches within the Amazon rainforest … [to supply] cattle to [their] slaughterhouses in the Amazon region' (Greenpeace, 2009). And short-term self-interest led to a number of reputable global brands and retailers, including 'Adidas, BMW, Carrefour, Eurostar, Ford, Honda, Gucci, IKEA, Kraft, Nike, Tesco, Toyota, [and] Wal-Mart', to engage in forms of global sourcing of raw materials and products which, in effect, constituted 'blind consumption', exposing them to the possibility of unwittingly purchasing goods from an 'Amazon-contaminated supply chain … [which] fuels deforestation and climate change' (Greenpeace, 2009).[6]

Dealing with the environmental consequences of our unsustainable consumption-driven way of life is made difficult by the fact that a number of the problematic consequences identified seem so abstract and remote, because they are geographically or temporally distant. As Giddens notes:

> No matter how much we are told about the threats, it is hard to face up to them, because they feel somehow unreal – and, in the meantime, there is a life to be lived, with all its pleasures and pressures. (2009: 2)

Compared to other currently troubling matters, and those anticipated to arise in the short term, the threat of climate change does not appear urgent. For governments there are routine, ongoing, and immediate pressures concerning the national economy, economic growth, employment, and material standards of living of citizens, as well as an extensive range of other matters that constantly demand attention; for commercial corporations it is profits, market share and position, stock values, brand image and the need to continually generate new products and services and cultivate consumer demand. In turn, for most members of the global consumer class while there may be awareness that global warming represents a growing problem, the threat does not, as yet, seem imminent, it lies beyond the horizon in what appears to be a relatively distant future. Any immediate environmental costs arising from global consumerism are being borne, for the most part, by distant others, those the globalization of economic life has placed out of sight and mind, those living in poorer countries working long hours for low pay to produce consumer goods for export markets in wealthy countries, predominantly in North America and Europe, and those trying to make a living by sorting through the various types of scrap, hazardous materials, and e-waste, the detritus of the consumer cycle that is harmful to human health and the environment and yet is increasingly being exported from consumer societies to Asia, 'the dustbin of the world's waste', and parts of West Africa (Vidal, 2004a:b; Greenpeace, n.d.). It is those individuals who have largely been excluded from the benefits of increasing consumption who are bearing the immediate social, economic, and environmental costs of rising global consumerism as the communities and landscapes in which they live are damaged by unsustainable production practices, excessive use of limited or relatively scarce resources leading to depletion, and contamination of air, water, and land from insufficiently regulated manufacturing processes and recycling of hazardous waste materials (Klein, 2001; Sklair, 2002; Tonkiss, 2006).

Concluding Remarks: Alternatives to a Social Logic of Consumerism

Alternative, more sustainable forms of consuming, including downsizing and downshifting to allow people more free time and autonomy (Gorz, 1982, 1983; Schor, 1998, 2004; Holt, 2005), as well as other forms of 'voluntary simplicity' and ethical forms of consumption designed to counter the emphasis placed on materialistic values within the prevailing 'social logic of consumerism' are growing in prominence (Jackson, 2009). There are increasingly encouraging signs that overworked, overspent, and over-indebted individuals experiencing 'disenchantment with the supposed blessings of consumerism' are beginning to explore other 'post-consumerist' versions of the good life (Soper and Thomas, 2006: 4). There are a growing number of communities attempting to live in a more sustainable manner (the Global Ecovillage Network, http://gen.ecovillage. org/, accessed 4 June 2009) and there is a global Transition Movement composed of towns, villages and communities in more than 30 countries around the world, which share the belief that an effective response to global warming requires a dramatic transformation of our way of life, one which will need to include locally developed community solutions to sustainability issues (http://transitiontowns.org/TransitionNetwork/Transition Network, accessed 4 June 2009; Bunting, 2009).

The alternatives to our resource and energy-intensive, materially acquisitive, consumption-driven way of life that are emerging constitute positive responses to the realization that our level of economic activity has already placed 'unsustainable burdens on the planet's ecosystems' (Jackson, 2009: 106) and that as a consequence 'compromises ... have to be made and ... difficult decisions ... have to be negotiated' (Giddens, 2009: 71). It is vital that there is recognition of the potential benefits to be derived from consuming differently, in particular an appreciation that curbing hyperconsumerism promotes the prospect of a significant improvement in the quality of the great majority of people's lives, and that incentives are offered to encourage movement towards more sustainable ways of living. As analysts have noted, no approach to the problematic ecological impact of our consumption-driven way of life 'based mainly upon deprivation is going to work' (Giddens, 2009: 11). To successfully overturn the social logic of consumerism is going to require more than promotion of 'altruistic compassion and environmental concern', as Soper and Thomas (2006: 4) have argued. Appeal to self-interest and the pleasure(s) to be derived from consuming differently, needs to be a prominent part of the argument against the excesses and damaging consequences of consumerism, but so also does a reaffirmation of the necessity of living within ecological limits, even if this should conflict with particular manifestations of self-interest. Expressions of self-interest preoccupied with immediate returns, with the prospect of short-term profit or enjoyment of familiar pleasures, have led to ways of living which have significantly increased the burdens on the planet's ecosystem. It is in the interest of all consumers, communities, and nations around the world to promote sustainable ways of living, to address the 'material profligacy of consumer society' (Jackson, 2009: 106), and begin to live within ecological limits.

Notes

1. The book *The New Green Consumer Guide* (Hailes, 2007) provides examples of the increasing range of advice available to potential green consumers. The American website GoodGuide.com (http://www.goodguide.com/, accessed 6 June 2009) draws on hundreds of databases and offers ratings for 'natural, green and healthy products' in respect of social, health and environmental impacts, with assessments covering the complete life cycle of products and all the various stages of industrial production. The site offers 'radical transparency' by revealing the multiple impacts of products, including treatment of workers, potentially problematic chemicals and toxins, and carbon footprints. ClimateCounts.org (http://climatecounts.org/scorecard_overview.php, accessed 12 June 2009) compares companies with their competitors in terms of their commitment to tackle climate change. Environmental Working Group (http://www.ewg.org/about, accessed 15 June 2009) founded in 1993 provides a number of resources for consumers and aims to reveal health problems, toxic contaminants, environmental damage, and natural resource implications associated with products and policies.

2. The Body Shop's identification of a new range of environmentally friendly men's grooming products as a further growth area is the latest in a long line of cosmetics and toiletries industry attempts to profitably exploit the 'gap in the marketing of men's relationship to their bodies' (Haugh, 1986: 78).

3. The 10th edition of the *Concise Oxford English Dictionary* defines 'greenwash' as:

> Disinformation disseminated by an organisation, etc., so as to present an environmentally responsible public image; a public image of environmental responsibility promulgated by or for an organisation, etc., but perceived as being unfounded or intentionally misleading.

The Greenwash Guide describes 'greenwash' as an explicit or implied 'environmental claim which is unsubstantiated (a fib) or irrelevant (a distraction). Found in advertising, PR or on packaging, and made about people, organizations, and products' (Futura Sustainability Communications, 2008: 3). See also the TerraChoice Environmental Marketing *Greenwashing Report* 2009, 'The "seven sins of greenwashing": environmental claims in consumer markets', (http://sinsofgreenwashing.org/findings/greenwashing-report-2009/, accessed 13 June 2009).

At a ceremony in Copenhagen on the 23rd May 2009, the eve of the World Business Summit on Climate Change, the Climate Greenwash Award went to Swedish energy company Vattenfall for 'its mastery of spin on climate change, portraying itself as a climate champion while lobbying to continue business as usual, using coal, nuclear power, and pseudo-solutions such as agrofuels and carbon capture and storage (CCS)'. The five other companies nominated for the award were, in rank order, Shell, Dong, ArcelorMittal, BP, and Repsol (http://www.climategreenwash.org/, accessed 29 May 2009).

4. Research indicates that a significant proportion of carbon emission savings arising from technological improvements in energy efficiency are cancelled out by what has been termed the 'rebound effect'. For example, industry savings on energy costs on building insulation and/or fuel economy in relation to private transport, when passed on to consumers in the form of lower prices leaves them with increased spending power and demand, which in turn leads to increases in production and consumption. It is estimated that 'total rebound effect is about 50% by 2030' and that energy efficiency policies will need to find ways of 'locking-in' energy savings and emission reductions 'otherwise they may be partly offset by more energy use' (Barker and Dagoumas, 2009; see also Schor, 2005; Sorrell, 2009) .

5. Scope undoubtedly exists for moving in the direction Gorz proposed, notably implementing a policy of time which would increase individual autonomy and enhance the quality of people's lives. Over the course of the twentieth century worker productivity increased substantially, indeed it more than doubled in America in the 50-year period following the end of World War II (Schor, 1992; Siegel, 2008). However, as impressive as the increases in productivity were they did not lead to more free time or greater autonomy, rather they fuelled rapidly rising levels of consumption and working hours actually increased (Schor, 1992: 2). The development from the early 1970s of neo-liberal capitalism further raised productivity and promoted 'flexibilization of working time', but the policies implemented served not to provide workers with the *option* of working less, rather the new working practices imposed 'new insecurities and inequalities' (Beck, 2000: 78, 80). And in America the income of the majority of workers 'stagnated or declined' and credit and debt financed consumption accelerated, 'increasing sixfold in twenty-five years' (Beck, 2000: 114, 74).

6. In August 2009 in response to a Greenpeace (2009) investigation and report on trade in beef and leather from farms in Brazil involved in illegal deforestation of the Amazon rainforest a number of global footwear brands including Adidas, Nike, Clarks, and Timberland announced a moratorium on leather from 'newly deforested areas … [and] demanded that suppliers bring in a stringent traceability system within a year, which will "credibly" guarantee the source of all leather'. The report also put pressure on major supermarket stores to check their beef supply chains to ensure produce was not coming from deforesting ranches in the Amazon region (Carrington and Phillips, 2009).

REFERENCES

Adbusters (n.d.) (2009) http://www.adbusters.org. Accessed 8 June 2009.

Adorno, T.W. (1991) *The Culture Industry: Selected Essays on Mass Culture*. London: Routledge.

Adorno, T.W. and Horkheimer, M. (1997[1944]) *Dialectic of Enlightenment*. London: Verso.

Adve, N. (2004) 'Rising struggles, falling water', *India Resource Center*. Available at: http://www.indiaresource.org/campaigns/coke/2004/risingstruggles.html. Accessed 23 September 2008.

Advertising Age (2008a) 'World's top 50 agency companies', *DataCenter*. Available at: http://adage.com/datacenter/datapopup.php?article_id=126706. Accessed 17 March 2009.

Advertising Age (2008b) *Global Marketers: Part 1 Global ad Spending by Marketer*, 22nd Annual Report. pp. 1–15. Available at: http://adage.com/images/random/datacenter/2008/globalmarketing2008.pdf. Accessed 17 March 2009.

Advertising Association (2007) 'Statistics'. Available at: http://www.adassoc.org.uk/html/statistics.html. Accessed 30 August 2007.

Advertising Association (2008) *The Advertising Statistics Yearbook* 2008. Available at: http://www.adassoc.org.uk/Ad_stats_yearbook_2008_-_8june08.pdf. Accessed 17 March 09.

Alcohol Concern (2004) *Advertising Alcohol: Fact Sheet Summary*. Available at: http://www.alcoholconcern.org.uk/files/20040506_085240_Advertising%20factsheet%20April%202004.pdf. Accessed 11 August 2008.

Allsop, M., Walters, A., Santillo, D. and Johnston, P. (2006) *Plastic Debris in the World's Oceans*, Greenpeace. Available at: http://www.unep.org/regionalseas/marinelitter/publications/docs/plastic_ocean_report.pdf. Accessed 2 May 2009.

Allwood, J.M., Laursen, S.E., de Rodriguez, C.M. and Bocken, N.M.P. (2006) *Well Dressed? The Present and Future Sustainability of Clothing and Textiles in the United Kingdom*. Cambridge: University of Cambridge Institute for Manufacturing. American Legacy Foundation. Available at: http://www.americanlegacy.org/whoweare.aspx. Accessed 10 August 2008.

Amis, J. and Cornwall, T.B. (eds) 2005 *Global Sport Sponsorship*. London: Berg.

Anderson, P. (2007) 'Jottings on the conjuncture', *New Left Review*, 48 (November–December). Available at: http://www.newleftreview.org/?view=2695. Accessed 23 April 2008.

Andoh, E. (1993) 'The Japanification of American fast food', *Mangajin*, 25 (April). Available at: http://www.mangajin.com/mangajin/samplemj/japnfctn/japnfctn.htm. Accessed 15 September 2008.

Anonymous (1999) 'Tobacco use: United States, 1900–1999', *Oncology*, 13 (12). Available at: http://www.cancernetwork.com/display/article/10165/81348. Accessed 9 August 08.

Aris, S. (1990) *Sportsbiz: Inside the Sports Business*. London: Hutchinson.

Armstrong, F. (2009) *The Age of Stupid*. Available at http://www.ageofstupid.net/the_film. Accessed 22 March 2009.

Arvidsson, A. (2006) 'Brand management and the productivity of consumption', in J. Brewer and F. Trentmann (eds), *Consuming Cultures, Global Perspectives: Historical Trajectories, Transnational Exchanges*. Oxford: Berg. pp. 71–94.

Bahro, R. (1984) *From Red to Green*. London: Verso.

Baker, A. (ed.) (2000) *Serious Shopping: Essays in Psychotherapy and Consumerism*. London: Free Association Books.

Baker, G. (2008) 'It's worse than we feared and there's more pain to come, but it will pass', *The Times*, 16 July: 6–7.

Baker, M. (2007) 'The problem with school "choice"', *BBC News*, March. Available at: http://news.bbc.co.uk/1/hi/education/6413811.stm. Accessed 1 August 2008.

Baran, P.A. and Sweezy, P.M. (1970[1966]) *Monopoly Capital: An Essay on the American Economic and Social Order*. Harmondsworth: Penguin.

Barber, B. (2007) *Consumed: How Markets Corrupt Children, Infantalize Adults, and Swallow Citizens Whole*. London: W.W. Norton.

Barker, T. and Dagoumas, A. (2009) 'The global macroeconomic rebound effect of energy efficiency policies: An analysis 2012–2030 using E3MG', UK Energy Research Centre, 4CMR, University of Cambridge, 14 May. Available at: http://www.landecon.cam.ac.uk/research/eeprg/4cmr/news/pdf/Rebound_Barker%20&%20Dagoumas_Rebound_14052009V3.pdf. Accessed 1 June 2009.

Barlow, M. and Clarke, T. (2002) *Blue Gold: The Fight to Stop the Corporate Theft of the World's Water*. London: Earthscan.

Baudrillard, J. (1998[1970]) *The Consumer Society: Myths and Structures*. London: Sage.

Bauer, N., Bower, A., Brunner, S., Edenhofer, O., Flaschland, C., Jakob, M. and Stern, N. (2009) *Towards a Global Green Recovery: Recommendations for Immediate G20 Action*. Report submitted to the G20 London Summit. Available at: http://www.pik-potsdam.de/global-greenrecovery. Accessed 2 April 2009.

Bauman, Z. (1992) *Intimations of Postmodernity*. London: Routledge.

Bauman, Z. (1998) *Work, Consumerism and the New Poor*. Buckingham: Open University Press.

Bauman, Z. (2000) *Liquid Modernity*. Cambridge: Polity Press.

Bauman, Z. (2004a) *Wasted Lives: Modernity and Its Outcasts*. Cambridge: Polity Press.

Bauman, Z. (2004b) 'The consumerist syndrome in contemporary society: An interview', with C. Rojek, *Journal of Consumer Culture*, 4 (3): 291–12.

Bauman, Z. (2007a) *Liquid Times: Living in An Age of Uncertainty*. Cambridge: Polity Press.

Bauman, Z. (2007b) *Consuming Life*. Cambridge: Polity Press.

BBC (2004) 'Store wars: fast fashion', 9 June. Available at: http://news.bbc.co.uk/1/hi/business/3086669.stm. Accessed 8 August 2009.

BBC (2006) 'Code for hospitals' patient ads', 20 November. Available at: http://news.bbc.co.uk/1/hi/health/6164214.stm. Accessed 4 August 2008.

BBC (2009a) 'US car scrappage scheme unveiled', 24 July. Available at: http://news.bbc.co.uk/1/hi/business/8167828.stm. Accessed 5 August 2009.

BBC (2009b) 'Go-ahead for new Heathrow runway', 15 January. Available at: http://news.bbc.co.uk/2/hi/uk_news/politics/7829676.stm. Accessed 28 February 2009.

BBC (2009c) 'Fast fashion from UK to Uganda', 20 February. Available at: http://news.bbc.co.uk/1/hi/uk/7899227.stm. Accessed 8 August 2009.

BBC Asia-Pacific News (2008) 'Record car ownership in Beijing'. Available at: http://news.bbc.co.uk/2/low/asia-pacific/7186635.stm. Accessed 24 April 2008.

BBC News Online (2004) Available at: http://news.bbc.co.uk/2/hi/business/4097471.stm. Accessed 30 August 2007.

Beck, U. (1992) *Risk Society: Towards a New Modernity*. London: Sage.

Beck, U. (2000) *The Brave New World of Work*. Cambridge: Polity Press.

Beck, U. (2005) *Power in the Global Age*. Cambridge: Polity Press.

Beck, U., Sznaider, N. and Winter, R. (eds) (2003) *Global America? The Cultural Consequences of Globalization*. Liverpool: Liverpool University Press.

Bell, B. (2006) 'Cola wars in Mexico', *In These Times,* October 6. Available at: http://www.inthesetimes.com/article/2840. Accessed 18 September 2008.

Bell, D. (1976) *The Cultural Contradictions of Capitalism*. New York: Basic Books.

Benady, A. (2008) 'End of consumerism', *Off-grid*. Available at: http://www.off-grid.net/2008/07/30/end-of-consumerism. Accessed 6 March 2009.

Bellah, R.N., Madsen, R., Sullivan, W.M., Swidler, A. and Tipron, S.M. (1996) *Habits of the Heart: Individualism and Commitment in American Life*. London: University of California Press.

Bernstein, J., McNichol, E. and Lyons, K. (2006) *Pulling Apart: A State-by-State Analysis of Income Trends*. Center on Budget and Policy Priorities and Economic Policy Institute. Washington DC. Available at: http://www.cbpp.org/1-26-06sfp.pdf. Accessed 14 November 2008.

Bevir, M. and Trentmann, F. (2008) 'Civic choices: Retrieving perspectives on rationality, consumption, and citizenship', in K. Soper and F. Trentmann (eds), *Citizenship and Consumption*. Basingstoke: Palgrave. pp. 19–33.

Bordwell, M. (2002) 'Jamming culture: Adbusters' hip media campaign against consumerism', in T. Princen, M. Maniates and K. Conca (eds), *Confronting Consumption*. London: MIT Press. pp. 237–53.

Bourdieu, P. (1998) *Acts of Resistance: Against the New Myths of Our Time*. Cambridge: Polity Press.

Bourdieu, P. (2003) *Firing Back: Against the Tyranny of the Market* 2. London: Verso.

Braudel, F. (1981) *The Structures of Everyday Life: Civilization and Capitalism, 15th–18th Centuries*, Vol 1. London: William Collins & Sons.

Braudel, F. (1974) *Capitalism and Material Life, 1400–1800*. New York: Harper & Row.

Breen, T.H. (2004) *The Marketplace of Revolution: How Consumer Politics Shaped American Independence*. New York: Oxford University Press.

Brewer, J. and Porter, R. (eds) (1993) *Consumption and the World of Goods*. New York: Routledge.

Brewer, J. and Trentmann, F. (2006) 'Introduction: Space, time and value in consuming cultures', in J. Brewer and F. Trentmann (eds), *Consuming Cultures, Global Perspectives: Historical Trajectories, Transnational Exchanges*. Oxford: Berg. pp. 1–17.

Bronner, S.J. (1989) 'Reading consumer culture', in S.J. Bronner (ed.), *Consuming Visions: Accumulation and Display of Goods in America 1880–1920*. London: W.W. Norton, pp. 13–53.

Brown, G. (2009) Speech to US Congress, Washington, 4 March. Available at: http://www.telegraph.co.uk/news/newstopics/politics/gordon-brown/4938252/Gordon-Browns-speech-to-Congress-the-full-text.html. Accessed 5 March 2009.

Brown, L.R. (2006) *Plan B 2.0: Rescuing a Planet under Stress and a Civilization in Trouble*. New York: W.W. Norton.

Bruner, L.M. (2002) 'Taming "wild" capitalism', *Discourse and Society*, 13 (2): 167–84.

Bruns, A. (2007) 'Produsage: Towards a broader framework for user-led content creation'. Paper presented at Creativity & Cognition Conference, Washington, DC, 14 June. Available at: http://produsage.org/presentations. Accessed 28 April 2009.

Bryman, A. (2004) *The Disneyization of Society*. London: Sage.

Bunting, M. (2004) *Willing Slaves: How the Overwork Culture is Ruling Our Lives*. London: HarperCollins.

Bunting, M. (2009) 'Beyond Westminster's bankrupted practices, a new idealism is emerging', 31 May. Available at: http://www.guardian.co.uk/commentisfree/2009/may/31/reform-transition-a-new-politics. Accessed 4 June 2009.

Burns, E. (2007) *The Smoke of the Gods: A Social History of Tobacco*. Philadelphia: Temple University Press.

Bush, G.W. (2001) 'Address to a joint session of congress and the American people', 20 September. Available at: http://www.whitehouse.gov/news/releases/2001/09/20010920-8.html. Accessed 7 November 2008.

Bush, G.W. (2006) Press conference, 20 December. Available at: http://www.whitehouse.gov/news/releases/2006/12/20061220-1.html. Accessed 7 November 2008.

Bush, G.W. (2008) Press conference, 15 July. Available at: http://www.whitehouse.gov/news/releases/2008/07/20080715-1.html. Accessed 16 July 2008.

Calder, L. (1999) *Financing the American Dream: A Cultural History of Consumer Credit*. Princeton, NJ: Princeton University Press.

Calvano, E. (2007) 'Destructive creation', SSE/EFI Working Paper Series in Economics and Finance No. 653, April. *Scandinavian Working Papers in Economics*. Available at: http://swopec.hhs.se/hastef/abs/hastef0653.htm. Accessed 10 August 2007.

Campbell, C. (1989) *The Romantic Ethic and the Spirit of Modern Consumerism*. Oxford: Blackwell.

Carrington, D. and Phillips, T. (2009) 'Shoe brands get tough on leather suppliers to save Amazon rainforest', *Guardian*, 4 August: 3.

Castells, M. (1996) *The Rise of the Network Society, Vol. 1, The Information Age: Economy, Society and Culture*. Oxford: Blackwell.

Castells, M. (1998) *End of Millennium, Vol. III. The Information Age: Economy, Society and Culture*. Oxford: Blackwell.

CBC News (2009) 'I want to grow trade not contract it: Obama', 19 February. Available at: http://www.cbc.ca/money/story/2009/02/19/obama-economy.html. Accessed 27 March 2009.

Chapelle, F.H. (2005) *Wellsprings: A Natural History of Bottled Spring Waters*. New Jersey: Rutgers University Press.

Chen, S. and Wolf, C. (2001) *China, the United States and the Global Economy*. Santa Monica, CA: Rand.

Chernenko, M., Khan, B.N., Almeida, C. and Merchant, J. (2009) *Marketing Plan 2009 for The Body Shop in the UK*. Available at: http://d.scribd.com/docs/eue8fowr6i158pctvdk.pdf. Accessed 6 March 2009.

China Daily (2008) 'McDonald's growing in China'. Available at: http://www.chinadaily.com.cn/bizchina/2008-09/08/content_7007412.htm. Accessed 15 September 2008.

China Daily (2004) 'China spends 32% more on ads'. Available at: http://bizchina.chinadaily.com.cn/openews.shtml?id=339. Accessed 1 September 2008.

Chomsky, N. (1999) *Profit over People: Neoliberalism and Global Order*. London: Seven Stories Press.

Chu, S. (2009) 'The man who could change the world', *The Climate Challenge Nobel Laureate Symposium, The Times*, 26 May: 8.

Churchill Insurance (2006) 'British women waste £7.3 billion on unworn clothes'. Available at: http://www.churchill.com/pressReleases/06012006.htm. Accessed 12 December 2008.

Clapp, J. (2002) 'The distancing of waste: Overconsumption in a global economy', in T. Princen, M. Maniates and K. Conca (eds), *Confronting Consumption*. London: MIT Press, pp. 155–76.

Clark, A. (2009) 'American debut: Topshop bites into the big apple', *Guardian*, 3 April: 25.

Clarke, J. (2006) 'Consumers, clients, or citizens? Politics, policy and practice in the reform of social care', *European Societies*, 8 (3): 423–42.

Clover, C. (2006) *The End of the Line: How Overfishing is Changing the World and What We Eat*. London: The New Press.

Clugston, C. (2008) 'Our American way of life is unsustainable – evidence', *Energy Bulletin*, 18 August. Available at: http://www.energybulletin.net/node/46276. Accessed 14 September 2008.

Coalition Against Coke Contracts (2006) 'Kerala throws out Coca-Cola and Pepsi', 9 August. Available at: http://caccuc.blogspot.com/2006/08/kerala-throws-out-coca-cola-and-pepsi. html. Accessed 23 September 2008.

Coca-Cola (2005) *News Release: Coca-Cola renews worldwide football association through Elite FIFA Partner Agreement.* Available at: http://www.thecoca-colacompany.com/presscenter/ nr_20051122_corporate_fifa_agreement.html. Accessed 1 October 2008.

Coca-Cola Per Capita Consumption (n.d.) Available at: http://www.thecoca-colacompany. com/ourcompany/ar/percapitaconsumption_north_america.html. Accessed 19 September 2008.

Coca-Cola Heritage (n.d.) 'The Chronicle of Coca-Cola: A global business'. Available at: http://www.thecoca-colacompany.com/heritage/chronicle_global_business.html. Accessed 9 September 2008.

Cockburn, A. (2005) 'Message in a bottle: How Coca-Cola gave back to Plachimada', *Counterpunch*, 16–17 April. Available at: http://www.counterpunch.org/cockburn04162005. html. Accessed 22 September 2008.

Cohen, D. (2007) 'Earth's natural wealth: An audit', *New Scientist*, 194 (2605). Available at: http://www.newscientist.com/article/mg19426051.200-earths-natural-wealth-an-audit. html?full=true. Accessed 25 May 2009.

Cohen, J. (1987) 'Effects of cigarette advertising on consumer behavior'. Available at: http:// tobaccodocuments.org/landman/2500082202-2253.html#images. Accessed 11 August 2008.

Cohen, M., Comrov, A. and Hoffner, B. (2005) 'The new politics of consumption: Promoting sustainability in the American marketplace', *Sustainability: Science, Practice and Policy*, 1 (1): 58–76. Available at: http://ejournal.nbii.org/archives/vol1iss1/0410-011. cohen.pdf. Accessed 1 March 2009.

Conca, K. (2002) 'Consumption and environment in a global economy', in T. Princen, M. Maniates and K. Conca (eds), *Confronting Consumption*. London: MIT Press, pp. 133–53.

Congressional Budget Office (2007) *Trends in Earnings Variability Over the Past 20 Years*, The Congress of the United States. Available at: http://www.cbo.gov/ftpdocs/80xx/ doc8007/04-17-EarningsVariability.pdf. Accessed 14 November 2008.

Corrigan, P. (1997) *The Sociology of Consumption*. London: Sage.

Credit Action (2006) 'Credit card holders affordability study'. Available at: http://www.credit action.org.uk/credit-card-holders-affordability-study.html. Accessed 2 December 2008.

Credit Action (2008) 'Debt statistics, November'. Available at: http://www.creditaction. org.uk/debt-statistics.html. Accessed 2 December 2008.

Crossik, G. and Jaumin, S. (eds) (1999) *Cathedrals of Consumption: The European Department Store 1850–1939*. Aldershot: Ashgate.

Curtis, P. and Lipsett, A. (2008) 'Fewer parents getting secondary school of their choice for children', *Guardian*, Tuesday 4 March. Available at: http://www.guardian.co.uk/ education/2008/mar/04/schools.publicschools. Accessed 13 January 2009.

Daly, H. (1996) *Beyond Growth: The Economics of Sustainable Development*. Boston, MA: Beacon Press.

Daly, H. (2008a) 'On a road to disaster', *New Scientist* Special Issue, *The Folly of Growth*, 200 (2678): 46–7.

Daly, H. (2008b) 'A steady-state economy', Sustainable Development Commission, 24 April: 1–10. Available at: http://www.sd-commission.org.uk/publications/downloads/Herman_ Daly_thinkpiece.pdf. Accessed 6 April 2009.

Davis, M. and Monk, D.B. (2007) 'Introduction', in M. Davis and D.B. Monk (eds), *Evil Paradises: Dreamworlds of Neoliberalism*. London: The New Press. pp. ix–xvi.

Dawson, M. (2005) *The Consumer Trap: Big Business Marketing in American Life*. Chicago, IL: University of Illinois Press.

DeAngelis, T. (2004) 'Consumerism and its discontents', *Monitor on Psychology*, 35 (6). Available at: http://www.apa.org/monitor/jun04/discontents.html.

DeCarlo, S. (2007) 'Executive pay: Big paychecks', *Forbes*. Available at: http://www. forbes.com/2007/05/03/ceo-executive-compensation-lead-07ceo-cx_sd_0503ceo compensationintro.html. Accessed 13 November 2008.

DEFRA (2007) *Waste Strategy for England 2007*, UK Department for Environment, Food and Rural Affairs, Cm 7086. Available at: http://www.defra.gov.uk/ENVIRONMENT/ waste/strategy/strategy07/pdf/waste07-strategy.pdf. Accessed 15 May 2009.

de Geus, M. (2009) 'Sustainable hedonism: The pleasures of living within environmental limits', in K. Soper, M. Ryle and L. Thomas (eds), *The Politics and Pleasures of Consuming Differently*. London: Palgrave Macmillan. pp. 113–29.

Demos (2006) 'America's growing economic divide: By the numbers', *Inequality.org*. Available at: http://www.demos.org/inequality/ByNumbersMay31.pdf. Accessed 20 February 2009.

Devlin, E., Eadie, D. and Angus, K. (2003) *Tobacco Marketing and Young People*. The Centre for Tobacco Control Research, The University of Strathclyde. Available at: http://www. tobaccopapers.com/casestudies/Yth-Smoking.pdf. Accessed 12 August 2008.

DiCaprio, L. (2008) *The 11th Hour*. Available at: http://wip.warnerbros.com/11thhour/ mainsite/site.html. Accessed 10 June 2008.

DiGregorio, S. (2009) 'No fish by 2048? The end of the line – interview with journalist Charles Clover', 1 May. *The Village Voice – Fork in the Road*. Available at: http://blogs.village-voice.com/forkintheroad/archives/2009/05/_photo_courtesy.php. Accessed 6 June 2009.

Doherty, D. and Etzioni, A. (2003) *Voluntary Simplicity: Responding to Consumer Culture*. Lanham, MD: Rowman & Littlefield.

Douglas, M. and Isherwood, B. (1979) *The World of Goods: Towards an Anthropology of Consumption*. New York: Basic Books.

Drobnick, J. (ed.) (2006) *The Smell Culture Reader*. London: Berg.

Durkin, T.A. (2000) 'Credit cards: Use and consumer attitudes 1970–2000', *Federal Reserve Bulletin*, September: 623–34. Available at: http://www.federalreserve.gov/pubs/ bulletin/2000/0900lead.pdf. Accessed 28 February 2008.

Durning, A. (1992) *How Much Is Enough? The Consumer Society and The Future of the Earth*. Worldwatch Institute. New York: W.W. Norton & Company Inc.

Edwards, A. (2007) 'Bottled water: Pouring resources down the drain?', *Environmental Ethics*, 1: 7–13. Available at: http://www.environmentalethics-sihe.co.uk/pdfs/ALYSARTICLE_ Edit.pdf. Accessed 23 September 2008.

Ehrenreich, B. (2008) 'The fall of the American consumer', *The Nation*, 11 March. Available at: http://www.thenation.com/doc/20080324/ehrenreich. Accessed 18 September 2008.

Elliott, L. (2009) 'It's not the bankers Labour is watching, it's you', *Guardian*, 11 May: 28.

Energy Information Administration (2009) 'US energy-related carbon dioxide emissions declined by 2.8 per cent in 2008', Official Energy Statistics from the US Government, 20 May. Available at: http://www.eia.doe.gov/neic/press/press318.html. Accessed 2 June 2009.

Engardio, P. (2005) 'A new world economy: The balance of power will shift to the East as China and India evolve', *Business Week*, 22 August. Available at: http://www.business-week.com/magazine/content/05_34/b3948401.htm. Accessed 22 April 2008.

Engstrom, R. and Carlsson-Kanyama, A. (2004) 'Food losses in food service institutions: Examples from Sweden', *Food Policy*, 29 (3): 203–94.

Etzioni, A. (2003) 'Introduction: Voluntary simplicity – psychological implications, societal consequences', in D. Doherty and A. Etzioni (eds), *Voluntary Simplicity: Responding to Consumer Culture*. Lanham, MD: Rowman & Littlefield. pp. 1–27.

Euromonitor International (2008) *Shopping for Pleasure: The Development of Shopping as a Leisure Pursuit*. London: Euromonitor International.

European Union (2007) 'Restructuring forum: The challenges of the automotive industry – Towards a European partnership for the anticipation of change', Brussels, 17 and 18 October. Available at: http://ec.europa.eu/employment_social/restructuring/docs/partnership_en.pdf. Accessed 18 March 2009.

European Union (2009) 'Annex 3: Guidance on scrapping schemes for vehicles'. Available at: http://ec.europa.eu/enterprise/automotive/pagesbackground/competitiveness/com_2009_104/annex_3.pdf. Accessed 18 March 09.

Evans, H. (1998) *The American Century*. New York: Alfred A Knopf.

Ewen, S. (2001) *Captains of Consciousness: Advertising and the Social Roots of the Consumer Culture*, 25th Anniversary Edition. New York: Basic Books.

Ewen, S. and Ewen, E. (1992) *Channels of Desire: Mass Images and the Shaping of American Consciousness*. Minneapolis, MN: University of Minnesota Press.

Faber, R.J. and O'Guinn, T.C. (1989) 'Compulsive buying: A phenomenological exploration', *The Journal of Consumer Research*, 16 (2): 147–57.

Farrell, D. et al. (2007) 'The "bird of gold": The rise of India's consumer market', McKinsey Global Institute. Available at: http://www.mckinsey.com/mgi/reports/pdfs/india_consumer_market/MGI_india_consumer_executive_summary.pdf. Accessed 23 April 2008.

Ferrier, C. (2001) 'Bottled water: Understanding a social phenomenon', Discussion paper commissioned by WWF. Available at: http://assets.panda.org/downloads/bottled_water.pdf. Accessed 22 September 2008.

FIFA (2006) '2006 FIFA World Cup in numbers'. Available at: http://www.fifa.com/aboutfifa/marketingtv/factsfigures/numbers.html. Accessed 3 October 2008.

Finch, J. (2008) 'This is the dawning of the age of austerity, says Asda', *Guardian*, 12 December: 37.

Fitzpatrick, M. (2005) 'What a waste – Japan faces up to food waste mountain', 2 June, *Just-food*. Available at: http://www.just-food.com/features_detail.asp?art=980. Accessed 9 December 2008.

Flanders, J. (2006) *Consuming Passions: Leisure and Pleasure in Victorian Britain*. London: Harper Press.

Flavin, C. and Engelman, R. (2009) 'The perfect storm', in L. Starke (ed.), *State of the World 2009: Into a Warming World*. A Worldwatch Institute Report on Progress Toward a Sustainable Society. New York: W.W. Norton & Co. pp. 5–12.

Fletcher, H. (2008) 'For sale, hardly worn: two million tonnes of clothes', *The Times, Times 2*, 15 December: 2–3.

Flynn, L.J. (2006) 'US: Growing worry for businesses: Old computers', *New York Times*, 4 April. Available at: http://www.corpwatch.org/article.php?id=13459. Accessed 9 December 2008.

Food navigator.com (2004) 'US wastes half its food', 26 November. Available at: http://www.foodnavigator-usa.com/news/ng.asp?id=56376. Accessed 9 December 2008.

Food and Agriculture Organisation of the United Nations (FAO) (2008) 'Number of hungry people rises to 963 million', *Newsroom*, 9 December. Available at: http://www.fao.org/news/story/en/item/8836/icode. Accessed 18 December 2008.

Foster, J.B. (2006) 'The household debt bubble', *Monthly Review*, 58 (1). Available at: http://www.monthlyreview.org/0506jbf.htm. Accessed 11 September 2008.

Frank, A.G. (1998) *ReOrient: Global Economy in the Asian Age*. Berkeley, CA: University of California Press.

Frank, T. (1998) *The Conquest of Cool: Business Culture, Counterculture and the Rise of Hip Consumerism*. London: University of Chicago Press.

Frank, T. (2001) *One Market Under God: Extreme Capitalism, Market Populism and the End of Economic Democracy*. London: Seeker & Warburg.

Franklin, P. (2006) 'Down the drain', *Waste Management World*, May–June: 62–65. Available at: http://www.container-recycling.org/assets/pdfs/media/2006-5-WMW-DownDrain.pdf. Accessed 23 September 2008.

Frean, A. (2009) 'One in five children is failing to get place at school of choice', *The Times*, 2 March: 5.

French, H. (2004) 'Linking globalization, consumption and governance', in L. Starke (ed.), *State of the World 2004: Progress Towards a Sustainable Society*. A Worldwatch Institute Report. London: Earthscan. pp. 144–61.

Friedman, M. (1982) *Capitalism and Freedom*. Chicago, IL: University of Chicago Press.

Friedman, B.M. (2006) *The Moral Consequences of Economic Growth*. New York: Vintage Books.

Friends of the Earth (2005) *Briefing Good Neighbours? Community Impacts of Supermarkets*. Available at: http://www.foe.co.uk/resource/briefings/good_neighbours_community. pdf. Accessed 14 August 2008.

Frost, R. (2002) 'Can Japanese brands go global?'. Available at: http://www.brandchannel. com/features_effect.asp?pf_id=130. Accessed 9 October 2008.

Futerra Sustainability Communications (2008) *The Greenwash Guide*. Available at: http://www.futerra.co.uk/downloads/Greenwash_Guide.pdf. Accessed 7 March 2009.

G20 (2009) 'London summit – leader's Statement 2nd April'. Available at: http://www.londonsummit.gov.uk/resources/en/PDF/final-communique. Accessed 3 April 2009.

Gabriel, Y. and Lang, T. (2006) *The Unmanageable Consumer*, 2nd edn. London: Sage.

Galbi, D. (2005) 'US annual advertising spending since 1919'. Available at: http://www.galbithink.org/ad-spending.htm. Accessed 6 August 2008.

Galbraith, J.K. (1963) *The Affluent Society*. Harmondsworth: Penguin.

Galbraith, J.K. (1969) *The New Industrial State*. Harmondsworth: Penguin.

Galbraith, J.K. (1975) *Economics and the Public Purpose*. Harmondsworth: Penguin.

Galbraith, J.K. (1985) *The Affluent Society*, 4th edn with a new introduction. London: Andre Deutsch.

Galbraith, J.K. (1992) *The Great Crash 1929*. London: Penguin Books.

Gardner, G. and Assadourian, E. (2004) 'Rethinking the good life', in L. Starke (ed.), *State of the World 2004: Progress Towards a Sustainable Society*. A Worldwatch Institute Report. London: Earthscan. pp. 164–79.

Gardner, G., Assadourian, E. and Sarin, R. (2004) 'The state of consumption today', in L. Starke (ed.), *State of the World 2004: Progress Towards a Sustainable Society*. A Worldwatch Institute Report. London: Earthscan. pp. 3–21.

Gardner, G. and Prugh, T. (2008) 'Seeding the sustainable economy', in L. Starke (ed.), *State of the World 2008: Special Focus – Innovations for a Sustainable Economy*. A Worldwatch Institute Report. New York: W.W. Norton. pp. 3–17.

Gardner, M.N. and Brandt, A.M. (2006) '"The Doctors' choice is America's choice": The physician in US cigarette advertisements, 1930–1953', *American Journal of Public Health*, 96 (2): 222–32.

Giddens, A. (1990) *The Consequences of Modernity*. Cambridge: Polity Press.

Giddens, A. (2009) *The Politics of Climate Change*. Cambridge: Polity Press.

Gillespie, E. (2008) 'Stemming the tide of "Greenwash"', *Consumer Policy Review*, 1 May. Available at: http://www.allbusiness.com/environment-natural-resources/environmentalism/11462838-1.html. Accessed 7 March 2009.

Giroux, H. (2003) 'Dystopian nightmares and educated hopes: The return of the pedagogical and the promise of democracy', *Policy Futures in Education*, 1 (3): 467–87.

Giroux, H. (2007) *The University in Chains: Confronting the Military–Industrial–Academic Complex*. Boulder, CO: Paradigm Publishers.

Gleick, P.H., Cooley, H., Cohen, M.J., Morikawa, M., Morrison, J. and Palaniappan, M. (2009) *World's Water 2008–9: The Biennial Report on Freshwater Resources*. Pacific Institute for Studies in Development, Environment and Security. London: Island Press.

Glickman, L. (ed.) (1999) *Consumer Society in American History: A Reader*. Ithaca, NY: Cornell University Press.

Global Footprint Network (2006) *National Footprint Accounts*, 2006 Edition. Available at: http://www.footprintnetwork.org.

Global Footprint Network (2008) 'World footprint: Do we fit on the planet?'. Available at: http://www.footprintnetwork.org/en/index.php/GFN/page/world_footprint. Accessed 11 February 2009.

Global Industry Analysts Inc. (2008) *Deodorants: A Global Strategic Business Report*. Available at: http://www.strategyr.com/Deodorants_Market_Report.asp. Accessed 8 August 2008.

Goleman, D. (2009) *Ecological Intelligence: Knowing the Hidden Impacts of What We Buy*. London: Allen Lane.

Gorz, A. (1982) *Farewell to the Working Class: An Essay on Post-Industrial Socialism*. London: Pluto Press.

Gorz, A. (1983[1975]) *Ecology as Politics*. London: Pluto Press.

Gorz, A. (1985) *Paths to Paradise: On the Liberation From Work*. London: Pluto Press.

Gorz, A. (1989) *Critique of Economic Reason*. London: Verso.

Gorz, A. (1999) *Reclaiming Work: Beyond the Wage-Based Society*. Cambridge: Polity Press.

Gray, J. (1999) *False Dawn: The Delusions of Global Capitalism*. London: Granta Books.

Green, J., McDowell, Z. and Potts, H.W.W. (2008) 'Does choose & book fail to deliver the expected choice to patients? A survey of patients' experience of outpatient appointment booking', *BMC Medical Informatics and Decision Making*, 8 (36). Available at: http://www.pubmedcentral.nih.gov/articlerender.fcgi?artid=2529277. Accessed 9 January 2009.

Greenpeace, (n.d.) 'Where does e-waste end up?'. Available at: http://www.greenpeace.org/international/campaigns/toxics/electronics/where-does-e-waste-end-up. Accessed 6 August 2009.

Greenpeace (2005) 'Toxic tech: Pulling the plug on dirty electronics'. Available at: http://www.greenpeace.org/raw/content/international/press/reports/toxic-tech-pulling-the-plug-o.pdf. Accessed 30 July 2009.

Greenpeace, (2009) 'Slaughtering the Amazon, summary'. Available at: http://www.greenpeace.org/raw/content/usa/press-center/reports4/slaughtering-the-amazon.pdf. Accessed 5 June 2009.

Grigsby, M. (2004) *Buying Time and Getting By: The Voluntary Simplicity Movement*. New York: State University of New York Press.

Guan, D., Peters, G., Weber, C.L. and Hubacek, K. (2009) 'Journey to world top emitter – an analysis of the driving forces of China's recent CO_2 emissions surge', *Geophysical Research Letters*, 36, L04709: doi:10.1029/2008GL036540.

Gunder Frank, A. (1998) *ReOrient: Global Economy in the Asian Age*. London: University of California Press.

Hailes, J. (2007) *The New Green Consumer Guide*. London: Simon & Schuster.

Hall, C. (2006) 'NHS to fund 40pc of private surgery', *Telegraph.co.uk*. Available at: http://www.telegraph.co.uk/news/uknews/1510704/NHS-%27to-fund-40pc-of-private-surgery%27.html. Accessed 5 August 2008.

Hall, S., Winlow, S. and Ancrum, C. (2008) *Criminal Identities and Consumer Culture: Crime, Exclusion and the New Culture of Narcissism*. Cullompton, Devon: Willan Publishing.

Halliday, J. (2009) 'US auto sales continued to drop in February', *Advertising Age*, March. Available at: http://adage.com/article?article_id=135014. Accessed 4 March 2009.

Hamilton, C. (2003) 'Downshifting in Britain: A sea change in the pursuit of happiness', The Australia Institute Discussion Paper No. 58. Available at: http://www.tai.org.au/file.php?file=DP58.pdf. Accessed 29 May 2009.

Hamilton, C. and Mail, E. (2003) 'Downshifting in Australia: A sea-change in the pursuit of happiness', The Australia Institute Discussion Paper No. 50. Available at: http://www.tai.org.au/documents/downloads/DP50.pdf. Accessed 26 May 2009.

Hamilton, C., Dennis, R. and Baker, D. (2005) 'Wasteful consumption in Australia', The Australia Institute Discussion Paper No. 77. Available at: http://www.tai.org.au/documents/downloads/DP77.pdf. Accessed 26 May 2009.

Hankyu Inc. (n.d.) 'Hankyu Department Stores Inc., Early History'. Available at: http://www.enotes.com/company-histories/hankyu-department-stores-inc/early-history. Accessed 21 April 2008.

Hansen, F., Rasmussen, J., Martensen, A. and Tufte, B. (eds) (2002) *Children, Advertising, and Media*. Copenhagen: Copenhagen Business School Press.

Harper, D., Fallon, S., Gaskell, K., Grundvig, J., Heller, C., Huhti, T. and Mayhew, B. (2005) *China*. London: Lonely Planet.

Hartman, J.W. (2008) *Center for Sales, Advertising and Marketing History*. Duke University Rare Book, Manuscript, and Special Collections Library. Available at: http://library.duke.edu/digital collections/eaa. Accessed 7 August 2008.

Harvey, D. (1989) *The Condition of Postmodernity*. Oxford: Blackwell.

Harvey, D. (2003) *The New Imperialism*. Oxford: Oxford University Press.

Harvey, D. (2005) *A Brief History of Neoliberalism*. Oxford: Oxford University Press.

Haugh, W.F. (1986) *Critique of Commodity Aesthetics: Appearance, Sexuality and Advertising in Capitalist Society*. Cambridge: Polity Press.

Hawkes, N. (2008) 'NHS hospitals can seek sponsors and advertise in fight to attract patients', *The Times*, 20 March. Available at: http://www.timesonline.co.uk/tol/life_and_style/health/article3587138.ece. Accessed 4 August 2008.

Hawkes, S. (2008) 'Primark sacks suppliers over use of child labour', *Timesonline*, 16 June. Available at: http://business.timesonline.co.uk/tol/business/industry_sectors/retailing/article4147524.ece. Accessed 24 June 2008.

Hawksworth, J. (2006) 'The world in 2050: Implications of global growth for carbon emissions and climate change policy', PriceWaterhouseCoopers. Available at: http://www.pwc.com/extweb/pwcpublications.nsf/docid/DFB54C8AAD6742DB852571F5006DD532/$file/world2050carbon.pdf. Accessed 12 April 2009.

Hays, C.L. (2004) *The Real Thing: Truth and Power at the Coca-Cola Company*. New York: Random House.

Health Insider (2007) 'Choose and Book use by GPs falls'. Available at: http://www.e-health-insider.com/news/item.cfm?ID=2636. Accessed 3 March 2009.

Heartfield, J. (2008) *Green Capitalism: Manufacturing Scarcity in an Age of Abundance*. London: Openmute.

Hemsley, S. (2007) 'The power of persuasion', *Guardian*, 21 May: 8.

Hertwich, E.G. (2005) 'Consumption and Industrial Ecology', *Journal of Industrial Ecology*, (19–2): 1–6.

Hindell, J. (2000) 'Japanese men smelling of roses', *BBC News Asia-Pacific*, 17 April. Available at: http://news.bbc.co.uk/2/hi/asia-pacific/716709.stm. Accessed 8 August 2008.

Hinsliff, G. and Smith, D. (2007) 'Arts supremo attacks Brown over funding', *Observer*, 8 April. Available at: http://politics.guardian.co.uk/arts/story/0,2052523,00.html. Accessed 10 August 2007.

Hirsch, F. (1995[1977]) *Social Limits to Growth*. London: Routledge.

Hoffman, J. (1992) *The Art and Science of Dumpster Diving*. Port Townsend, WA: Loompanics Unlimited.

Holt, D. (2005) 'An interview with Juliet Schor', *Journal of Consumer Culture*, 5 (5): 5–21.

Hoover Institution (2006) 'Facts on policy: Consumer spending'. Available at: http://www.hoover.org/research/factsonpolicy/facts/4931661.html. Accessed 11 September 2008.

Hopkins, K. (2008) 'Credit crunch: Lowest ever consumer confidence', *Guardian*, 9 July. Available at: http://www.guardian.co.uk/business/2008/jul/09/creditcrunch.economics. Accessed 30 July 2008.

Hutt, W. (1940) 'The concept of consumers' sovereignty', *Economic Journal*, 50 (197): 66–77.

Iacoviello, M. (2005) 'Household debt and income inequality, 1963–2003', Economics Department, Working Papers in Economics, Boston College, pp. 1–43. Available at: http://escholarship.bc.edu/cgi/viewcontent.cgi?article=1173&context=econ_papers. Accessed 28 November 2008.

IIAR (2008) 'Compulsive shopping and spending', Illinois Institute for Addiction Recovery. Available at: http://www.addictionrecov.org/spendaddict.aspx. Accessed 9 December 2008.

Illich, I. (1985[1973]) *Tools for Conviviality*. London: Marion Boyars.

Interbrand, (2008) *Best Global Brands* 2008. Available at: http://www.interbrand.com/images/BGB_reports/BGB_2008_EURO_Format.pdf. Accessed 15 March 2009. pp. 1–85.

International Air Transport Association (IATA) (2008) 'Economic briefing: The impact of recession on air traffic volumes'. Available at: http://www.iata.org/NR/rdonlyres/7E25AD13-E0AD-4166-ABD8-CFA192D51AB4/0/IATA_Economics_Briefing_Impact_of_Recession_Dec08.pdf. Accessed 28 February 2009.

International Cooperative Alliance (n.d.) Available at: http://www.ica.coop/coop/index.html. Accessed 9 June 2009.

International Institute for Sustainable Development (IISD) (1999) 'Ten hot SD issues for the Millennium', *Developing Ideas Digest Issues*, January/February http://www.iisd.org/didigest/jan99/default.htm. Accessed 18 August 2008.

International Monetary Fund (2009) 'World economic outlook'. Available at: http://www.imf.org/external/pubs/ft/survey/so/2009/RES012809A.html. Accessed 13 February 2009.

International Scientific Congress (2009) 'Climate change: Global risks, challenges and decisions', University of Copenhagen, 10–12 March. Available at: http://climatecongress.ku.dk/newsroom/congress_key_messages. Accessed 20 March 2009.

IOC Athens (2004) 'Marketing report'. Available at: http://www.olympic.org/uk/organisation/facts/introduction/100years_uk.asp. Accessed 3 October 2008.

Irwin, R. (2001) 'Painting South Africa red'. Available at: http://www.brandchannel.com/features_effect.asp?fa_id=40. Accessed 18 September 2008.

Jackson, T. (2008a) 'The challenge of sustainable lifestyles', in L. Starke (ed.), *State of the World 2008: Special Focus – Innovations for a Sustainable Economy*. A Worldwatch Institute Report. New York: W.W. Norton. pp. 45–60.

Jackson, T. (2008b) 'What politicians dare not say', *New Scientist* Special Issue *The Folly of Growth*, 200 (2678): 42–3.

Jackson, T. (2009) *Prosperity Without Growth? The Transition to a Sustainable Economy*. London: Sustainable Development Commission. Available at: http://www.sd-commission.org.uk/publications/downloads/prosperity_without_growth_report.pdf. Accessed 31 March 2009.

Jameson, F. (1991) *Postmodernism, Or The Cultural Logic of Late Capitalism*. London: Verso.

Jargon, J. (2008) 'Kraft reformulates Oreo, scores in China', *The Wall Street Journal*, 1 May. Available at: http://s.wsj.net/article/SB120958152962857053.html. Accessed 16 September 2008.

Jaumain, S. and Crossick, G. (1999) *Cathedrals of Consumption: The European Department Store 1850–1939*. Aldershot: Ashgate.

Jenkins, S. (2008) 'In banks we trust should not be the mantra for 2009', *Guardian*, 31 December: 29.

Jhally, S. (2000) 'Advertising at the edge of the apocalypse', in R. Anderson and L. Strate (eds), *Critical Studies in Media Commercialism*. New York: Oxford University Press. pp. 27–39.

Johnson, D. and Shipp, S. (n.d.) 'Trends in inequality using consumer expenditures: 1960–1993', Bureau of Labor Statistics, Washington, DC. Available at: http://www.bls.gov/ore/pdf/st950100.pdf. Accessed 20 February 2009.

Jordan, C. (2003–2005) 'Intolerable beauty: Portraits of American mass consumption'. Available at: http://www.chrisjordan.com. Accessed 21 March 2008.

Jordan, C. (2006–2009) 'Running the Numbers: An American self-portrait'. Available at: http://www.chrisjordan.com. Accessed 12 June 2009.

Jordan, C. (2007) 'Running the numbers an interview by Nicole Pasulka', *Morning News*, 23 July. Available at: http://www.themorningnews.org/archives/galleries/running_the_numbers/11rtn.php. Accessed 12 March 2008.

Jordan, C. (2009) 'Running the numbers II: Portraits of global mass culture'. Available at: http://www.chrisjordan.com/current_set2.php?id=9. Accessed 15 May 2009.

Just-auto, (2009) 'UK: West European car sales plunged 25.4% in January'. Available at: http://www.just-auto.com/article.aspx?id=97898. Accessed 4 March 2009.

Kalish, I. (2005) 'China's consumer market: Opportunities and risk', *Deloitte Research*. Available at: http://www.bglegis.com/China_Consumer.pdf. Accessed 29 September 2008.

Kalish, I. (2007) 'China & India: Comparing the world's hottest consumer markets', *Deloitte Consumer Business*. Available at: http://www.deloitte.com/dtt/cda/doc/content/China%20and%20India_July%202007.pdf. Accessed 29 September 2008.

Kamat, A. (2002) 'Water profiteers', *India Resource Center*, 28 May. Available at: http://www.indiaresource.org/issues/water/2003/waterprofiteers.html. Accessed 23 September 2008.

Kamdar, M. (2007) *Planet India: The Turbulent Rise of the World's Largest Democracy*. London: Pocket Books.

Kaplan, J. (2008) 'The gospel of consumption and the better future we left behind', *Orion Magazine*, May/June. Available at: http://www.orionmagazine.org/index.php/articles/article/2962. Accessed 28 April 2009.

Kasser, T. (2009) 'Shifting values in response to climate change', in L. Starke (ed.), *State of the World 2009: Into a Warming World*. A Worldwatch Institute Report on Progress Toward a Sustainable Society. New York: W.W. Norton. pp. 122–5.

Kaye, J. and Argenti, P.A. (2004) 'Coca-Cola India', Tuck School of Business, Dartmouth College. Available at: http://mba.tuck.dartmouth.edu/pdf/2004-1-0085.pdf. Accessed 23 September 2008.

Keane, M. and Spurgeon, C. (2004) 'Advertising industry and culture in post-WTO China', *Media International Australia*, 111 (5): 104–17.

Kellner, D. (1992) 'Popular culture and the construction of postmodern identities', in S. Lash and J. Friedman (eds), *Modernity and Identity*. Oxford: Blackwell, pp. 141–77.

Kiley, D. (2007) 'Best global brands', Special Report, *Business Week*, 6 August: 56–64. Available at: http://www.ourfishbowl.com/images/press_releases/businessweek_bgb07_article.pdf. Accessed 4 March 2008.

Klein, N. (2001) *NoLogo*. London: Flamingo.

Klein, N. (2007) *The Shock Doctrine: The Rise of Disaster Capitalism*. London: Allen Lane.

Koran, L.M., Faber, R.J., Aboujaoude, E., Large, M.D. and Serpe, R.T. (2006) 'Estimated prevalence of compulsive buying behavior in the United States', *American Journal of Psychiatry*, 163 (October): 1806–12.

Kowinski, W.S. (1985) *The Malling of America: An Inside Look at the Great Consumer Paradise*. New York: William Morrow & Company.

Kozinn, A. (1993) 'Critic's notebook: On remembered joys of the LP recording', *New York Times*, 12 July. Available at: http://query.nytimes.com/gst/fullpage.html?res=9F0CE7D61F38F931A25754C0A965958260&sec=&spon=&pagewanted=all. Accessed 19 September 2008.

Labour Behind the Label (n.d.) Available at: http://www.labourbehindthelabel.org. Accessed 15 April 2008.

Lane, R.E. (2000) *The Loss of Happiness in Market Democracies*. New Haven, CT: Yale University Press.

Lane, P. (2008) 'Fun, games and money, the business of sport', *The Economist*, 31 July. Available at: http://www.economist.com/specialreports/displaystory.cfm?story_id=11825627. Accessed 1 October 2008.

Lash, S. and Urry, J. (1994) *Economies of Signs and Space*. London: Sage.

Laville, S. and Smithers, R. (2007) 'War over school boundaries divides Brighton', *Guardian*, 1 March. Available at: http://www.guardian.co.uk/uk/2007/mar/01/schooladmissions.topstories3. Accessed 1 August 2008.

Layard, R. (2003) 'Happiness: Has social science a clue?', Lionel Robbins Memorial Lectures 2002/3', 3–5 March, London School of Economics. Available at: http://cep.lse.ac.uk/events/lectures/layard/RL030303.pdf. Accessed 15 December 2008.

Layard, R. (2005) *Happiness: Lessons From A New Science*. London: Allen Lane.

Leach, W. (1989) 'Strategists of display and the production of desire', in S.J. Bronner (ed.), *Consuming Visions: Accumulation and Display of Goods in America* 1880–1920. London: W.W. Norton, pp. 99–132.

Leach, W. (1993) *Land of Desire: Merchants, Power, and the Rise of a New American Culture*. New York: Pantheon Books.

Leake, J. (2009) 'I'm a planet-saving kinda guy: Interview with Tony Blair', *Sunday Times*, 5 July: 5.

Lears, J. (1989) 'Beyond Veblen: Rethinking consumer culture in America', in S.J. Bronner (ed.), *Consuming Visions: Accumulation and Display of Goods in America* 1880–1920. London: W.W. Norton, pp. 73–97.

Lebow, V. (1955) 'Price competition in 1955', *Journal of Retailing*, XXXI (1): 5–10.

Leiss, W., Kline, S., Jhally, S. and Botterill, J. (2005) *Social Communication in Advertising: Consumption in the Mediated Marketplace*, 3rd edn. Abingdon: Routledge.

Levine, J. (2007) *Not Buying It: My Year Without Shopping*. London: Pocket Books.

Levitt, T. (1983) 'The globalization of markets', *Harvard Business Review*, 61 (5–6): 92–102.

Leys, C. (2006a) 'Not safe in their hands', *Red Pepper*, March. Available at: http://www.redpepper.org.uk. Accessed 8 June 2006.

Leys, C. (2006b) 'The great NHS "deficits" con', *Red Pepper*, May. Available at: http://www.redpepper.org.uk/toc/x-may2006-toc.html. Accessed 8 June 2006.

Loab, A.P. (1995) 'Birth of the Kettering doctrine: Fordism, Sloanism and the discovery of tetraethyl lead', *Business and Economic History*, 24 (1): 72–87. Available at: http://www.h-net.org/~business/bhcweb/publications/BEHprint/v024n1/p0072-p0087.pdf. Accessed 5 May 2009.

London Greenpeace (1998) '"What's wrong with the Body Shop?" Campaign leaflet', Available at: http://www.mcspotlight.org/beyond/companies/bodyshop.html. Accessed 1 March 2009.

Lopez, J. (2000) 'Economic stagnation set to continue in Japan', *World Socialist Web Site*. Available at: http://www.wsws.org/articles/2000/jun2000/jap-j03.shtml. Accessed 1 May 2009.

Lovejoy, T. (2009) 'Climate change's pressures on biodiversity', in L. Starke (ed.), *State of the World 2009: Into a Warming World*. A Worldwatch Institute Report on Progress Toward a Sustainable Society. New York: W.W. Norton. pp. 67–70.

Lovelock, J. (2009) *The Vanishing Face of Gaia*. London: Allen Lane.

Lovins, A.B., Lovins, L.H. and Hawken, P. (1999) 'A road map for natural capitalism', *Harvard Business Review*, 77 (3): 145–58. Available at: http://www.natcap.org/images/other/HBR-RMINatCap.pdf. Accessed 22 May 2009.

Low, K.E.Y. (2005) 'Ruminations on smell as a sociocultural phenomenon', *Current Sociology*, 53 (3): 397–417.

Luce, H.R. (1941) *The American Century*. New York: Farrar & Rinehart.

Luttwak, E. (1999) *Turbo Capitalism: Winners & Losers in the Global Economy*. London: Orion Business Books.

Lyotard, J.F. (1993) *Political Writings*. London: UCL Press.

Lyotard, J.F. (1984[1979]) *The Postmodern Condition: A Report on Knowledge*. Manchester: Manchester University Press.

Macalister, T. (2009) 'BP sheds 620 jobs at solar power business', *Guardian*, 2 April: 26.

Macartney, J. (2009) 'China's exports slide as global crisis extends its reach', *The Times*, 12 March: 53.

Macy's Inc. (n.d.) 'Macy's: A History'. Available at: http://www.macysinc.com/company/his_macys.asp. Accessed 21 April 2008.

Madslien, J. (2008) 'Tata: a growing global giant', *BBC News*. Available at: http://news.bbc.co.uk/1/hi/business/7313059.stm. Accessed 24 April 2008.

Maguire, J. (1999) *Global Sport: Identities, Societies, Civilizations*. Cambridge: Polity Press.

Mail Online, (2007) 'Model figures: Kate Moss helps Topshop lift sales by 10%'. Available at: http://www.dailymail.co.uk/news/article-489645/Model-figures-Kate-Moss-helps-Topshop-lift-sales-10.html. Accessed 29 August 2008.

Malcolm, J.D. (2001) *Financial Globalisation and the Opening of the Japanese Economy*. London: Routledge.

Mallaghan, P. (2008) 'The digital shop window: Gimmick or godsend?', *Screens.tv*. Available at: http://www.screens.tv/article/1139/The_digital_shop_window:_gimmick_or_god send%3F.html. Accessed 29 August 2008.

Maniates, M. (2002) 'In search of consumptive resistance: The voluntary simplicity movement', in T. Princen, M. Maniates and K. Conca (eds), *Confronting Consumption*. London: MIT Press. pp. 195–235.

Marcuse, H. (1968) *One Dimensional Man: The Ideology of Industrial Society*. London: Sphere Books.

Marquit, M. (2007) 'Interest in "going green" fuels big oil attempts to look eco-friendly', *The Panelist*, 24 August. Available at: http://thepanelist.com/Hot_Topics/Alternative_Energy/_20070824536. Accessed 7 March 2009.

Martindale, D. (2003) 'Burgers on the brain', *New Scientist*, 177 (2380). Available at: http://www.organicconsumers.org/foodsafety/fastfood032103.cfm#burgers. Accessed 11 August 2008.

Marx, K. (1963[1852]) *The Eighteenth Brumaire of Louis Bonaparte*. New York: International Publishers Co. Inc.

Marx, K. (1973[1857–8]) *Grundrisse: Foundations of the Critique of Political Economy*, translated with a Foreword by Martin Nicolaus. Harmondsworth: Penguin.

Marx, K. and Engels, F. (1976[1845]) *Collected Works, Volume 5, 1845–1847*. London: Lawrence and Wishart.

Marx, K. and Engels, F. (1968[1848]) *The Communist Manifesto*. Harmondsworth: Penguin.

Matthews, A., Cowburn, G., Rayner, M., Longfield, J. and Powell, C. (2004) *The Marketing of Unhealthy Food to Children in Europe*, a report of Phase 1 of the 'Children, obesity and associated avoidable diseases' project, Belgium: European Heart Network. pp. 1–21. Available at: http://www.ehnheart.org/files/English-141257A.pdf. Accessed 23 April 2009.

Matos, G. and Wagner, L. (1998) 'Consumption of materials in the United States, 1900–1995', *Annual Review of Energy and the Environment*, 23: 107–22.

Mayhew, B. (2004) *Shanghai*. London: Lonely Planet.

McChesney, R.W. (1999) 'Noam Chomsky and the struggle against neoliberalism', *Monthly Review*, April. Available at: http://www.chomsky.info/onchomsky/19990401.html. Accessed 7 February 2009.

McDonald's (2008) 'Canada 2008 FAQs'. Available at: http://www.mcdonalds.ca/en/aboutus/faq.aspx. Accessed 15 September 2008.

McDougall, D. (2008) 'The hidden face of Primark', *Observer*, 22 June. Available at: http://www.guardian.co.uk/world/2008/jun/22/india.humanrights. Accessed 24 June 2008.

McKendrick, N., Brewer, J. and Plumb, J.H. (1983) *The Birth of a Consumer Society: The Commercialization of Eighteenth Century England*. London: Hutchinson.

McNeal, J.U. (1999) *The Kids Market: Myths and Realities*. Ithaca, NY: Paramount Market Publishing.

McQueen, R. (1998) *The Eatons: The Rise and Fall of Canada's Royal Family*. Toronto: Stoddart Publishing.

Medical News Today (2009) 'Doctors still having problems with choose and book, British Medical Association research shows'. Available at: http://www.medicalnewstoday.com/articles/136841.php. Accessed 3 March 2009.

Mencimer, S. (2001) 'Theocracy in America: What gentile life in Mormon Utah can teach us about church and state', *Washington Monthly*, April. Available at: http://www.washingtonmonthly.com/features/2001/0104.mencimer.html. Accessed 21 April 2008.

Meyerson, H. (2008) 'The mall of America', *Washingtonpost.com*, 21 February: A15. Available at: http://www.washingtonpost.com/wp-dyn/content/article/2008/02/20/AR2008022002269.html. Accessed 23 April 2008.

Miles, S. (1998) *Consumerism as a Way of Life*. London: Sage.

Miller, P. and Rose, S. (1997) 'Mobilizing the consumer: Assembling the subject of consumption', *Theory, Culture and Society*, 14 (1): 1–36.

Mises, L. Von (1996[1949]) *Human Action*, Bettina B Greaves. Irvington: Foundation for Economic Education. Available at: http://www.mises.org/humanaction/chap15sec4.asp. Accessed 18 July 2008.

Mishel, L. (2006) 'CEO-to-worker imbalance grows', *Economic Snapshots*, Economic Policy Institute. Available at: http://www.epi.org/content.cfm/webfeatures_snapshots_20060621. Accessed 4 March 2008.

Mishel, L., Bernstein, J. and Allegretto, S. (2006/2007) *The State of Working America*. Economic Policy Institute. New York: Cornell University Press.

Mitchell, R.E. (2007) *Thorstein Veblen's Contribution to Environmental Sociology: Essays in the Political Ecology of Wasteful Industrialism*. New York: Mellen Press.

Mitchell, R.E. (2001) 'Thorstein Veblen: Pioneer in environmental sociology', *Organization and Environment*, 4 (14): 89–408.

Modern Advertising (2007) Available at: http://english.maad.com.cn/content.asp?articleid=100#. Accessed 6 August 2008.

Monbiot, G. (2000) *The Captive State: The Corporate Takeover of Britain*. London: Macmillan.

Monbiot, G. (2006) *Heat*. London: Allen Lane.

Monbiot, G. (2007) 'Eco-junk', *Guardian*, 24 July. Available at: http://www.monbiot.com/archives/2007/07/24/eco-junk. Accessed 2 February 2009.

Monbiot, G. (2008) 'This is what denial does', *Guardian*, 14 October. Available at: http://www.monbiot.com/archives/2008/10/14/this-is-what-denial-does. Accessed 18 March 2009.

Monbiot, G. (2009) 'Scrap it', *Guardian*, 10 March. Available at: http://www.monbiot.com/archives/2009/03/10/scrap-it. Accessed 18 March 2009.

Montgomerie, J. (1997) 'The logic of neo-liberalism and the political economy of consumer-debt led growth', in S. Lee and S. McBride (eds), *Neo-Liberalism, State Power and Global Governance*. Dordrecht: Springer, pp. 157–72.

Moore, M. (2009) 'Goodbye GM', *Huffington Post*. Available at: http://www.huffingtonpost.com/michael-moore/goodbye-gm_b_209603.html. Accessed 5 June 2009.

Mortished, C. (2008) 'Sorry Asia, you smell: the not-so-subtle ploy to sell three billion deodorants', *The Times*, 26 May: 5.

Moreton, C. (2006) 'Landfill crisis: What a waste', *Independent*, 22 January. Available at: http://www.independent.co.uk/environment/landfill-crisis-what-a-waste-524082.html. Accessed 13 May 2009.

Murphy, V. (2003) 'Mecca Cola challenges US rival', *BBC News Online*, 8 January. Available at: http://news.bbc.co.uk/1/hi/world/middle_east/2640259.stm. Accessed 10 September 2008.

Myers, D.G. (2007) 'Happiness'. Available at: http://www.davidmyers.org/Brix?pageID=48. Accessed 11 November 2008.

Mygatt, E. (2006) 'Fueled by developing Asia, global economy continues to expand'. Eco-Economy Indicators, *Earth Policy Institute* 12 October. Available at: http://www.earth-policy.org/index.php?/indicators/C53/. Accessed 3 July 2009.

Nair, C. (2008) 'The limits of growth – Part II', Yale Global Online, 24 November. Available at: http://yaleglobal.yale.edu/display.article?id=11645. Accessed 27 March 2009. pp. 1–4.

Nash, J. (2007) 'Consuming interests: Water, rum, and Coca-Cola from ritual propitiation to corporate expropriation in Highland Chiapas', *Cultural Anthropology*, 22 (4): 621–39.

Nationwide (2009) 'Nationwide consumer confidence index in partnership with TNS', January. Available at: http://www.nationwide.co.uk/NR/rdonlyres/E7FABB29-D8E9-4D3D-8FAB-C0ABD2F3F0A2/0/January_NCCI_4February2008.pdf. Accessed 3 March 2009.

Netherlands Environmental Assessment Agency (2007) 'Global CO_2 emissions: increase continued in 2007'. Available at: http://www.pbl.nl/en/publications/2008/GlobalCO2emissionsthrough2007.html. Accessed 2 June 2009.

New York Times (2006) 'Coca-Cola Profit up 10% on Strength in Overseas Markets', 20 April, Available at: http://www.nytimes.com/2006/04/20/business/20cokehtml. Accessed 2 July 2009.

New Scientist (2008) *The Folly of Growth:* Special Issue, 200 (2678).

NHS Direct (n.d.) 'Patient Choice'. Available at: http://www.nhsdirect.nhs.uk/articles/article.aspx?articleId=572. Accessed 5 August 2008.

Nielsen, A.C. (2008) 'Consumer confidence, concerns and spending intentions: A global Nielsen consumer report'. Available at: http://www2.acnielsen.com/reports/index_consumer.shtml. Accessed 30 May 2008.

Nordhaus, T. and Shellenberger, M. (2007) *Break Through: From the Death of Environmentalism to the Politics of Possibility*. New York: Houghton Mifflin.

Nugent, H. (2006) 'Dinner has come so far it has put the climate in danger', *The Times*, 21 July: 28.

Ofcom, (2004) *Child Obesity – Food Advertising in Context*. Available at: http://www.ofcom. org.uk/research/tv/reports/food_ads/report.pdf. Accessed 22 August 2008.

Offer, A. (2006) *The Challenge of Affluence: Self-Control and Well-Being in the United States and Britain since 1950*. Oxford: Oxford University Press.

Olympic Sponsorship (n.d.) 'TOP Programme: Coca-Cola'. Available at: http://www. olympic.org/uk/organisation/facts/programme/coke_uk.asp. Accessed 1 October 2008.

O'Mahony, B. (2003) 'US and British consumer confidence hit new lows', *Irish Examiner*, 29 March. Available at:http://archives.tcm.ie/irishexaminer/2003/03/29/story489194688. asp. Accessed 30 July 2008.

Optimum Population Trust (n.d.) Available at: http://www.optimumpopulation.org. Accessed 25 March 2009.

Packard, V. (1960) *The Hidden Persuaders*. Harmondsworth: Penguin.

Packard, V. (1963) *The Waste Makers*. Harmondsworth: Pelican Books.

Pagnamenta, R. (2009) 'Green energy feels the chill in harsh economic climate', *The Times*, 11 April: 34–5.

Palmer, K. (2008) 'The end of credit card consumerism', *US News.com, Business & Economy*. Available at: http://www.usnews.com/articles/business/economy/2008/08/08/the-end-of-credit-card-consumerism.html. Accessed 10 February 2009.

Parker, R. (2005) *John Kenneth Galbraith: His Life, His Politics, His Economics*. Chicago, IL: University of Chicago Press.

Parnell, K. (2002) 'Could automative processor obsolescence be history?', *Xilinx*, White Paper (v1.0), 25 October. Available at: http://www.xilinx.com/bvdocs/whitepapers/ wp169.pdf. Accessed 9 December 2008.

Paxton, W. (2002) 'Wealth distribution – the evidence', *Institute for Public Policy Research*, Centre for Asset-based Welfare – Evidence Report. Available at: http://www.ippr.org. uk/uploadedFiles/projects/Wealth%20Distribution.pdf. Accessed 28 February 2008.

Pearce, F. (2006) *When the Rivers Run Dry: Water – The Defining Crisis of the Twenty-First Century*. Boston, MA: Beacon Press.

Pendergrast, M. (2000) *For God, Country and Coca-Cola: The Definitive History of The Great American Soft Drink and The Company That Makes It*. New York: Basic Books.

Penty, A. (1922) *Post-industrialism*. London: Allen and Unwin.

Persky, J. (1993) 'Retrospectives – consumer sovereignty', *Journal of Economic Perspectives*, 7 (1): 183–91.

Pew Research Center (2006) 'Luxury or necessity? Things we can't live without: The list has grown in the past decade', *Pew Research Center: A Social Trends Report*. Available at: http://pewresearch.org/assets/social/pdf/Luxury.pdf. Accessed 12 November 2008.

Philo, G. and Miller, D. (eds) (2001) *Market Killing: What the Free Market Does and What Social Scientists Can Do About It*. London: Longman.

Polanyi, K. (2001[1944]) *The Great Transformation: The Political and Economic Origins of Our Time*. Boston, MA: Beacon Press.

Porritt, J. (2007) Interview. Available at: http://www.smartplanet.com/news/people/ 10000120/interview-consume-less-live-better-says-jonathon-porritt.html. Accessed 10 June 2008.

Porritt, J. (2009) 'Political policies for a sustainable future', Environmentally Sustainable Populations Conference: The scientific case for population policy, *Optimum Population*

Trust, 26 March. Available at: http://www.optimumpopulation.org/opt.events.html. Accessed 24 July 2009.

Princen, T. (2002) 'Consumption and its externalities: Where economy meets ecology', in T. Princen, M. Maniates and K. Conca (eds), *Confronting Consumption*. London: MIT Press. pp. 23–42.

Princen, T., Maniates, M. and Conca, K. (eds) (2002) *Confronting Consumption*. London: MIT Press.

Propper, C., Damiani, M., Leckie, D. and Dixon, J. (2006) 'Distance travelled in the NHS in England for inpatient treatment', *Centre for Market and Public Organisation* Working Paper Series No. 06/162, Bristol Institute of Public Affairs, University of Bristol. Available at: http://www.bristol.ac.uk/cmpo/publications/papers/2006/wp162.pdf. Accessed 9 January 2008.

Raff, D.M.G. and Summers, L.H. (1987) 'Did Henry Ford pay efficiency wages?', *Journal of Labor Economics*, 5 (4): 57–86. Part 2, *The New Economics of Personnel*.

Rauch, E. (2000) 'Productivity and the workweek'. Available at: http://swiss.csail.mit.edu/~rauch/worktime. Accessed 5 June 2008.

Renner, M. (2004) 'Moving towards a less consumptive economy', in L. Starke (ed.), *State of the World 2004: Progress Towards a Sustainable Society*. A Worldwatch Institute Report. London: Earthscan. pp. 96–119.

Renner, M. (2009) 'Global auto industry in crisis', *Worldwatch Institute*, 18 May. Available at: http://webmail.port.ac.uk/gw/webacc?action=Item.Read&User.context=on 2hrbQh7li6jkaJu1&Item.drn=20832z2z0&merge=msgitem&Url.Folder.type=Folder. UNIVERSAL. Accessed 22 May 2009.

Renouard, J. (2007) 'The predicaments of plenty: Interwar intellectuals and American consumerism', *The Journal of American Culture*, 30 (1): 54–67.

Richards, M. (2008) *Improving Access to Medicines for NHS Patients*. A Report for the Secretary of State for Health. Available at: http://www.dh.gov.uk/en/Publicationsandstatistics/Publications/PublicationsPolicyAndGuidance/DH_089927. Accessed 9 January 2009.

Richards, J. and Burgess, J. (2009) 'Britain's biggest shopping centres: A story in data', *The Times Magazine*, 14 February: 27.

Ritzer, G. (1995) *Expressing America: A Critique of the Global Credit Card Society*. Thousand Oaks, CA: Pine Forge Press.

Ritzer, G. (1998) *The McDonaldization Thesis: Explorations and Extensions*. London: Sage.

Ritzer, G. (2005) *Enchanting A Disenchanting World: Revolutionizing the Means of Consumption*, 2nd edn. London: Pine Forge Press.

Roach, S.S. (2007) 'You can almost hear it pop', *New York Times*, 16 December. Available at: http://www.nytimes.com/2007/12/16/opinion/16roach.html?_r=1&oref=slogin. Accessed 10 September 2008.

Robbins, R.H. (1999) *Global Problems and the Culture of Capitalism*. Boston, MA: Allyn and Bacon.

Robertson, R. (1990) 'Mapping the global condition: Globalization as the central concept', *Theory, Culture and Society*, 7 (2–3): 15–30.

Robertson, R. (2001) 'Globalization theory 2000+: Major problematics', in G. Ritzer and B. Smart (eds), *Handbook of Social Theory*. London: Sage, pp. 458–71.

Rojek, C. (2004) 'The consumerist syndrome in contemporary society: An interview with Zygmunt Bauman', *Journal of Consumer Culture*, 4 (3): 291–312.

Ross, R. (2008) *Clothing: A Global History*. Cambridge: Polity Press.

Roszak, T. (1972) *Where the Wasteland Ends: Politics and Transcendence in Post-Industrial Society*. New York: Doubleday.

Rothbard, M.N. (2001) *Money, Economy and State: A Treatise on Economic Principles*. Auburn, AL: The Ludwig von Mises Institute.

Roubini, N. (2008) 'The coming financial pandemic, *National Post*, 5 March. Available at: http://www.nationalpost.com/news/story.html?id=350930. Accessed 10 September 2008.

Rovell, D. (2005) *First in Thirst: How Gatorade Turned the Science of Sweat into a Cultural Phenomenon*. New York: Amacom Books.

Rovell, D. (2006) 'Investors fret about nike's star endorsements', *MSN Money*. Available at: http://articles.moneycentral.msn.com/Investing/CNBC/TVReports/NikeStarEndorsements. aspx. Accessed 15 August 2008.

Ryan, J.C. and Durning, A.T. (1997) *Stuff: The Secret Lives of Everyday Things*, NEW Report No. 4. Seattle, WA: Northwest Environment Watch.

Sassatelli, R. (2007) *Consumer Culture: History, Theory and Politics*. London: Sage.

Satterthwaite, D. (2009) 'The implications of population growth and urbanization for climate change', *Environment and Urbanization*, 21 (2): 545–67.

Schaefer, A. and Crane, A. (2005) 'Addressing sustainability and consumption', *Journal of Macromarketing*, 25 (1): 76–92.

Scherr, S.J. and Sthapit, S. (2009) 'Farming and land use to cool the planet', in L. Starke (ed.), *State of the World 2009: Into a Warming World*. A Worldwatch Institute Report on Progress Toward a Sustainable Society. New York: W.W. Norton. pp. 30–50.

Schlereth, T.J. (1989) 'Country stores, county fairs, and mail-order catalogues: Consumption in rural America', in S.J. Bronner (ed.), *Consuming Visions: Accumulation and Display of Goods in America 1880–1920*. London: W.W. Norton, pp. 339–75.

Schlosser, E. (2001) *Fast Food Nation: The Dark Side of the All American Meal*. London: Allen Lane.

Schmidt, C. (2007) 'Making smoking history worldwide', *Harvard Public Health Review*, Spring/Summer. Available at: http://www.hsph.harvard.edu/review/spring07/spr07tobacco.html. Accessed 13 August 2008.

Schor, J. (1992) *The Overworked American: The Unexpected Decline of Leisure*. New York: Basic Books.

Schor, J. (1995) *A Sustainable Economy for the 21st Century*. New York: Seven Stories Press.

Schor, J. (1998) *The Overspent American: Why We Want What We Don't Need*. New York: Basic Books.

Schor, J. (2002) 'Understanding the new consumerism: Inequality, emulation and the erosion of well-being'. Available at: http://webhost.ua.ac.be/psw/pswpapers/PSWpaper%20 2002-02%20schor.pdf. Accessed 13 March 2009.

Schor, J. (2004a) *Born to Buy: The Commercialized Child and the New Consumer Culture*. New York: Scribner.

Schor, J. (2004b) 'The politics of consumption: An interview with Denis Soron', *Aurora Online*. Available at: http://aurora.icaap.org/index.php/aurora/article/view/13/24. Accessed 7 April 2009.

Schor, J. (2005) 'Prices and quantities: Unsustainable consumption and the global economy', *Ecological Economics*, 55 (3): 309–20.

Schroeder, R. (2007) 'US consumer credit rises in August', *MarketWatch*. Available at: http://www.marketwatch.com/news/story/economic-report-us-consumer-credit/ story.aspx?guid=%7B68E0E9B6-9CFB-4192-8188-C601EDB2DAA2%7D. Accessed 11 September 2008.

Schumacher, E.F. (1973) *Small is Beautiful: Economics as if People Mattered*. New York: Harper & Row.

Schumpeter, J.A. (1954[1918]) 'The crisis of the tax state', *International Economic Papers*, 4: 5–38.

Schumpeter, J.A. (1975[1942]) *Capitalism, Socialism and Democracy*. New York: Harper.

Schwartz, B. (2005) *The Paradox of Choice: Why More Is Less*. New York: Harper Perennial.

Schwenninger, S.R. (2002) 'America's consumption trap', *New America Foundation*, 31 August. Available at: http://www.newamerica.net/publications/policy/americas_consumption_trap. Accessed 10 September 2008.

Seaton, M. (2006) 'The scramble for schools'. *Guardian*, g2, 14 March. pp. 6–9.

Sedlmaier, A. (2005) 'From department store to shopping mall: New research in the transnational history of large-scale retail', *Economic History Yearbook*. Berlin: Akademie Verlag. pp. 9–16.

Sennett, R. (2001) 'Street and office: Two sources of identity', in W. Hutton and A. Giddens (eds), *On the Edge: Living with Global Capitalism*. London: Vintage.

Shah, A. (2005) 'Behind consumption and consumerism: Effects of consumerism'. Available at: http://www.globalissues.org/TradeRelated/Consumption.asp. Accessed 30 July 2008.

Shah, A. (2006) 'Behind consumption and consumerism: Obesity'. Available at: http://www.globalissues.org/TradeRelated/Consumption/Obesity.asp. Accessed 31 July 2008.

Shah, A. (2008a) 'Children as consumers'. Available at: http://www.globalissues.org/article/237/children-as-consumers#Advertisingtochildrenisbigbusiness. Accessed 30 April 2009.

Shah, A. (2008b) 'Consumption and consumerism'. Available at: http://www.globalissues.org/issue/235/consumption-and-consumerism. Accessed 10 October 2008.

Shah, A. (2008c) 'World military spending'. Available at: http://www.globalissues.org/article/75/world-military-spending. Accessed 9 December 2008.

Shankar, A., Whittaker, J. and Fitchett, J.A. (2006) 'Heaven knows I'm miserable now', *Marketing Theory*, 6 (4): 485–505.

Sheumaker, S. and Wajda, S.T. (2007) *Material Culture in America: Understanding Everyday Life*. Santa Barbara, CA: ABC-CLIO.

Shepherd, J. (2009) 'School admission figures show 92,000 children missing out on first choice', *Guardian*, 12 March. Available at: http://www.guardian.co.uk/education/2009/mar/12/school-admissions-first-choice. Accessed 14 March 2009.

Shen, S. (2007) 'McDonald's goes slow in China franchising', *International Herald Tribune*, 7 February. Available at: http://www.iht.com/articles/2007/02/07/bloomberg/sxmcdo.php. Accessed 18 September 2008.

Shenkar, O. (2005) *The Chinese Century: The Rising Chinese Economy and Its Impact on the Global Economy, the Balance of Power, and Your Job*. Upper Saddle River, NJ: Wharton School Publishing/Pearson Education Inc.

Shove, E. and Warde, A. (1998) 'Inconspicuous Consumption: The Sociology of Consumption and the Environment', published by the Department of Sociology, Lancaster University, http://www.comp.lancs.ac.uk/sociology/papers/Shove-Warde-Inconspicuous-Consumption.pdf.

Siegel, C. (2008) 'More time or more stuff'. Available at: http://www.sierraclub.org/sustainable_consumption/downloads/MoreTimeMoreStuff.pdf. Accessed 11 November 2008.

Simms, A., Moran, D. and Chowla, P., (2006) *The UK Interdependence Report: How the World Sustains the Nation's Lifestyles and the Price it Pays*. London: New Economics Foundation. Available at: http://www.neweconomics.org/gen/uploads/f2abwpumbr1-wp055y2l10s5514042006174517.pdf. Accessed 22 February 2009.

Simms, A., Johnson, V., Smith, J. and Mitchell, S. (2009) *The Consumption Explosion*. The *Third UK Interdependence Report*, London, New Economics Foundation, http://www.neweconomics.org/gen/uploads/qxva43auphuy4x45yk433355240922009112524.pdf.

Sklair, L. (2002) *Globalization: Capitalism and Its Alternatives*. Oxford: Oxford University Press.

Skousen, M. (2007) 'Which drives the economy: Consumer spending or saving/investment?', *Initiative for Policy Dialogue*. Available at: http://www2.gsb.columbia.edu/ipd/j_gdp.html. Accessed 2 December 2008.

Slade, G. (2007) 'Waste: Commentary: Ten thousand songs in your pocket. Ten thousand years in a landfill', *Mother Jones*, March/April. Available at: http://www.motherjones.com/commentary/columns/2007/03/iwaste.html. Accessed 19 August 2008.

Slade, G. (2006) *Made to Break: Technology and Obsolescence in America*. London: Harvard University Press.

Slater, D. (1997) *Consumer, Culture and Modernity*. Cambridge: Polity Press.

Smart, B. (1992) *Modern Conditions, Postmodern Controversies*. London: Routledge.

Smart, B. (ed.) (1999) *Resisting McDonaldization*. London: Sage.

Smart, B. (2002) 'Accounting for anxiety: Economic and cultural imperatives transforming university life', in D. Hayes and R. Wynyard (eds), The *McDonaldization of Higher Education*. London: Bergin and Garvey. pp. 43–56.

Smart, B. (2003) *Economy, Culture and Society: A Sociological Critique of Neo-Liberalism*. Buckingham: Open University Press.

Smart, B. (2005) *The Sport Star: The Cultural Economy of Sporting Celebrity*. London: Sage.

Smart, B. (2007a) '(Dis)interring postmodernism, or a critique of the political economy of consumer choice', in J. Powell and T. Owen (eds), *Reconstructing Postmodernism: Critical Debates*. New York: Nova Science Publishers. pp. 167–86.

Smart, B. (2007b) 'Not playing around: Global capitalism, modern sport and consumer culture', *Global Networks*, 7 (2): 113–34.

Smart, B. (2009) 'Made in America: The unsustainable all-consuming global free-market "utopia"', in P. Hayden and C. el-Ojeili (eds), *Globalization and Utopia*. London: Palgrave. pp. 157–83.

Smith, A. (1976[1776]) *An Inquiry into the Nature and Causes of the Wealth of Nations*, edited by R.H. Campbell, A.S. Skinner and W.B. Todd, Oxford: Clarendon Press.

Smith, D. (2007) 'Stop shopping … or the planet will go pop', *The Observer*, Sunday 8 April. p. 8. Available at: http://www.guardian.co.uk/politics/2007/apr/08/greenpolitics.observerpolitics. Accessed 14 August 2008.

Smith, E. (2007) 'Sales of music, long in decline, plunge sharply', *The Wall Street Journal*, 21 March. Available at: http://online.wsj.com/article/SB117444575607043728.html?mod=home_ whats_news_us. Accessed 19 August 2008.

Snyder, L.B., Milici, F.F., Slater, M., Sun, H. and Strizhakova, Y. (2006) 'Effects of alcohol advertising on drinking among youth', *Archives of Pediatric and Adolescent Medicine*. 160: 18–24.

Soper, K. (2007a) 'Re-thinking the good life: The citizenship dimension of consumer disaffection with consumerism', *Journal of Consumer Culture*, 7 (2): 205–29.

Soper, K. (2007b) 'The other pleasures of post-consumerism', *Soundings*, 35 (March): 31–40. Available at: http://www.lwbooks.co.uk/journals/articles/soper.html. Accessed 23 October 2008.

Soper, K. (2008a) Paper to Sustainable Development Commission Meeting on 'Living well (within limits) – exploring the relationship between growth and wellbeing', 24 July. Available at: http://www.sd-commission.org.uk/publications/downloads/kate_soper_thinkpiece.pdf. Accessed 3 April 2009.

Soper, K. (2008b) '"Alternative hedonism" and the citizen-consumer', in K. Soper and F. Trentmann (eds), *Citizenship and Consumption*. Basingstoke: Palgrave Macmillan. pp. 191–205.

Soper, K. (2009) 'Introduction: The mainstreaming of counter-consumerist concern', in K. Soper, M. Ryle and L. Thomas (eds), *The Politics and Pleasures of Consuming Differently*. London: Palgrave Macmillan. pp. 1–21.

Soper, K. and Thomas, L. (2006) '"Alternative hedonism" and the critique of "consumerism"', Cultures of Consumption Working Papers Series. Available at: http://www.consume.bbk.ac.uk/working_papers/SoperAHWorkingPaperrevised.doc. Accessed 6 November 2008.

Soros, G. (2008) *The New Paradigm for Financial Markets: The Credit Crisis of 2008 And What It Means.* New York: Public Affairs.

Sorrell, S. (2009) 'The rebound effect: Mechanisms, evidence, and implication', *UK Energy Research Centre*, 4CMR University of Cambridge, 14 May. Available at: http://www.landecon.cam.ac.uk/research/eeprg/4cmr/news/pdf/Rebound_Steve%20Sorrell.pdf. Accessed 1 June 2009.

Spencer, J. (2007) 'China pays steep price as textile exports boom', *Wall Street Journal Online*, 22 August: A1. Available at: http://online.wsj.com/public/article/SB118580938555882301.html. Accessed 27 August 2007.

Srivastava, A. (2008) 'Coca-Cola continues unethical and dishonest practices in India', *India Resource Center,* 12 September. Available at: http://www.indiaresource.org/campaigns/coke/2008/kaladeraunethical.html. Accessed 25 September 2008.

Starke, L. (ed.) (2004) *State of the World: Progress Towards A Sustainable Society.* A Worldwatch Institute Report. London: Earthscan.

Starke, L. (ed.) (2008) *State of the World 2008: Special Focus – Innovations for a Sustainable Economy.* A Worldwatch Institute Report on Progress Toward a Sustainable Society. New York: W.W. Norton.

Starke, L. (ed.) (2009) *State of the World 2009: Into a Warming World.* A Worldwatch Institute Report on Progress Toward a Sustainable Society. New York: W.W. Norton.

Stearns, P.N. (2001) *Consumerism in World History: The Global Transformation of Desire.* London: Routledge.

Stern, N. (2007) *Stern Review: The Economics of Climate Change,* Executive Summary. Available at: http://www.gruene.ch/d/pdf/klima_stern_report.pdf. Accessed 12 April 2009.

Stiglitz, J. (2002) *Globalization and Its Discontents.* London: Penguin.

Strauss, S. (1924) 'Things are in the saddle', *Atlantic Monthly*, November: 577–88.

Stuart, T. (2009) *Waste: Uncovering the Global Food Scandal.* London: Penguin.

Sustainable Consumption Roundtable (2006) *I Will If You Will: Towards Sustainable Consumption.* London: Sustainable Development Commission. Available at: http://www.sd-commission.org.uk/publications/downloads/I_Will_If_You_Will.pdf. Accessed 12 March 2009.

Sutherland, M. and Sylvester, A.K. (2000) *Advertising and the Mind of the Consumer*, 2nd edn. London: Kogan Page.

Svoboda, S. (1995) 'Note on the trash crisis', National Pollution Prevention Center for Higher Education, University of Michigan. Available at: http://www.umich.edu/~nppcpub/resources/compendia/CORPpdfs/CORPtrash.pdf. Accessed 13 May 2009.

Swanson, L.A. (1990) 'Advertising in China: Viability and structure', *European Journal of Marketing*, 24 (10): 19–31.

Talberth, J. (2008) 'A new bottom line for progress', in L. Starke (ed.), *State of the World 2008: Special Focus – Innovations for a Sustainable Economy.* A Worldwatch Institute Report. New York: W.W. Norton. pp. 18–31.

Tammemagi, H.Y. (1999) *The Waste Crisis: Landfills, Incinerators and the Search for a Sustainable Future.* New York: Oxford University Press.

Teel, S.J. (ed.) (2000) 'Economic impact of the Coca-Cola system on China', Peking University, Tsinghua University and University of South Carolina. Available at: http://mooreschool.sc.edu/export/sites/default/moore/research/presentstudy/Coca-Cola/China/china.full.aug.pdf. Accessed 25 September 2008.

Telegraph.co.uk (2007) 'Thousands join queue to dress like Kate'. Available at: http://www.telegraph.co.uk/fashion/main.jhtml?xml=/fashion/2007/05/01/efmoss01.xml. Accessed 28 August 2008.

The Body Shop (n.d.) (2008) http://www/thebodyshop.co.uk/_en_gb/services/affiliates.aspx. Accessed 6 March 2009.

The Climate Group Report (2009) *Technology for a Low Carbon Future.* Available at: http://www.theclimategroup.org/assets/resources/Technology_for_a_low_carbon_future_report.pdf. Accessed 28 July 2009.

The Conference Board (2008) 'The consumer confidence press release'. Available at: http://www.conference-board.org/economics/ConsumerConfidence.cfm. Accessed 2 December 2008.

The Conference Board (2009) 'The consumer confidence press release'. Available at: http://www.conference-board.org/economics/ConsumerConfidence.cfm. Accessed 3 March 2009.

The Economist (2008) 'Sponsorship form'. Available at: http://www.economist.com/special reports/displaystory.cfm?story_id=11825607. Accessed 1 October 2008.

The Economist (2009) 'Troubled tigers: Asia needs a new engine of growth'. Available at: http://www.economist.com/printedition/displayStory.cfm?Story_ID=13022067. Accessed 13 February 2009.

The Kings Fund (2006) 'Local variations in NHS spending priorities'. Available at: http://www.kingsfund.org.uk/publications/briefings/local_variations.html. Accessed 4 August 2008.

The Register (2006) 'Slow start for choose and book'. Available at: http://www.theregister.co.uk/2006/02/17/choose_and_book_takeup. Accessed 3 March 2009.

Tilly, C. and Kennedy, M. (2007) 'Challenging Coke's thirst for water: The Apizaco story', *Grassroots International*, 2 July. Available at: http://www.grassrootsonline.org/blog/challenging-cokes-thirst-water-apizaco-story. Accessed 19 September 2008.

Toffler, A. (1983) *The Third Wave.* London: Pan Books.

Tonkiss, F. (2006) *Contemporary Economic Sociology: Globalization, Production, Inequality.* Abingdon: Routledge.

Toops, D. (2005) 'Top ten power brands', *Foodprocessing.com.* Available at: http://www.foodprocessing.com/articles/2005/562.html?page=7. Accessed 16 September 2008.

Toosi, M. (2002) 'Consumer spending: An engine for US job growth', *Monthly Labour Review*, 125 (11): 12–22. Available at: http://www.bls.gov/opub/mlr/2002/11/art2full.pdf. Accessed 28 February 2008.

Tucker, R. (2002) 'Environmentally damaging consumption: The impact of American markets on tropical ecosystems in the twentieth century', in T. Princen, M. Maniates and K. Conca (eds), *Confronting Consumption.* London: MIT Press, pp. 177–95.

Tweedie, N. (2008) 'Recession forces many to give up private schools', *Telegraph.co.uk.* Available at: http://www.telegraph.co.uk/education/educationnews/3508764/Recession-forces-many-to-give-up-private-schools.html. Accessed 3 March 2009.

University of Alabama Media Relations (2001) 'When more doctors smoked Camels'. Available at: http://main.uab.edu/show.asp?durki=46398. Accessed 12 August 2008.

UNICEF (n.d.) 'Child protection from violence, exploitation and abuse'. Available at: http://www.unicef.org/protection/index_childlabour.html. Accessed 20 February 2009.

United Nations Development Programme (1998) *Human Development Report: Consumption for Human Development.* Available at: http://hdr.undp.org/en/reports/global/hdr1998. Accessed 8 September 2008.

United Nations Development Programme (2006) *Human Development Report: Beyond Scarcity: Power, Poverty and the Global Water Crisis.* Available at: http://hdr.undp.org/en/media/HDR06-complete.pdf. Accessed 10 April 2009.

United Nations Environment Programme (UNEP) (1992) 'Rio declaration on environment and development'. Available at: http://www.unep.org/Documents.Multilingual/Default.asp?DocumentID=78&ArticleID=1163. Accessed 27 March 2009.

United Nations Environment Programme (UNEP) (2006) 'Basel Conference addresses electronic wastes challenge'. Available at: http://www.unep.org/Documents.Multilingual/Default.asp?DocumentID=485&ArticleID=5431&l=en. Accessed 30 July 2009.

UN Wire (2002) 'Bush outlines alternative plan to Kyoto Protocol', United Nations Foundation. Available at: http://www.unwire.org/unwire/20020215/23928_story.asp. Accessed 17 February 2009.

US Department of Agriculture (2005) 'Orange juice – production, consumption, exports, and imports statistics'. Available at: http://indexmundi.com/en/commodities/agricultural/orange-juice. Accessed 9 May 2009.

US Federal Reserve (2008a) 'Statistical release G 19 "Consumer credit"'. Available at: http://www.federalreserve.gov/releases/G19/hist/cc_hist_sa.html. Accessed 27 November 2008.

US Federal Reserve (2008b) 'Statistical release Z1 "Flow of funds accounts of the United States: Flows and outstandings 2nd Quarter 2008"'. Available at: http://www.federalreserve.gov/releases/z1/Current/z1.pdf. Accessed 28 November 2008.

US Federal Reserve Board (2008c) 'Consumer credit'. Available at: http://www.federalreserve.gov/releases/g19/Current. Accessed 14 November 2008.

Van Wee, B., Moll, H.C. and Dirks, J. (2000) 'Environmental impact of scrapping old cars', *Transportation Research, Part D*, 5: 137–43. Available at: http://ivem.eldoc.ub.rug.nl/FILES/ivempubs/publart/2000/TranspResDvWee/2000TranspResDvWee.pdf. Accessed 18 March 2009.

Veblen, T. (1994[1899]) *The Theory of the Leisure Class*. London: Penguin Books.

Veblen, T. (2005[1904]) *The Theory of Business Enterprise*. New York: Cosimo Classics.

Veblen, T. (2006[1923]) *Absentee Ownership – Business Enterprise in Recent Times: The Case of America*. London: Transaction Publishers.

Ventour, L. (2008) 'The food we waste', WRAP Food waste report v2. Available at: http://www.wrap.org.uk/downloads/The_Food_We_Waste_v2__2_.59e3199e.5635.pdf. Accessed 14 August 2008.

Vidal, J. (2004a) 'The UK's new rubbish dump: China', *Guardian*, 20 September. Available at: http://www.guardian.co.uk/society/2004/sep/20/environment.china. Accessed 6 August 2009.

Vidal, J. (2004b) 'Poisonous detritus of the electronic revolution', *Guardian*, 21 September. Available at: http://www.guardian.co.uk/society/2004/sep/21/environment.uknews. Accessed 6 August 2009.

Vidal, J. (2005) 'More than 30% of our food is thrown away – and it's costing billions a year', *Energy Bulletin*, April 15, published by The *Guardian* (UK). Available at: http://www.energybulletin.net/5350.html. Accessed 10 June 2009.

Virmani, A. (2005) *Tripolar World: India, China and US*, Indian Council for Research on International Economic Relations. Available at: http://www.icrier.org/pdf/Tripolar Wrld_IHC5.pdf. Accessed 10 June 2009.

Vries, J. de (1993) 'Between purchasing power and the world of goods: Understanding the household economy in early modern Europe', in J. Brewer and R. Porter (eds), *Consumption and the World of Goods*. New York: Routledge, pp. 85–132.

Waldman, A. (2003) 'Sizzling economy revitalizes India', *New York Times*, 20 October. Available at: http://query.nytimes.com/gst/fullpage.html?res=9E07E7D7103EF933A1 5753C1A9659C8B63. Accessed 23 April 2008.

Walker, R. (2008) *I'm With the Brand: The Secret Dialogue Between What We Buy and Who We Are*. London: Constable.

Wang, J. (2008) *Brand New China: Advertising, Media and Commercial Culture*. London: Harvard University Press.

Wang, T. and Watson, J. (2009) 'Trade, climate change, and sustainability', in L. Starke (ed.), *State of the World 2009: Into a Warming World*. A Worldwatch Institute Report on Progress Toward a Sustainable Society. New York: W.W. Norton. pp. 88–9.

Wansink, B., Brasel, S.A. and Amjad, S. (2000) 'The mystery of the cabinet castaway: Why we buy products we never use', *Journal of Family and Consumer Science*, 92 (1): 104–8.

War on Want (2006a) *Fashion Victims: The True Cost of Cheap Clothes at Primark, Asda and Tesco*. Available at: http://www.waronwant.org/Fashion+Victims+13593.twl. Accessed 30 July 2008.

War on Want (2006b) *Coca-Cola: The Alternative Report*. Available at: http://wow.webbler.org/downloads/cocacola.pdf. Accessed 25 September 2008.

War on Want (2007) *Let's Clean Up Fashion: 2007 Up-date*. Available at: http://www.waronwant.org/Fashion+Victims+13593.twl. Accessed 30 July 2008.

Warde, A. (1997) *Consumption, Food and Taste*. London: Sage.

Warner, J. (2007) 'India: Where the credit crisis is but distant thunder', *Independent*, 12 December. Available at: http://www.independent.co.uk/news/business/analysis-and-features/india-where-the-credit-crisis-is-but-distant-thunder-764604.html. Accessed 24 April 2008.

Watson, J.L. (2003) 'Introduction: Transnationalism, localization and fast foods in East Asia', in R. Robertson and K.E. White (eds), *Globalization: Critical Concepts in Sociology, Vol. 4, Culture and Identity*. London: Routledge. pp. 127–57.

Watson, J.L. (ed.) (2006) *Golden Arches East: McDonald's in East Asia*, 2nd edn. Stanford, CA: Stanford University Press.

Watt, N. (2007) 'Carry on flying, says Blair – science will save the planet', *Guardian*, 9 January. Available at: http://www.guardian.co.uk/business/2007/jan/09/theairlineindustry.greenpolitics/print. Accessed 16 December 2008.

Watts, J. (2009) 'China says western nations responsible for its CO_2 emissions', *Guardian*, 18 March: 17.

Weber, M. (1970[1906]) 'Capitalism and rural society in Germany', in *From Max Weber: Essays in Sociology*, ed. H.H. Gerth and C. Wright Mills. London: Routledge & Kegan Paul, pp. 363–85.

Weber, M. (1976) *The Protestant Ethic and the Spirit of Capitalism*. London: George Allen & Unwin.

Weissman, R. and Hammond, R. (2000) 'International tobacco sales', *Foreign Policy in Focus*, 3 (17). Available at: http://www.fpif.org/briefs/vol3/v3n17tob.html, Accessed 10 August 2008.

Weller, C.E. (2008) 'Economic snapshot for April 2008', *Center for American Progress*. Available at: http://www.americanprogress.org/issues/2008/04/econ_snapshot.html. Accessed 2 December 2008.

WWhich? (2006) 'Childcatchers report on the marketing of food to children'. Available at: http://216.239.59.104/search?q=cache:79HZ2LXVt5cJ:www.oxha.org/knowledge/publications/which_childcatchers_rpt_jan06.pdf+children+catchers+and+advertising+&hl=en&ct=clnk&cd=1. Accessed 31 July 2008.

White, L. (1988) *Merchants of Death: The American Tobacco Industry*. New York: Beech Tree.

White, M. and Wintour, P. (2004) 'Public services: the choice', *Guardian*, 24 June. Available at: http://www.guardian.co.uk/politics/2004/jun/24/uk.schools. Accessed 2 May 2009.

Whiteside, T. (1971) *Selling Death: Cigarette Advertising and Public Health*. New York: Liveright.

Wilk, R. (2001) 'Consuming morality', *Journal of Consumer Culture*, 1 (2): 245–60.

Williams, A. (2007) 'Buying into the green movement', *New York Times*, 1 July. Available at: http://www.nytimes.com/2007/07/01/fashion/01green.html?_r=2&oref=slogin. Accessed 23 May 2009.

Williams, R. (1976) *Keywords: A Vocabulary of Culture and Society*. Glasgow: Fontana.

Williams, R. (1980) *Problems in Materialism and Culture*. London: Verso.

Williams, Z. (2006) *The Commercialisation of Childhood*. London: Compass. Available at: http://clients.squareeye.com/uploads/compass/documents/thecommercialisationofchildhood.pdf. Accessed 31 July 2008.

Wilson, A. and Boehland, J. (2005) 'Small is beautiful: US house size, resource uses and the environment', *Journal of Industrial Ecology*, 9 (1–2): 277–87. Available at: http://mitpress.mit.edu/journals/JIEC/v9n1_2/jiec_9_1-2_277_0.pdf. Accessed 25 March 2009.

Winge, T. (2008) '"Green is the new black": Celebrity chic and the "green" commodity fetish', *Fashion Theory: The Journal of Dress, Body and Culture*, 12 (4): 511–24.

Winters, L. (2006) *Health Impact Assessment of the Patient Choice Agenda*, Observatory Report Series No. 62, Liverpool Public Health Observatory. Available at: http://www.liv.ac.uk/PublicHealth/obs/root/liverpool%20public%20health%20observatory/publications/observatory%20report%20series/HIA_of_Patient_Choice_Final_Report_%202006.pdf. Accessed 9 January 2009.

Wolff, E. (2003) 'The wealth divide: The growing gap in the United States between the rich and the rest', *The Multinational Monitor*, 24 (5). Available at: http://multinationalmonitor.org/mm2003/03may/may03interviewswolff.html. Accessed 28 February 2008.

World Advertising Trends (2007) 'Top ten countries by advertising expenditure 2006'. Available at: http://www.warc.com/LandingPages/Data/Adspend/AdspendByCountry.asp. Accessed 6 August 2008.

World Health Organization (2002) *Fact Sheets: Smoking Statistics*. Available at: http://www.wpro.who.int/media_centre/fact_sheets/fs_20020528.html. Accessed 11 August 2008.

World Health Organization (2004) *The Tobacco Atlas*. Available at: http://www.who.int/tobacco/statistics/tobacco_atlas/en/print.html. Accessed 11 August 2008.

Worldwatch Institute (2004) *State of the World 2004: Progress Towards a Sustainable Society*. London: Earthscan.

Worldwatch Institute (2006) *State of the World 2006: Special Focus – China and India*. New York: W.W. Norton.

WRAP (2006) 'New funding to tackle UK's six million tonnes of food waste', 11 December. http://www.wrap.org.uk/wrap_corporate/news/new_funding_to.html. Accessed 8 August 2009.

Yan, Y. (2001) 'McDonald's in Beijing: The localization of Americana', in D. Miller (ed.), *Consumption: Critical Concepts in the Social Sciences*. London: Taylor & Francis. pp. 335–53.

Yang, E. (2001) 'Coca-Cola: Think local, act local', *The Monroe Street Journal*. Available at: http://media.www.themsj.com/media/storage/paper207/news/2001/11/12/Corporate/Coca Cola.Think.Local.Act.Local._143767.shtml. Accessed 26 September 2008.

ZenithOptimedia (2004) 'Best prospects for advertising since 2000'. Available at: http://www.zenithoptimedia.com/about/news/pdf/Adspend%20Forecast%20Update%20Dec%202004.doc. Accessed 15 March 2009.

ZenithOptimedia (2007) *Global ad Market to Accelerate in 2008 Despite Credit Squeeze*. Available at: http://www.anes.it/area/ZenithOptimedia.pdf. Accessed 1 September 2008.

ZenithOptimedia (2008a) *Western Markets Continue to Slow, but Surging Developing Markets Propel Healthy World Growth in Ad Expenditure.* Available at: http://www.zenithoptimedia. com/gff/pdf/Adspend%20forecasts%20June%202008.pdf. Accessed 6 January 2009.

ZenithOptimedia (2008b) 'No growth in global adspend in 2009'. Available at: http:// www.zenithoptimedia.com/gff/pdf/Adspend%20forecasts%20December%202008.pdf. Accessed 13 January 2009.

Zhao, B. (1997) 'Consumerism, Confucianism, communism: Making sense of China Today', *New Left Review*, I, 222 (3–4): 43–59.

Zhou, Q. (2004) *What Kind of God: A Survey of the Current Safety of China's Food.* Berlin: Reportage Literature.

Zhou, Q. (2006a) 'China's food fears (part one)', *Chinadialogue.* Available at: http://www. chinadialogue.net/article/show/single/en/374. Accessed 15 September 2008.

Zhou, Q. (2006b) 'China's food fears (part two)', *Chinadialogue.* Available at: http://www. chinadialogue.net/article/show/single/en/379-China-s-food-fears-part-two. Accessed 15 September 2008.

Zivalich, L. (2006) 'Hey big spender', *Paradigm*, 11 (1): 6–7. Available at: http://www. addictionrecov.org/paradigm/P_PR_W06/paradigmW06.pdf. Accessed 10 May 2009.

INDEX

CPSIA information can be obtained
at www.ICGtesting.com
Printed in the USA
LVHW102349131218
600121LV00003B/1/P

9 781847 870506